Against the Stream

Critical Essays on Economics

AGAINST THE STREAM

STREAM

Critical Essays on Economics

GUNNAR MYRDAL

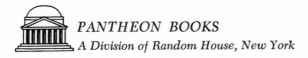

PANTHEON BOOKS
A Division of Random House, New York

Library of Congress Cataloging in Publication Data
Myrdal, Gunnar, 1898–
Against the Stream: Critical Essays on Economics.

Includes bibliographical references.
   1. Economics. 2. Social sciences. I. Title.
HB71.M87   330   73–4753
ISBN 0–394–48682–X

Portions of this book were first published in *American Economic Review, Journal of Social Issues,* and *Journal of Social Policy.*

Grateful acknowledgment is made to the following:

Encyclopaedia Britannica, for permission to reprint excerpts from "The World Poverty Problem" by Gunnar Myrdal, from *Britannica Book of the Year 1972.* Copyright © 1972 by Encyclopaedia Britannica, Inc., Chicago, Illinois.

Academic Press, for permission to reprint "Twisted Terminology and Biased Ideas" by Gunnar Myrdal, from *International Economics and Development: Essays in Honor of Raul Prebisch,* edited by Luis De Marco. Copyright © 1972 by Academic Press, Inc.

Manufactured in the United States of America by
The Book Press, Brattleboro, Vermont

FIRST EDITION

9 8 7 6 5 4 3 2

PREFACE

THE AUTHOR of this little book has been for a couple of years between major research undertakings. In spring 1970 I finished *The Challenge of World Poverty*,[1] which contains the policy conclusions of *Asian Drama*[2] and of my further studies of the plight of the peoples in underdeveloped countries. In the fall of 1973 I am committed to begin work on *An American Dilemma Revisited: The Racial Crisis in the United States in Perspective*, a topic about which I have been brooding over the years. In the intervening period— one of relative repose—I permitted myself to give way to the temptation of reading papers of a general character, dealing with matters I had earlier studied more intensively. A few of them are reprinted in the present volume.

They were all written in response to a particular question raised by a particular audience. When I wrote them, I had no intention of bringing them together in a book. They do not follow a plan and do not cover a defined set of topics. Most of them have a personal touch that will perhaps be unexpected in a book on the type of problems I treat. This may be more easily forgiven when I add that I shall never take time to write my memoirs in the ordinary sense. When I look back over my life, I am more interested in the problems I as a student have been struggling with than in situations I have been in and people I have met. I might even consider this little book a substitute for the memoirs I shall never write.[3]

I have, of course, done some editing and, in particular, tried to cut down repetitions. There are some left, which is unavoidable in a collection of essays. I would also remind the reader that, as James Bryce once explained in his own defense, certain things need to be said repeatedly, particularly when they are set in different contexts and seen from different points of view.

As I look back over my working life, it appears as if I had spread my efforts over a very wide and disparate field. But when I look at what I have published over almost half a century, I sense an inner consistency. It is as if I have been building an edifice where every new story stands upon the one before. References I have made in these very general essays—or could have made if I were not afraid of overburdening the reader's interest—in many cases go back to my earliest writings.

Though I have occasionally found reasons to change my views even on important matters, I have never felt the need to go back and cover the whole field again. When, for instance, after having produced *The Political Element in the Development of Economic Theory,* I found by further study that the idea displayed in that book—that there was a solid and "objective" economic theory—was mistaken and that value premises were needed already for establishing facts and not only for drawing policy conclusions, this did not distract from the validity of the main findings in the book. The analysis of the doctrinal development of economic theory from earliest time, and the way it had been distorted by the biases of the time, still stands. I had only to add my new insights that economic theory can never be neutral and, in the positivist sense, "objective."

In the subtitle I call the papers "critical," for I certainly feel critical of many prevalent approaches and theories in present-day writings in economics. Many of my earlier writings were also critical of what was then conventional wisdom. At the same time, I feel very deeply that I am working in the great tradition that began in the eighteenth century. That this is not a *contradictio in adjecto* was made clear already in the early book of mine I have mentioned above.

More particularly, I hold, like the classical and even the first generation of the neo-classical authors, that economics is a moral science in the meaning clarified by John Stuart Mill in his earliest works, "political economy," as it was commonly called even two generations ago. Our predecessors proceeded from the conception that there were objective values that could be known and could be laid as basis both for the study of facts and for policy conclusions. The "welfare theory" then developed by the first generation of neo-classical authors had thus its logical foundation upon the utilitarian moral philosophy, which, in turn, rested on the hedonistic associational psychology.

Modern establishment economists have retained the welfare theory from the earliest neo-classical authors, but have done their best to conceal and forget its foundation upon a particular and now obsolete moral philosophy. They have thus succeeded in presenting what appears to be an amoral economic theory, and they are often proud of stressing this as "professionalism." In *The Political Element in the Development of Economic Theory* I demonstrated the superficiality and logical inconsistency of this modern welfare theory, and I showed later, in *An American Dilemma*, that in all economic research there is a need from the beginning to the end to work with explicit value premises.

When thereafter in many fields of study I have tried to apply this insight, and worked under the discipline of stating my value premises and justifying their selection, I have restored the character of economics to that of a moral science. Economic policy conclusions can rationally be inferred from these value premises, and the facts ascertained from the viewpoint of the same value premises.

Finally, I hope that my frank and uninhibited style, long an inveterate habit, will be endured by my readers on the rationale that progress in social science lies through controversy, which should be sharpened and not veiled.

GUNNAR MYRDAL

The Stockholm University Institute for International
Economic Studies

January, 1973

Contents

Against the Stream

Critical Essays on Economics

Chapter 1

CRISES AND CYCLES IN THE DEVELOPMENT OF ECONOMICS[1]

1. Establishment Economics

IN MY CONCEPTION of economic science and its development, one implied assumption is that in every period there
tends to be a body of approaches and theories which
dominate the scene, even though there are always aberrants
and occasionally also outspoken rebels.

Those adhering to the dominant body form an establishment; their writings enjoy prestige; they quote each other
and usually nobody else, least of all rebels—when there
happen to be economists who dare to question in a radical
fashion the approaches and theories the establishment economists have in common. Thus they tend to create around
themselves a space often amounting to an isolation, and
not only toward other social science disciplines. Within
their group some individual researchers are by general ac-
claim raised to prominence. But even the thousands of lesser
fellow workers achieve status from belonging to the establishment and laboring loyally within its confines. The same
happens, of course, in the other social sciences, although I
believe that the forces of conformity are especially strong
in economics.

Innovation and originality are certainly appreciated, but mainly if they are of the additive and amending type. There is room for a certain amount of controversy, though it must not concern the basic structure of established approaches and theories. More generally, what gives status in the academic world and opens up positions in the research and teaching institutions of our craft and also opportunities for being called upon to advise governments, organizations, and businesses, is to work within the set pattern and to demonstrate acumen and inventiveness by embroidering upon it. To these even materially important rewards should be added the force of tradition. It has been said that no vested interests are stronger than those rooted in ingrained thoughtways and preconceptions.

Within establishment economics there are always schools that differ in various respects. Sometimes they are in the nature of different subdisciplines. Some students direct their work toward problems other than those of pure and general theory—for instance, economic history, business management, or relations in the labor market. By observing a mutually respected distance, these schools mostly live at peace with one another and do not really challenge each other.

The central economic theory is traditionally held in highest esteem, and the workers in the other subdisciplines feel happy when they can find a connecting line. When economists within that line of economic theory disagree, which they often do, there is usually enough of a common basis of thought not to create serious disturbance within the camp. The disagreements help protect them from seeing that together they form an establishment. This is an attitude parallel and, indeed, related to their common naïveté in keeping themselves unaware of how their research is conditioned by other forces than the search for truth, that is, the serious problem of biases.

In the present context I shall not enter further into the problems of the causal mechanism that keeps establishment economics together and tends to perpetuate its dominance (see Chapter 3, Sections 4 and 5). I shall confine myself to pointing out the importance within this mechanism of the interests and prejudices that are socially, economically, and politically powerful in the surrounding society. All knowledge—like all ignorance—tends to be opportunistic, when not critically scrutinized. It is inherent in the nature of an establishment that it protects itself forcefully against that type of critical scrutiny by ignoring as long as possible criticism from outside its narrow group.

But conformity is now and then broken. Such a crisis implies a disestablishment of the establishment—until a new orthodoxy has come into being. The result is a development that tends to become cyclical. A crisis and the ensuing shift of research approaches are normally not simply an autonomous development of our science but are caused by the external forces of change in the society we are studying and living in as participants.

2. The Keynesian Revolution

Thus the so-called Keynesian revolution was in my opinion not so much the effect of a book and the proliferation of other books and articles in its wake. These literary manifestations of nonconformism becoming general enough to be experienced as a crisis in the development of economic science were themselves largely brought about by, and in any case gained importance from, economic and political changes in society: the unfortunate economic situation in Britain during the Twenties and early Thirties with high and persistent unemployment, and the Great Depression in the United States from the beginning of the Thirties, plus the ripening at about the same time of ongoing trends of change of the organizations in the labor market and of the political power structure within these countries, which generally gave workers and people in the lower income brackets greater influence.

Though the younger among us can now perhaps not understand it fully, particularly as many of the older ones have been interested in covering up the trail, before the Great Depression in America economists in general actually believed in Say's law of the equality, or even identity, of aggregate supply and demand. I recall how once in the late Twenties I spent hours trying unsuccessfully to demonstrate to an older American friend and colleague of mine, who was a very prominent and accomplished member of the established school of economists, how it was possible for these two elements to show a difference.

Practical people, untrained in economic theory—and not only the cranks—had themselves never really believed in Say's law, or even understood it. The situation was a little like when my youngest daughter started school and came home reporting to her parents that it was only the teacher who did not know how children are begotten. In every parliament there had for a very long time been members of different political parties suggesting that workers should be put to work by public enterprise when demand for labor slackened, and there had even been businessmen who shared this opinion. But the inherited and still prevalent theory was that unemployment should be cured by pressing down wages and not by creating more demand for labor by direct policy interventions in the markets for labor or for goods and services.

The adherence of economists to Say's law corresponded, of course, to the policy inclinations toward non-interventionist *laissez-faire* of established economics at that time, which, in turn, fitted the interests and prejudices that had politically dominated their societies. During the Depression, and under the changed institutional and political conditions in the United States in the Thirties, as even earlier in crisis-ridden Britain, the Keynesian revolution had to come as a theoretical rationalization and justification of changed policy inclinations.

It was mainly an Anglo-American occurrence. In Sweden, where we grew up in the tradition of Knut Wicksell, Keynes's works were read as interesting and important contributions along a familiar line of thought, but not in any sense as a revolutionary breakthrough. We were astounded, for instance, that it took Pigou twenty years to catch on.

Wicksell had published his trail-blazing writings around the turn of the century. Sweden was not at that time ahead of the Anglo-Saxon countries in regard to political influence of the workers but, on the contrary, was rather lagging in this respect. General suffrage was not won until the aftermath of World War I. Nor did Wicksell write under conditions of what was then considered extraordinarily high unemployment. When he bluntly criticized Say's law and took his whole departure from that criticism, he did not focus his further arguments on unemployment.

This demonstrates that science occasionally does make room for important contributions independent of the conditions in the surrounding society, though it does not happen very often. But for a long time the Wicksellian—pre-Keynesian—new theoretical approach lived its isolated life among some economists in Sweden, without having any influence on policy. In Sweden, too, it was the Depression, and the democratization of the political system that had meanwhile taken place, that made the unorthodox Wicksellian theory relevant—mainly among the younger in our profession, while our older colleagues conservatively kept to the beaten track. But the existence of Wicksell's theory made it possible for us in Sweden to be a little ahead of our Anglo-Saxon colleagues in presenting the new theory and working out guidelines for policy.

3. American Institutionalism

I should now like to discuss a cycle in the development of economics, proceeding on what I consider a deeper level than the one where the so-called Keynesian revolution moved. When my wife, Alva Myrdal, and I first came to America at the very end of the Twenties for a year as Rockefeller Fellows, the "wind of the future" was institutional economics. This was then the *New Economics,* as I remember a collection of essays was called. The approach was conceived to be in a line with three great American economists: Veblen, Commons, and Mitchell, of whom the latter two were still living and active. (As I then observed, this was a too narrow and provincial account of the new school's ancestry. Generally speaking, no country can be so provincial as a big country.)

In this movement Columbia, under Mitchell, played the same role that Harvard, with Alvin Hansen at the head, played in the later Keynesian revolution. At that time I was utterly critical of this new orientation of economics. I was in the "theoretical" stage of my own personal development as an economist. I even had something to do with the initiation of the Econometric Society, which was planned as a defense organization against the advancing institutionalists.

My writings up till then had been in the great neoclassical tradition of economics, which I had tried to develop further by introducing the anticipations into the Walras model.[2] It is true that I had also settled scores with the "welfare" theory and other similar metaphysical ingredients in the established structure of economic theory, such as the "utility" concept and all its escapist synonyms.

This type of immanent criticism aroused little interest among the institutionalists, who seemed to be even more unaware of the *Political Element in the Development of*

Economic Theory, to quote the title of a book of mine published at that time.[3] (I recall a long conversation I had with Mitchell in the fall of 1929. He had devoted much study to the history of economics and was giving a course on that at Columbia. I felt almost desperate when I failed even to get him to see my point.)

But the courageous trend in the late Twenties toward an institutional approach had a brief existence in the United States. What I believe nipped it in the bud was the worldwide economic depression. Faced by this great calamity, we economists of the "theoretical" school, accustomed to reason in terms of simplified macro-models, felt we were on top of the situation, while the institutionalists were left in the muddle. It was at this stage that economists in the stream of the Keynesian revolution adjusted their theoretical models to the needs of the time, which thus gave victory much more broadly to our "theoretical" approach.

Even the additional difficulty of having to work with explicit value premises—tested for relevance, significance, feasibility, and logical consistency—which through my work on the value problem I had found to be a necessary logical requirement, turned out to be rather a simple matter, exactly because of the Depression. That depression was theoretically much simpler to handle than the present worldwide "stagflation," where high or even rising unemployment goes together with inflation rather than deflation (see next chapter).

Policy goals converged.[3a] In Sweden, where I was working in the early Thirties, the common interest was to stop the deflation and cause prices to rise again, making profitable business, more investments, and fuller employment possible. This could all be brought about through utilizing the currency devaluation forced upon us, plus large-scale public investments and an underbalanced budget. For rationalizing that type of policy by a consistent theory, we young economists in Sweden were prepared by Knut Wicksell's works about the cumulative processes away from *Monetary Equilibrium*,[4] which lived with us as a tradition.

This was the time when Erik Lindahl, Bertil Ohlin, and I turned to monetary problems and so lived in an era that Professor G. L. S. Shackle has named *The Years of High Theory*.[5] Mainly through circumstance—the currency depreciation in 1931 was forced upon us and was not part of policy, the terms of trade turned to Sweden's advantage, and exports moved up—but also to some extent due to economic policy, guided by our theory, Sweden, in spite of a large labor conflict in 1933, climbed rather rapidly out of the depths of the Depression. In an appendix to the budget of January 1933, I had given the theoretical justifications for an expansionary policy in terms you would now call Keynesian.[6]

I should add that this new policy line in Sweden at that time was interesting mainly from the point of view of the theory we expounded and which was accepted as a principle of government policy. The principle was not carried out vigorously enough—the actual expansionary fiscal policy put into effect, for instance, was much too moderate.

4. The Equality Issue

But I turned to other problems, where my theoretical equipment served me less well. The political climate in Sweden had changed rather radically, and I was personally in full sympathy with that development. In 1932 a Labor government was elected, and it has remained in power in that conservative country for forty years, through the vagaries of elections every second year and the calamities caused by World War II.

There was then in Sweden a strong quest for egalitarian social reforms. Alva Myrdal and I wrote a book on popula-

tion and family policy in 1934,[7] which resulted in the setting
up of Royal Population Commissions in all the Scandinavian
countries and in Britain. Particularly in Sweden, it opened
an era of social reform, systematically focused on the welfare of children and the family.

A main thesis underlying this new phase of my work was
that well-planned egalitarian reforms would be preventive,
prophylactic, and thus productive. The fact that forty years
of steadily speeded up social reform has not stopped economic growth and progress, as the older economists were
continually warning, but that in Sweden these forty years
have proved an outstanding success even in "economic"
terms, has now in hindsight given a pragmatic confirmation
that we were right, even though behind this development
were also other forces. Even if economic growth has tended
to stagnate in the last few years, this is definitely not due to
the social reform policy, but to the fact that the development toward "stagflation" has now even reached Sweden.

At the beginning of this era, although we did not have
slums in the American sense, over half of the families in
Swedish cities lived in two-room or even smaller apart-
ments. There were still groups in the nation so poor they
were undernourished;[8] the school system left masses of
people with only an insufficient elementary education;
health protection and medical care were not freely available for people in all income strata. Corresponding to these
deficiencies in the social and economic order, direct taxes
on income and wealth were then in Sweden even lower
than they are still today in the United States.

So I came to work on the equality issue, first in Sweden,
then from 1938 in the United States—my *American
Dilemma* was not a study of the Negroes but of the American society from the viewpoint of the most disadvantaged
group—and in the last couple of decades in the world, ever
more definitely focusing my research on the great majority
of poverty-stricken masses in the underdeveloped countries.

Traditional economic theory, more explicitly from John Stuart Mill on, had made a distinction between two types of problems: those of production (including exchange) and those of distribution. As I had already shown during my "theoretical" period, this distinction is illogical for the purposes for which it was used, as production and distribution are interrelated within the same macro-system (Chapter 8, Sections 5 and 6).

Moreover, from Mill onward, the distinction had been used by economists as a means to escape from the problems of distribution by concentrating on those of production, usually with only a general reservation in regard to distribution and then thinking about distribution as a simple matter of money incomes. This reflected a bias in economic theory which is still with us, not least in research on underdeveloped countries, implying the view that egalitarian reforms are necessarily costly in terms of economic growth, and very definitely not productive. This view has continually been argued on speculative grounds. Even in regard to developed countries, very little empirical evidence has been provided, even for such simple "economic" interrelationships as the effect of a change in income distribution on savings, labor output, and efficiency.

The question of equality had consistently been kept in the background. This, in turn, is related to the fact that as soon as distribution is brought into focus, the type of general theory in "economic" terms, which had served us so well when dealing with problems of balance and growth during the Great Depression, becomes insufficient. All the "non-economic" factors—political, social, and economic structure, institutions and attitudes, indeed all interpersonal relations—have to be included in the analysis.

5. Out of Step Again

Through the types of problems I came to deal with, I became an institutional economist, after having been in my youth one of the most ardent "theoretical" economists. This change of interest was, as I pointed out, in its turn dependent on the political development in my home country, where again, as earlier in relation to the Keynesian revolution, we happened to be in the van, particularly compared with the United States.

And again I was out of step with the development of economics as it evolved in the United States and elsewhere in the developed countries—and largely also in the underdeveloped and even the Communist countries—after the brief spurt of institutionalism in the Twenties. Now the highest prestige was given over to ever more esoteric theoretical constructs in terms of the "economic" factors, preserving even the empty "welfare theory." Without any intention on my part, I happened to remain a rebel, following a different, and indeed a contrary, cycle to the common one.

The concept of the development of economics as following a cyclical movement implies, of course, that anybody out of step with the main trend can be looked upon as either a backward person who has not succeeded in catching on, or as a person ahead of his time, pointing the way the trend will have to move. It will probably come as no surprise to anybody when I state that I strongly believe in the second. More precisely, I believe we are going to see a rapid development of economic science in the institutional direction, and that much that is now hailed as most sophisticated theory will in hindsight be seen to have been a temporary aberration into superficiality and irrelevance.

Indeed, I believe that the next ten or fifteen years will see a radical redirection of our research efforts toward institutional economics. A basic cause is the rise to political importance of the equality issue in the United States as in the world at large. This issue cannot be dealt with in narrowly conceived "economic" terms. On a logical level my criticism against establishment economics is that while pretending strict, precise, and rigorous reasoning, there is often systematic carelessness about assumptions and concepts implied, which too often are neither logically consistent nor adequate to reality.

6. In Underdeveloped Countries

In regard to the study of the development problems of underdeveloped countries, which is continually taking an ever larger share of our research resources, I believe that we have mishandled these problems. (I shall argue this more closely in Chapters 5 and 6 and shall also touch upon these problems in several other chapters in this book.) In particular, we have kept away from interesting ourselves in the need in underdeveloped countries for radical egalitarian reforms, which from my studies I have found necessary for rapid and steady development by raising productivity.

We are now in a period of transition. I am hopeful about the future of our work in this field. As I used to say, facts kick, even if belatedly when observed through the glasses of inadequate categories, in this case taken over from our analysis of the play of the "economic" factors in the developed countries. A new approach will be institutional, focusing also on the equality issue and taking into due account social and economic stratification, the political forces anchored in these institutions and in peoples' attitudes, and the productivity consequences of consumption when levels of living are extremely low.

7. In Developed Countries

Equally, in regard to the analysis of the economic development of developed countries, I believe we are reaching the end of an era of economic research, and I noticed signs of the approaching catharsis in some of the papers and discussions at the meeting of the American Economic Association, where I made these remarks. In our ever more complex societies—characterized by the rise of importance of very large corporations, many of them multinational, their tendency to become conglomerates, the growth and strengthening of organizations, not only in the labor market, administered prices, and so on—the inherited categories of our science in terms of markets and aggregates are increasingly inadequate to the reality we are studying.

Definitely, the equality issue will rise to supreme political importance. That this is true in regard to the relations between poor and rich countries, the general public is beginning to become aware. But even in regard to the national economy of individual developed countries the importance of the equality issue is rising. The huge problems of the slums in the United States cannot be foreseen to disappear simply by "economic growth." That they create a demand for radical policy interventions is now becoming generally understood among competent observers, as is also that a failure to solve them can endanger social peace and the continuation of an orderly democratic society.

But even a society at the other extreme like Sweden, where the inequalities from the outset were less accentuated and where for decades the reforms toward the democratic welfare state have accelerated, we find the equality issue rising to ever greater urgency. Technological and institutional developments tend to cause new inequalities and to accentuate old ones. And it is as if everything previously accomplished by social reform has only whetted the appetite for more. Further reform stands as socially and politically necessary.

The problem of equality concerns all social relationships in the broadest sense. That one set of these relationships is to economic productivity is, at the same time, very clear. An important aspect of the poverty problem in the United States is thus that a large part of the labor force growing up in the slums becomes an "underclass" that is not "in demand," because it is not up to the standards of modern society. We might note in passing how the existence of so-called "structural unemployment," about which social workers and other researchers nearer the ground of reality were talking, was denied, or in any case neglected, by most American economists, at least until a few years ago.

I feel that economic science is up against a serious crisis, in my view very much more revolutionary in regard to our research approaches than ever was the Keynesian revolution of more than three decades ago, which, as far as fundamental approach is concerned, merely vindicated and slightly altered our old "theoretical" approach. As always, under the pressure of what is becoming politically important in the society in which we live, we will respond by redirecting our research approaches.

8. The Future of Economics

I am well aware that I am often considered almost not a part of the profession of establishment economists, though sometimes given credit for what I did during the first decade of my working life. I am even referred to as a sociologist. And by that, economists usually do not mean anything flattering. Another, in some respects, like-minded rebel, Galbraith, who in addition writes a beautiful and forcible English, is often handled even more rudely by sometimes being classified by his colleagues as a journalist. But we insist on remaining economists.

Let me end by making a personal declaration as to why I look upon this coming redirection of research as a proper task for economists. Economics has for two centuries been the "political" science, in the proper sense of this word. We have all been planners, even those of us whose conclusions were for non-interference. However deep down in detail and into particular micro-problems we go, we have never been afraid of taking the macro-view or of formulating policy proposals for a country or even the whole world.

I can understand that colleagues in the other social sciences may feel that we economists have inherited a slightly paranoid approach to the world's problems. They can raise their warning fingers that we should not forget this or that. But they have never had the guts to present a development plan themselves, or even to challenge seriously our approaches, theories, and planning. Put any economist in the capital of an underdeveloped country and give him a few assistants, and he will in no time produce a plan. No political scientist, statistician, sociologist, psychologist, or what have you, would ever think of behaving in this way.

Paranoid or not, this type of approach is socially useful. For this is what is needed in every country. This is what politics is about. I have, therefore, no doubt at all that it is economists who will continue to play first fiddle in the study of underdeveloped countries. Even in regard to the increasingly complex problems of developed countries, which have to be dealt with from an institutional approach, we shall be pressed to take the lead and to offer coordinating solutions that can be translated into policies. We need therefore to preserve our courage to take the broader view but, at the same time, to become better informed about the complicated pattern of social relationships, which cannot be confined to the sphere of our abstract "economic" factors.

Throughout my life I have been aware of, and in principle

been sympathetic to, the strivings toward interdisciplinary research. Very little has come out of these attempts, as we are all aware. On the whole, what we have witnessed has been an ever more effective gap between the various social sciences and sometimes between subdisciplines within them.

My feeling is that what we need in the social sciences— besides ever more specialized research in all our different fields and, at the same time, whatever usefulness we can produce by interdisciplinary encounters—is transdisciplinary research. By this I mean that at least a few should widen their scope and master facts and factual relationships outside their own field as it is traditionally delimited. And it must be done without lowering standards of expertise.

The reorientation of economics in the institutional direction clearly implies transdisciplinary research in this sense. And I hold, moreover, that the slightly paranoid tendency inherited by us economists to take the macro-view and not to shun planning for a whole country and the world makes this more natural to us than to our colleagues in the other disciplines we would then be invading.

More generally, I believe that the borderlines between disciplines should be transgressed. Research should be focused on areas of specific problems, not confined to the separate disciplines as they have become established for the purposes of teaching and specialization in research. In time, this orientation toward problem areas, which is already on its way, will imply a rather radical reorganization of our universities.

Chapter 2

"STAGFLATION"[1]

LET ME ADD a comment on the aftermath in the postwar period of the so-called Keynesian revolution in the Thirties, which I dealt with in the beginning of the first chapter. In its time, it implied a forceful strengthening of the "theoretical" approach in economics and the virtual crushing of the then advancing institutional school in the United States. The explanation I gave for this was the simple character of the Great Depression. Interests and goals, as I pointed out, converged.

1. Keynesianism as Establishment Economics

The Keynesian approach, which had gradually become establishment economics, was certainly heavily biased toward seeing the normal tendency of every economy to fall into a depression, characterized by deflation and unemployment. Keynes's own theory had been anything but "general," as the title of his book implies. In that particular respect, Wicksell's earlier theory was theoretically superior. It implied the notion of "monetary equilibrium," away from which there could be a cumulative process directed either toward inflation or deflation. This more general model we

in the Swedish school of younger economists had inherited,
though, of course, in the first years of the Thirties we too
had focused our analysis more specifically on the means of
overcoming a deflationary development which stood out as
the practical problem.

Against this background it is understandable that during
the war economists had rather commonly expected a new
depression of the old type once the war was over. We then
also drew an analogy to what happened after World War I.
For a time, I shared in that expectancy and even argued
this view in a small book appearing in early 1944, *Warning
for Peace Optimism.*[2] Having confessed my initial mistake,
I may be permitted to add that less than a year later I
expressed the contrary view that we had to look forward
instead to a continuing inflation after the war (in an interview and speaking as chairman of the Swedish Postwar
Planning Commission).

I mention these things as a partial explanation of why,
on the whole, even after the war, economists did not, for a
long time, recognize the general tendency to inflation in
all countries as the main problem. From the economic profession came little or no critique against the common tendency of government spokesmen—for instance, at the
London, Geneva, and Havana ITO Conferences (1947–
1948)—continually to concentrate on the need to prepare
to fight deflation and depression, while almost everywhere
inflation had already become the problem. In fact, economists themselves played important roles as members of government delegations at all these conferences and in preparing for them in the various countries.

By their non-general Keynesian approach, which, as I
pointed out at the time, had implied an adjustment to the
experiences and dominant policy inclinations during the
Depression, economists were now generally unprepared to
warn against inflation and even to analyze it intensively

when it occurred. Memories of the Great Depression were still alive. Also, for decades, there had been little experience in "orderly" countries of rapid inflation in peacetime.

But at the same time, this slowness to recognize what had become and was to remain the main postwar problem, namely inflation, was again in the nature of an adjustment to the then dominant political forces in the various countries.

2. The Legacy of the War Years

During the war, as during all previous wars, the printing press and forced savings had to a large extent been relied upon to finance the tremendously increased public expenditures. Winning the war—or managing to stay out of it, as Sweden succeeded in doing—was the all-consuming concern.

And during the war people got accustomed to public expenditures of a much greater magnitude without seeing to it that they were paid for by keeping down private consumption by means of sufficiently increased taxation. In the United States the war and the way of financing it did succeed finally where the New Deal had failed in overcoming the depression and unemployment—as we see it now, because its policy was not Keynesian, or not enough so.

Indeed, the war had changed attitudes toward public expenditure in a fundamental way. Everyone who lived through those years can testify to that psychological change. I believe that this change in attitudes was of paramount importance for what was going to happen. After the war there was felt in all countries a need for huge expenditures of an investment type: in Europe, for reconstruction purposes; in all countries, high armament expenditures, felt to be necessary in the political climate of the cold war; in

most countries, though differently, for a rapid expansion of
public services that required high initial costs, such as
roads, hospitals, and schools.

Taxes had been rising after as well as during the war,
though not enough to have the nations pay fully for the
increased expenditures through a sufficient check on the
rise in private consumption. This pattern of fiscal policy
was retained as a legacy from the war. I do believe that, in
a fundamental sense, this failure in fiscal policy was the
basic cause of the continuing inflationary development.

The governments, and likewise the economists who did
not insist on fiscal balance, then responded to the powerful
political forces among the constituencies of voters everywhere, who wanted rising expenditures in the various fields
but at the same time desired rising private consumption and,
if not lower taxes, taxes not raised sufficiently to maintain
monetary equilibrium. To have people pay instead by
forced saving (implied in allowing prices to rise) in many
ways also eased the situation for the ministers of finance
by automatically pressing higher progressive rates of income taxation downward in the income strata. The steady
stream of American dollars, in the beginning made possible
by a huge American exchange surplus and later on by a
similarly huge deficit, replenished the reserves of the central banks, permitting and even spurring monetary expansion.

Rates of interest were initially kept at a low level, as they
had been during the Depression, motivated by the Keynesian approach. Sometime during the Fifties, that policy
line was abandoned, and "monetary policy" placed on a par
with fiscal policy. Interest rates were permitted to go up.
But, since prices were continually rising, the "real" interest
rates were still very low and occasionally even negative.
As long as inflation was permitted to go on, it was politically impossible to raise the real interest rates, as this would

have created gross inequalities and even chaos in the credit market, where so many obligations were running with fixed nominal interests. The "monetary policy" in many countries had therefore from time to time to be transformed into credit controls and restrictions, a development which led to a sort of planning of the worst type: having to be carried out by the banking bureaucracy, usually without clear directives. As getting a loan implied a gift, "connections" in the widest sense of the word became important, ordinarily favoring the upper income strata.

These are huge generalizations, with many individual deviations, and they best fit the Anglo-Saxon countries, France, and the Scandinavian countries and only later the defeated Western countries, Germany and Italy, after they had reached a measure of economic stability.

3. Effects of Inflation

Only gradually was ongoing inflation experienced as a problem, and few economists made an early move to analyze that problem in any depth. Some of them even invented reasons why a measure of inflation was needed to speed up economic growth and stabilize economic development. Practically nobody tried seriously to spell out the thesis (from even pre-Keynesian economics) that inflation has arbitrary, unintended, and therefore undesirable effects on resource allocation and the distribution of incomes and wealth.

As inflation gathered momentum, a number of additional undesirable effects, not sufficiently noted in classical economic literature, became increasingly important. Rising prices, plus the individual's uncertainties about the size of the rises to be expected, rob people of a yardstick for measuring their demands and supplies, their consumption, savings, and investments. They create deep-seated unrest in all relationships, from those between citizens and government to those between husband and wife.

Relations to the foreign exchange front were seen as crucial, but it was not made clear that the great insecurity in regard to balance of payments that became the rule for almost all countries had its roots in the common pattern of lack of internal monetary stability.

The long-time attitude of relative indulgence on the part of economists toward the ongoing inflation was, of course, in the beginning a legacy from the Keynesian approach, which paid one-sided attention to the dangers of deflation. But when the desirability of a stable currency even later did not tempt economists to intensive study, a main cause of this was that such a goal seemed increasingly unattainable. Usually they have been satisfied to focus their attention on the need not to fall out of step with what was happening in other countries and so not to endanger their foreign exchange balance. But another cause has been that under modern conditions such study would have meant they had to come to grips with a wide variety of institutional factors, which they have not been well trained to deal with.

4. Why Inflation Tends to Accelerate

Wicksell's early theory of the cumulative process away from equilibrium implied laying stress on the anticipations as a main driving force, particularly in regard to prices of real capital goods but also of other goods and services. In this respect again, the early Swedish school had a better grip on the problem than Keynes and most of his followers, who did not start out by giving an explicit role to anticipations in their models.

When we now look back at what has actually happened

in the postwar era, we have to recognize, besides anticipations, a large number of other factors that spur inflation.
They are all of an institutional character and are thus less
easily accounted for in simple theoretical models.

The gains to be gotten from owning goods and from going
into debt, and the corresponding losses of keeping savings
in cash or in banks during an inflation, are ideas only gradually grasped by the people at large. But as these effects
of inflation become increasingly understood, the change in
popular attitude will tend to accelerate an ongoing inflation.
Increasingly, people—not only the very rich but ordinary
middle-class people getting to own a mortgaged house and
some other durable goods—are thus developing an economic interest in further inflation.

Moreover, since wages and social security payments are
continually being adjusted to compensate for rising prices,
the people who feel themselves hurt by inflation are growing ever fewer.

The entire system of organizations in a society is in all
countries grossly biased, and this becomes increasingly
important as organizations are also becoming stronger.
People are becoming organized as income earners of various
sorts or as profit takers, while organizations defending the
general and common interest of all as consumers are weak
in all countries.

The interests of salary-earning employees and of profit-
earning employers are not always conflicting. While within
an ongoing inflationary development the former rationally
have to count on higher costs of living and to press for
higher wages, the latter can in the same way often count
on higher prices for their products or services. When inflation is worldwide, this also applies to export industries.
This is, of course, one of the forces behind the cost-push
effects in an inflationary process, but they are apt to operate with different and changing strength depending on the
institutional setup and the power relations.

It is easy to see that the great uncertainty about how prices will develop, and the irritation and unrest thereby created, tend to make people in all groups and organizations more eager to press their demands and, in particular, to crave compensation whenever other groups have succeeded in raising their incomes. Meanwhile the fear of inflation, that to some extent also prevails among the public, has a different force, depending upon, among other things, the various countries' different experiences in recent decades.

The income tax laws, to take still another example, ordinarily favor expenditures that would not be profitable, except for the rules about tax exemptions—for instance, for repairs to buildings which not only maintain but may increase their capital value—and particularly the rules permitting low incomes or negative incomes in some enterprises to be withdrawn from the earnings in others. Contrary to a commonly held opinion, occasionally even expressed by economists, that high taxes discourage risky investments, the truth is that even investments having only a slight chance of yielding a long-term return become profitable when taxes are high. And this effect, which would spur inflation even at stable prices, becomes stronger in an ongoing inflationary development, and then tends to accelerate that development.

These are only a few abstract illustrations of the general thesis that in modern society the tendency of inflation to become cumulative and to accelerate is rooted in a wide and complex institutional reality.

5. In Retrospect

I am afraid that we must regard the development in respect to international and national monetary balance in the postwar era as having been a complete failure.

Internationally, this has led to a situation in which everybody now agrees that the realignment of exchange rates and the widening of the band of flexibility reached in December 1971 by the agreement between the "Group of Ten" highly developed countries is nothing more than a temporary stopgap solution, and one that has already been broken by new sterling depreciations.

A more permanent arrangement must amount to a consensus between all the Western countries and Japan on a great number of things: not only on exchange rates and rules for their alteration, but also on an agreed code for responsible internal financial and economic policies, particularly in regard to the movement of interest rates. These are important for short-term capital movements and must be coordinated and synchronized. Some additional control over such capital movements must be agreed upon and also some way of funding the huge United States dollar debts to the central banks. And such an agreement can no longer, in my opinion, take the form simply of a permanent set of rules of the Bretton Woods type, but will have to consist of only some very general agreed-upon principles for the guidance of a continuous *ad hoc* process of reaching agreements on adjustments. This last point is generally missed in the very lively discussion among economists that is now going on. Meanwhile the danger of some degree of currency and trade war is not averted.

The basic problem concerns the internal policy of the various individual countries. In all of them inflation tends to accelerate because of the institutional factors I have exemplified under Section 4 above. As no country can permit unrestrained inflation, checks have then to be applied.

To check an ongoing inflation with a tendency to accelerate is a very different thing from preserving a stable currency. The result will most often be a high and sometimes rising level of unemployment, while prices are continuing to rise, though less rapidly than otherwise. This is what has been called "stagflation," which is either an actual reality or a threat in all countries. Quite ordinarily, the development will in time tend to take on the character of the kind of "stop-go-stop" that has characterized the British economy in particular for a long time now.

6. "Stagflation"

From the point of view of economic theory, the course toward "stagflation," caused by the tendency of inflation to accelerate and the political necessity not to let it run wild, is characterized by a conflict between goals: mainly stability of the purchasing power of the currency, foreign exchange balance, and full employment. The first thing to observe is that this situation is fundamentally different from that during the Great Depression, when there was a convergence of these goals. And this was the basis for realism when applying the simple Keynesian theoretical approach. What is now required is a very much more complicated theory that also, as I pointed out, has to work with a great number of institutional factors, all of which could be safely disregarded forty years ago.

Therefore, we cannot be satisfied today with the simple type of theory we could then agree upon and lay as a basis for rather straightforward policy directives. This is my main assertion, and I believe it to be fully substantiated. To go further and try critically to characterize in general terms the huge literature in this field would be a Herculean task, but I shall nevertheless make a few points. As I have recently been devoting myself to quite different problems, I have to base my observations on my routine cursory study of journals and quite a few new books.

In accommodating to the obvious conflict between main goals, the general tendency has been to give little importance to the first goal but rather to accept as normal and natural that prices should go up, though not too rapidly. The discussion of international liquidity, for instance, leading to the creation of the Special Drawing Rights, has generally assumed, without much query, that exchange reserves should be augmented to meet the needs raised by the growth in international trade, which is continually subject to inflation due to rising prices.

Very few economists have felt it worthwhile to investigate the various effects, exemplified under Section 3 above, of an ongoing inflation. And still fewer have devoted intensive research to the corresponding policy problem of how, without unduly increasing unemployment, a national economy could restore, and thereafter maintain, monetary equilibrium with a stable value of the currency. This represents a resignation to the social and political forces that are driving inflation forward.

As I also illustrated under Section 4 above, these forces are rooted in a set of complex institutional factors, besides a common desire in all our countries to have public expenditure without paying for it fully by holding down private consumption. In studying the process of inflation, economists in the post-Keynesian tradition have ordinarily relied upon overly simplified models, for instance relating unemployment directly to inflation and the rise in wages (the Philips curve). The crude quantity theory, sponsored by Milton Friedman, that has gained so many adherents particularly in the United States, quite obviously excludes consideration even of many "economic" factors which already, according to the simple Keynesian approach, were known to have importance, and can therefore not be correct. Correlations are not explanations, and besides they can be as spurious as the high correlation during a long period in Finland between foxes killed and divorces.

Much more research needs to be directed toward analyzing in depth the causal mechanism of driving forces in the inflationary process. Such an analysis of an inflationary

movement must come to concern itself much more with
the institutional factors exemplified above, and it will then
shift character. I see everywhere in recent literature scattered efforts to do this, though ordinarily inhibited and
frustrated by the common adherence to simplified model
thinking. It is in this direction, however, that we have to
proceed further and more systematically. Relative success
in any income policy will depend largely upon mastering
institutional factors that have had little place either in the
Keynesian or the post-Keynesian approaches.

As these institutional factors tend to give an inflationary
process its cumulative and accelerating character, it is to
be expected that the evil tendency to "stagflation" will
become ever more common, checked only for short intervals
by attempts to interfere by means of "income policies,"
which are difficult to apply effectively and the result of
which usually is a subsequent jump upward in both wages
and prices. The deeper reasons to feel skeptical of the success of such policies in the long run are, of course, as I said
before, that more and more people in all nations are becoming aware that they profit from inflation, while those
who suffer from it are on the decrease.

And "monetary policies," which could well be what the
medical profession calls "minor curatives" when maintaining
an already reached monetary balance, are rather ineffective
in an ongoing inflationary process and are then sometimes even counter-productive. Incidentally, while in general statements few economists avoid placing "monetary
policies" on a par with fiscal policies, which has become a
sort of ritual, there is very little intensive research being
done on how interest rates and other credit policies actually
influence savings, enterprise, and investment in various
fields.

Those who are really hurt, however, by an inflationary
process which is not stopped but only held in check for a

longer or shorter period are the unemployed and, indirectly, all others who have to pay for their support. I do not find it improbable that, in a development toward continuing or even intensified "stagflation," matters may become so unsatisfactory that people generally can be persuaded to want to stop inflation altogether. Such a change in the political climate would then give economists the opportunity to stress again the primary goal for monetary policy of preserving an unchanged value of the currency and to direct research on the policy means by which that result could be attained. They would have to include as a main feature the restoration of fiscal balance by keeping public expenditure within the limits of the restriction of private consumption, or to state it the other way round, to limit private consumption by taxation enough to pay for the expenditures.

7. Conclusions

This is, however, in the realm of speculation. What I have wanted to demonstrate more specifically by this brief note is, first, that the Keynesian approach, once it had become establishment economics, initially and for a considerable time caused delay in adjusting theory to the new reality. To be "behind its time" in this sense is the regular methodological weakness of establishment economics.

Secondly, the foregoing pages have also pointed to how narrowly the political climate has constantly limited the horizon of economists.

Thirdly, and most important, I have pointed to one more field, in which development necessitates a more institutional approach, as well as the increasing weight of the equality issues stressed in the last chapter. And I would add that inflation and still more "stagflation" are themselves apt to raise such issues, since, in many ways, not only in regard to the unemployed, this type of monetary development will create and accentuate inequalities.

A new approach is needed to again give weight to the primary goal of monetary equilibrium and a stable value of the currency. In regard to international relations, this more demanding goal for national economic policy would remove the fear of runaway price inflation and an eventual forced devaluation. On the contrary, a country following such a policy in the present world would have to foresee the need to revaluate its currency, which usually meets less resistance abroad and creates less of a problem. Such a redirection of policy would imply, and need, a change of economic theory equally radical as when Wicksell two generations ago, and Keynes and others one generation ago, broke with Say's law and its implied policy intention not to interfere in the working of the market forces.

There are many facts in my own country, Sweden—the wider elbow room we ought to feel that we have, because of the higher and relatively more equal levels of income and living, the uniquely perfect organization of the labor market that has brought working days lost by labor conflicts to an international minimum, and, as I should like to believe, the relatively higher rationality in political attitudes in all economic and social strata—that would make it more possible there for economists to open new perspectives in research, as sometimes they have done in this and other fields in past time.

But now, as forty years ago, in order to become instrumental in causing policy change, they would need a minister of finance, a government, a parliament, and behind them a people that were prepared to back such a more exacting policy. As I see it, this does not exonerate the economists from their responsibility. They can have an influence on the political climate, as I and others have had in bygone times, for instance on social policy in the Thirties.

Economists have a duty to be ahead of their time and not only to adjust—with a nagging and less deep-boring criticism—to the ongoing development. In this case, this would mean that they should decline to accept as necessary the ongoing inflation, which intermittently leads to a rise in unemployment and relative economic stagnation while inflation goes on.

The duty to stand up against the trend of our time by redirecting research is implied in the old, and in my view correct, name for our discipline: political economy. In this particular case, this would imply among other things a stress on the requirement that if a nation wants public services and, indeed, a rapid increase and improvement in them, it be prepared to scale down its demand for private consumption, particularly of a lot of industrial products that are less necessary in comparison with the public consumption demand. That such a redirection of demand goes together with all serious efforts to improve our environment shall be discussed in Chapter 11. For many reasons that shall be touched on in Chapter 10, the rise in gross national product, as now very inadequately calculated, should then not be permitted to retain its position as the main development goal.

There is at present great unanimity that the "quality of life" shall be raised, but no group and few individuals are prepared to abstain, in order to reach that goal, from wanting to raise their consumption. They are all involved in a fierce competition and a striving for compensation that makes the space for the quality of life ever narrower. These same attitudes of people in all social classes are driving forces behind inflation, though at the same time all complain about the rising prices (Chapter 11, Sections 11 and 12). Neither a higher "quality of life" nor a stable value of the currency can be achieved without a rather radical change of people's attitudes.

The rationality of a broad settlement among all groups

in a nation where, under recognition of the demand for greater equality, the cravings for higher incomes are tempered, is obvious. The constant experience that in an ongoing inflation rises in income to be extracted from un-hampered competition become fictitious, should help toward accomplishing this broad settlement.

Chapter 3

THE PLACE OF VALUES
IN SOCIAL POLICY[1]

1. Valuations

LET ME START this chapter on the valuation basis of social policy by a negative assertion in contradiction of the title given me for the paper upon which the chapter is based. To stress the subjectivity of the valuation process, I deliberately use the word "valuations" and avoid the term "values"—which is so popular in all social sciences, not only in sociology and anthropology—except in the combination "value premises," used when certain valuations have been defined and made explicit for use in research.[2]

The use of the term "values" invites confusion between valuations in a subjective sense, the object of these valuations, and indeed often the whole social setting of valuations. The term "values" also often contains a hidden value premise, namely that a "value" that is believed to exist is *eo ipso* valuable in some objective sense; this usually implies a bias of the *laissez-faire* variety.

The term "values," finally, carries the association of something solid, homogeneous, and fairly stable, while in reality valuations are regularly contradictory, even in the mind of a single individual, and also unstable, particularly in modern society. Human behavior is typically the result of compromises between valuations on different levels of generality.

If this view was accepted, we would perhaps expect great changes in the valuations underlying social policy as, in the course of time, the welfare state develops in a country. In particular, the valuations in each country could be expected always to show lasting divergencies between not only individuals but also different social groups and political parties. In any case, we would take for granted that there would be great discrepancies between different civilizations and big changes over long periods of time.

2. Over the Ages

Let me comment on the last assumption first. At least in regard to valuations on the higher and more general level, I have come to doubt it. I have been fascinated to discover that over the ages the great world religions, including, on a purified doctrinal level, even Hinduism, and the grand philosophies attached to these religions have all been egalitarian in principle and thus endorsed the fundamental valuation basic even to modern social policy.[3]

Why and how did it happen, that this shining, idealistic vision of the dignity of the individual human being, of his basic right to equality of opportunity and also his right to assistance when in need, came to be developed so early and everywhere? And how did it survive so many centuries of blatant inequality and oppression? I do not know the answer to these questions. I should like to see sociologically oriented historians of ideas devote study to the problem of causation.

When the closely interrelated[4] secular philosophies of natural law and utilitarianism established themselves throughout the Western world in the seventeenth and eigh-

teenth centuries, they followed the same line. This became
the more important as all the social sciences and, in particular, economics branched off from these Enlightenment
philosophies. They came to include and, in fact, elaborated
the doctrine of equality and actually afforded theoretical
"proofs" of it.

The proofs do not stand scrutiny. Indeed, what distin-
guishes valuations from beliefs and theories about reality is
that they cannot be proved or disproved, but merely exist as
social facts. This has never been honestly recognized, at least
not by the economists who still labor with a value theory
and a welfare theory, which at root are always metaphysical
in the sense of the Enlightenment philosophies.

As facts, however, these egalitarian valuations should be
expected to have had their importance for social policy. All
social speculation in the Western world from that time on
has had ultra-radical policy premises at its very roots. But
the whole development of economic theory from the classics until today must largely be explained as determined
by the need felt to isolate and render innocuous these
radical policy premises at the basis of economic theory.[5] In
England the so-called "radical school" from Bentham on
was radical in all fields except the economic one. This was,
of course, an adjustment to the political power situation in
England in that period and the opportunistically biased
way of thinking in a society so dominated.

When the conditions for an egalitarian social policy were
gradually created, this was the effect of a changed political
power situation as the masses of the people were gradually
granted suffrage, and of the increased strength of the organizations in the labor market. A role was also played by
the long series of intensive social surveys, a field of realistic
empirical research in which England was pioneering just
as much as in economic theory. The works of Marx and
Engels and also various other writings and activities in the

"Marxian" tradition were important, as was "the new liberalism" inaugurated by John Stuart Mill much more than a hundred years ago.

All these impulses were in their different ways in line with the doctrine of equality remaining at the basis of all social and, in particular, economic speculation right from the Enlightenment period.

3. "Created Harmony"

In modern times, when social policy has been expanding rapidly and has made all the developed countries into welfare states, there is quite clearly in the several countries a rather great convergence of valuations basic to this development. My experience of research, and also intermittently of politics, leads me, in particular, to see in each of these countries a remarkable degree of accordance and even conformity in the development of valuations underlying social policy, arising as a result of political development itself—what I have called "created harmony," in contra-distinction to the liberalistic assumption of a pre-existing harmony of interest that was basic to the thinking of natural law and utilitarianism.[6]

In Sweden, for instance, where the Labor Party has been in power for forty years, huge social reforms have been instituted at a steady and, in fact, accelerating pace. It is true that until recently there was regularly considerable resistance to the reforms from the political parties to the right. But equally regularly, once a reform legislation had been decided and enacted, the criticism died down, and a sort of *ex post* national consensus became established.

This was the case, for instance, in regard to the old-age pension system, which is now gradually assuring every aging Swede not only a basic pension but, up to a rather high income level, an annual income in real terms amounting to two-thirds of his average income during his fifteen best years. In spite of the fact that the government bill was carried by a majority of only one vote in Parliament, this huge reform, once it was on the statute book, was no longer questioned by any party.

Even more than that, political parties to the right are now increasingly active in themselves proposing improvements of the old-age pension system, for instance by wanting to lower the pensionable age. Sweden has become what a political science colleague of mine has called "the service state." The meaning of this term is that all political parties are now competing with each other in proposing ever more social reforms.

It has fallen to the Labor Party, as traditionally carrying government responsibility, to try to educate the electorate to accept the fact that they cannot increase public consumption, particularly in the heavily capital-intensive services, and at the same time increase their private consumption at the same rate without lapsing into inflation.

The ordinary man in all our countries is inclined to demand more and better public services of the type mentioned and at the same time higher retained income for his private consumption. The fact that the Labor Party in Sweden has still had only partial success in getting the people to understand and accept that they have to choose and cannot get a great deal for nothing is the ultimate cause of rising prices, and this, in turn, constantly sets the limit for the progress of further social reforms.

The election in 1970, fought by political parties who were all generous in proposing further egalitarian reforms, created the political climate for an immediate reform activity of such scope that no responsible government could undertake it. This situation will certainly endanger the Labor Party's hold over the electorate at a future election. People may feel that it is no longer necessary to vote the Labor ticket in order to ensure the continuation of the reform policies which up till now have been the party's main appeal. But the Labor Party can derive consolation from the fact that a change of government, which would put it in opposition, will not stop the reforms. The other parties are equally, and in fact more, overcommitted.

Sweden, of course, is an extreme case. But I see much the same socio-political mechanism at work in other developed countries. The Republican Party, when it came to power in the United States under Eisenhower, did not attempt to reverse the reforms carried out by the preceding Democratic regimes' New Deal and Fair Deal, although in various respects these programs had been fought by the majority of Republicans in Congress, joining together with the non-liberal Democrats from the South. Instead, the Republican Administration continued that same policy in a cautious way.

The present Nixon Administration certainly did not indulge in President Johnson's exuberant rhetoric about the "Unconditional War on Poverty" and the creation of the "Great Society." But at first it actually liquidated little of what had been inaugurated during the Johnson regime. And in spite of the heavy costs of the Vietnam war and the inflation caused by the unwillingness of the Americans to pay for that war and for the moon flights and other unproductive "conspicuous public consumptions," the Republican government attempted to create a new image of itself by proposing to take radical measures against poverty. Satisfying the peculiar American quest for stilted eloquence, President Nixon competed by promising a "Second American Revolution."

As Nixon now starts out on his second term as president, he places himself more determinedly than ever as leader of political reaction even in internal problems. The connection with United States foreign policy, and particularly with the course of the gruesome Vietnam war, shall be discussed in Chapter 14. I do not believe, however, that this reaction will be lasting. The American nation will again find its way to the imperatively necessary social reforms (Chapter 14, Section 13).

I realize that in Britain the present Conservative government shows signs of reversing the further development of the welfare state. Among many other things, the low rate of Britain's increase in productivity and her high unemployment coincident with inflation can explain such a retreat. Nevertheless, I doubt that this reversal will go far. I do not believe it can be anything more than, at most, a temporary halt.

In Germany, the Brandt government is firmly committed to overcoming the relative backwardness of that country's welfare position up till now. Their greatest difficulty is also the inflationary trend, which the government must seek to overcome in order to take radical steps toward perfecting the welfare state. But the movement will go on.

To summarize, as far as the developed countries are concerned, I see the welfare state as more than an achieved situation. Dynamically, it has become an almost immutable trend. Its further development can be slowed down for a time and occasionally even reversed. But after such a stop it can be expected to continue its course. By doing so, whatever struggles there are about specific items of reform, one of the results of the development is a broad national valuation consensus, though in specific cases such a consensus is first arrived at when a reform is already instituted.

4. Productivity of Social Reform

Economists in the classical and neo-classical line traditionally came to assume a conflict between economic growth and egalitarian reforms. They took it for granted that a price had to be paid for the reforms in terms of a lower productivity of the national economy.

As I pointed out in Chapter 1, Section 4, they did so on speculative grounds. In fact, until now, very little empirical research has been devoted to proving this abstract assumption. Even for developed countries we still lack detailed empirical studies of even such elementary things as how the savings ratio, labor input, and labor efficiency react to different degrees of equality in the distribution of income and wealth.

Meanwhile, large-scale egalitarian reform policies have been set in motion in all developed countries, and this reform activity has on the whole been escalating ever since World War I. The important thing to note is that not only the economists and all conservatives, who generally offered resistance at least initially, but even the radical propagators of these reforms generally accepted the traditional common assumption that a somewhat lower rate of economic progress was a price that had to be paid for the egalitarian reforms.

The reforms were regularly argued simply in terms of achieving greater social justice. The importance of this valuation was gradually becoming so widely accepted that political conditions were created for the reforms to pass through the parliaments. These reforms were coming to be considered worth their price.

Only in countries that are the most advanced as welfare states, and only in very recent times, has the idea emerged that welfare reforms, instead of being costly for a society, were actually laying a basis for a more steady and rapid economic growth. Historically, this idea has been an afterthought.

To attempt empirical study of the effects on economic growth of social reforms has been of interest mostly to a few sociologists, social workers, and statisticians, while economists have tended to stick to their speculative theory about the antagonism between welfare and progress— though stressing it less, for many earlier predictions have not come true. This type of empirical study has nowhere reached deeply into the problems. It is of great importance that such studies be carried out.

Meanwhile, there is broad historical evidence for the view that, on the whole, social reforms have been an investment in economic progress rather than a drag on it from a national point of view. As the welfare state develops, political and popular discussion, influenced by earlier reforms not having had the ruinous effects often predicted, are actually, though without much sophistication or even explicitness, now coming to assume this new and different theory. This change in thinking about the advancing reform activity then provides a spur to the continuation and acceleration of social reforms, or rather releases the reform activity from inhibitions.

A very important element in the development of social reforms and the thinking about them was when, particularly in Sweden from the Thirties onward, the reforms became increasingly directed toward the welfare of the family and children. Such reforms could be advocated in terms of being "preventive" or "prophylactic," i.e., saving the individual and society from future costs and/or increasing future productivity.[7]

Such arguments could most easily be applied to reforms in the fields of housing, nutrition, and more broadly, health and education. The rapid increase in reforms to protect the handicapped and help them become better adjusted to industrial society belongs to the same category, as do the reforms in the treatment of young offenders in order to prevent them from relapsing.

Income redistributional reforms protecting the level of living of families with children and, in particular, under-privileged families, can also be advocated as being in this sense productive. Indeed, even old-age pensions and other policies to provide for the aging can be defended from the point of view of family welfare, as in modern urbanized society individual families are no longer able to care for them without great deprivation.

But the argument applies with particular force when the reforms imply contributions in kind and not in cash, as occurs often in health and education and in many other fields of modern welfare policy. What is actually happening in the most advanced welfare states is a stress on the "socialization of consumption" as distinct from the old socialist policy-proposals for socialization of large-scale industry and high finance.

The result of Social Democratic rule in Sweden has been large-scale social reforms, but practically no nationalization of industry and commerce—though, of course, there have been increasing and strengthened controls protecting the public interest in industrial and commercial developments. Sweden stands now as the one country among the developed nations where business is almost entirely left in private hands, even more so than in the United States, with its absolutist faith in private enterprise. The exceptions are mainly public enterprises inherited from decades and centuries ago, long before the Social Democratic party came to power. These included in Sweden's case railways and generally what in the United States are called public utilities, though they are privately owned.

The above remarks should underline my request for empirical studies of the economic effects of egalitarian social reforms. They should be carried out in terms of cost/benefit analysis. In anticipation of such deeper studies we can, however, establish the fact that in Sweden the welfare state, which has been developing rapidly for almost forty years under a single-minded Labor government, has also been a remarkable economic success. Economically, the country has reached a level that is not far below and might be higher than that of the United States (see Chapter 10, Section 6, and Chapter 14, Section 8).

This development can, of course, not be credited entirely to the vigorous social reform activity. Other factors—the full employment policy, the free trade policy that has helped to keep industrial management alert and energetic, the perfected organization of the labor market that has kept workdays lost because of conflicts down to insignificant total figures—and many other conditions and developments, partly due to good luck, have been primary causes.

Nevertheless, this remarkable economic progress would imply a confirmation of the new theory that the body of social reforms has been productive or that in any case it has not hindered economic growth. When in recent years the Swedish economy has tended not to expand very fast, no competent person has put the blame on the social reforms. It is clear that the cause has rather been failures of the general economic policies that have brought Sweden also the frustration of "stagflation" dealt with in the last chapter.

It is true that with the progressive system of taxation the burden of paying for social reforms falls more heavily on people in the higher income brackets. This is part of the redistributional effect of the reforms. In fact, taxation even in the middle income strata has had to be raised. Particularly when, as often, it assumes heavy initial investment, public consumption cannot be increased without lowering the rate of increase of private consumption—otherwise there will be inflation, which means that it is paid for by forced saving.

These choices have to be made. If they are made in favor of continuing social reform activity, that does not necessarily and, I believe, not normally imply a lower rate of increase in a nation's economic growth, but quite likely the opposite.

5. *The Underdeveloped Countries*

The problems of the relationship between development and egalitarian reforms in underdeveloped countries will be dealt with in Chapters 5 and 6. After the war and the avalanche of decolonization, the ideals of modernization were adopted almost everywhere as a sort of state religion. A prominent role among these ideas was played by the egalitarian doctrine. There is a strong flavor of the Enlightenment philosophy coloring most public pronouncements in these countries concerning the goals for planned development.

In sharp contrast to these declarations for greater equality stands the fact that almost everywhere in the non-Communist underdeveloped countries actual development has moved toward increasing inequality. Even when egalitarian reforms have been legislated for in some of these countries, they have not been carried out, or they have been permitted to work in the interest of the not-so-poor.

Economists—both indigenous and Western ones—have commonly, at least until very recently, overlooked this paradox, or even rationalized it by holding that these extremely poor countries cannot afford to think in terms of social justice and to pay the price for egalitarian reforms which they assume would hamper economic growth. Even in this respect, the situation shows similarities to the late Enlightenment period in Europe, when the very radical policy premises for economic theory were put away and concealed, while the actual policies, and also the policy proposals of the economists, moved in the conservative direction.

Contrary to most of my economist colleagues, at least until very recent years, I hold to the view, founded on study, that a primary precondition for rapid and steady development in these countries is that the drift toward increasing inequality be stopped and turned into a movement toward greater equality. The reasons for believing that social reforms, if well planned and effectively implemented, are productive are even stronger in the poor and usually very inegalitarian underdeveloped countries. If the present trend toward increasing inequality is not stopped and reversed, development will be hampered and frustrated. In underdeveloped countries, where, to stress only one flagrant fact, large masses of people are undernourished, growth models which abstract from the productivity effects of consumption are very much more misleading than in developed countries.

It is apparent that the explanation of this paradox—the contradiction between the often emphatic declarations in favor of greater equality and the trend toward greater inequality—must relate to the distribution of power in the underdeveloped countries. I shall come back to this problem in Chapter 6.

6. Policies in Developed Countries Toward the Underdeveloped Ones

Alfred Marshall—that great eclectic master of economic science, whose mind was always so sensitive to questions of conscience—wrote just after World War I:

> . . . the notion of national trade has been bound up with the notion of solidarity between the various members of a nation. . . .

> We are indeed approaching rapidly to conditions which have no close precedent in the past, but are perhaps really more natural than those which they are supplanting—conditions under which the relations between the various industrial strata of a civilized nation are being based on reason rather than tradition. . . .

> . . . it is becoming clear that this [Great Britain] and
> every other Western country can now afford to make in-
> creased sacrifices of national wealth for the purpose of
> raising the quality of life throughout their whole popula-
> tion. A time may come when such matters will be treated
> as a cosmopolitan rather than national obligation; but that
> time is not in sight. For the practical purpose of the pres-
> ent and the coming generation, each country must, in the
> main, dispose of her own resources, and bear her own
> burdens.

The generations of which Marshall wrote have now passed
or are passing.

Meanwhile, social reforms in the developed countries
have rapidly advanced. The welfare state came into being
in a world ridden by international crises, one rising on the
crest of another, beginning with World War I.[8] The state had
to interfere in the working of the market forces in order to
preserve internal stability. Undoubtedly, this necessity for
continuous interference was one of the contributing forces
in the rapid development of the welfare state. Taboos were
broken. And when the state had to interfere, it had at that
late time become natural that the weaker sections of society
should be protected. But this relationship of social reforms
to international crises contributed greatly, at the same time,
to making the welfare state nationalistic.

Now that, after World War II, the problems of international inequalities can no longer be dealt with by the
richer countries in the customary complacent mood, it is
not primarily because of changed valuations. It is not
simply the case that people have now become more com-
passionate for their fellow human beings all over the world.
What has happened is that the misery of those far away
has been brought home to the peoples of the richer countries. Opportune ignorance no longer protects their consciences.

Against the sounding board of the intergovernmental organizations within the United Nations, where the governments of the underdeveloped countries are now the great majority of members, their complaints and their demands are raised. The international secretariats have documented the gap, and the widening gap, in income and levels of living between the developed and the underdeveloped nations. And the duty of the former to the latter, both to give aid and to reform their trading policies in a more favorable and, to begin with, less discriminatory way, is becoming recognized as a general proposition, a valuation on the higher level of our ideals.

And so the welfare state is hesitantly and very slowly being widened to be conceived of as a welfare world. To what extent this gradual and far from universal development of what is in the minds of people has been propelled by the doctrine of equality as formulated in the era of Enlightenment in the Western world and accepted as almost a state religion in the underdeveloped countries, I do not know. But it seems clear to me that, in the total absence of this inherited ideological valuation basis, it would have been impossible even to formulate the request that rich nations should aid poor nations and take consideration of them in their commercial policies.

We should next note how very commonly the type of valuation that would fit the concept of the welfare world is concealed, if not bluntly denied, almost everywhere.[9] Other motives in terms of self-interests are propounded instead.

As in the very early stages of the development of the welfare state in the Western nations, so now in the world at large we can witness the spread of the idea that aid to the poor nations constitutes a sort of insurance against revolt on their part. For this reason, aid would be in the interest of the rich nations.

In Chapter 9, Sections 3 and 4, I shall comment on this glib theory that the poor nations must be aided in order to preserve peace in the world.

When aid in the United States is justified as being "in the best interests of the United States," these interests are more specifically defined primarily in the coarser terms of political, strategic, and military advantages to the United States in the cold war. Both in the United States and in most other developed countries, additional national interests propounded as reasons for aid are those of continued cultural domination (France in particular) and, even more generally, commercial advantages.

7. The Importance of Motivation

It is my thesis that when, in recent years, willingness to aid has faltered both in the United States and in most other developed countries and, therefore, globally, the explanation is that the arguments focused on the self-interest of the developed nations are not believed by, and, even more important, do not appeal to, the common people who make up the bulk of the electorate in all these countries. It is only natural that the disastrous course of United States foreign and military policies toward underdeveloped countries, particularly in Asia and Latin America, to which most American aid has been directed, has made the reduction of aid steep in that country.

In a small country like Sweden, which has had no colonies for more than a century, it took a long time before the need to aid the underdeveloped countries became recognized. But now the trend is toward a rapid increase in aid commitments to underdeveloped countries (an annual increase of 25 per cent in the last few years). Something similar is now happening in a few other countries similarly placed.

If only for geographical reasons, it is difficult, even impossible, to get the Swedes to fear an onslaught by the poor nations, if they are not aided. Sweden is, moreover, not participating in the cold war, and the Swedes feel no political, strategic, and military necessity for getting the underdeveloped countries on their side. There is, of course, no ambition on the part of the Swedes to spread their own language or culture. Old-established free-trade traditions in commercial policy have prevented the Swedes, who are conservative in this respect, from seeking to give their industrialists commercial advantages from aid. Sweden consequently has not tied aid to deliveries from her own country, as almost every other country has done.

In Sweden the only motive that could effectively be presented to the people has been human solidarity and compassion toward the needy.

With some hesitation, I have touched on the difference between the two countries which I personally feel as nearest. I have done so to illustrate a thesis. It is my firm conviction, not only as a moralist but as an economist having studied these problems, that this is the only motivation that holds, and it is what we have to stress if we want to reverse the global trend toward decreasing aid to the underdeveloped countries. The Swedes do not differ from people in other developed nations.

It is true, however, that the unbroken and successful advance of the welfare state at home has been a favorable condition for this development of foreign policy. It is a very long time since anybody in Sweden suggested that a motive for aid to poor people might be that it was a form of insurance for the better-off in our nation. No element of such self-interest is ever now invoked as a motive for domestic social reforms. In addition, the fact that, despite all remaining inadequacies, the really needy at home are a relatively small and steadily shrinking minority makes it less possible than, for instance, in the United States to

argue that charity begins at home, in the sense that aid
should be limited by national boundaries.

I should add that I fear that Sweden's aid to underdeveloped countries may falter in following through its rising
trend, possibly even breaking general commitments undertaken by government and parliament. But I am not seeking
the explanation for this in a change in the valuation basis.

The explanation is rather that Sweden has not managed
to stop an accelerating inflation. As I hinted in Chapter 2,
Section 6, the result has been "stagflation." With this comes
a strained financial situation, forcing the Minister of Finance to look for budgetary savings. Even the social reform policy at home has to be curtailed, and a situation of
actual competition with foreign aid is then created. Also the
effect that inflation has of causing widespread unrest in
all social relations at home, noted in Chapter 2, Section
3, regularly leads to a more selfish direction of people's
interests.

The aid problem will be taken up again in Chapter 6,
Sections 11–14.

8. The Vision of the Welfare World

In the distant future perspective, I believe, however, that
the human valuations that in the developed countries have
brought us on the road toward the welfare state cannot
halt at national boundaries. Nothing less than a welfare
world corresponds to the valuations upon which our domestic social policy has been founded.

I cannot be defeatist on this score. Before World War
II hardly anyone saw a common responsibility on the part
of all the developed nations to aid underdeveloped countries. Now such a responsibility is gradually becoming
recognized as a general proposition—though very niggardly
implemented and hidden behind a concoction of flimsy

ideas about self-interest. And this has happened within a space of time that is short, historically speaking. Perhaps for this reason we should not feel disheartened about the prospect of these international relations gradually developing in line with the valuations which have given us the still rapidly developing domestic welfare state.

THE NEED FOR A SOCIOLOGY AND PSYCHOLOGY OF SOCIAL SCIENCE AND SCIENTISTS[1]

IN A STUDY of the development problems of the underdeveloped countries in South Asia, published five years ago,[2] the Prologue had the title "The Beam in Our Eyes"; the subtitle of its first section was "A Plea for a Sociology of Knowledge." The theme was further developed in a later book focused on the policy conclusions of my earlier studies of the development problems in underdeveloped countries.[3] It was there followed out systematically in regard to specific main issues, charging the economic literature on these problems with opportunistic biases on a gross scale. Later, in condensed form, I presented my criticism of conventional economic writings on underdeveloped countries in an introductory feature article, "The World Poverty Problem," which I was requested to write for the 1972 Yearbook of Encyclopaedia Britannica,[4] and which reappears in this volume as Chapters 5 and 6.

1. The Argument

In my plea to sociology—and I would now add social psychology—the argument was briefly the following. The behavior of human beings in all spheres of life, and how they are motivated and then conditioned by their inherited constitution, their life experiences, and the entire social environment in which they live, are increasingly brought under scientific observation and analysis. We have studies on businessmen, their wives, farmers, blue- and white-collar workers, civil servants, congressmen, local political bosses, criminals, prostitutes, and all sorts of groups placed in their various geographical and social surroundings. Only about the peculiar behavior of our own profession do we choose to remain naïve. How we as scientists operate in seeking to establish knowledge is largely shielded from the searchlight of empirical study.

But social scientists are, of course, not different from other human beings. In our search for truth, and in the direction of our research interests, the particular approach we are choosing, the explanatory models and theories we are constructing and the concepts we use, and, consequently, the course we follow in making observations and drawing inferences, we are influenced by individual personality traits and, besides that, by the mighty tradition in our disciplines and by the play of interests and prejudices in the society in which we live and work. The evolution of our sciences cannot be seen as autonomous, but is continually influenced by the inner and external forces I hinted at. These forces may easily lead to that type of systematic, though unintentional, falsification of our conception of reality, which I call biases. They then become inimical also to our efforts to reach rational policy conclusions.

The almost complete lack of scientific inquiry on the

research behavior of ourselves cannot be defended by a greater difficulty of carrying out studies in this field. The corpus delicti, our writings, is on the table. And for the rest, it should not be more difficult to get at the other forces influencing us in our work besides our intention to seek true knowledge, than, for instance, to study, as has been done, how the behavior of business executives is not determined simply by their desire to maximize profits. The concept "economic man" of the classical economists has long since been discarded as inadequate to reality—except by a few of the most ardent "welfare theorists." Meanwhile the "scientific man" is not even defined. He exists only implicitly in the form of a virtual taboo on raising the psychological and sociological problems of how our research activity is conditioned.

The force of this irrational taboo is demonstrated, for instance, in the fact that economists, even when they review my works, do not so much as mention the accusations I have persistently made against bias in the literature. Still less do they attempt to refute these charges.

2. On the Level of Logic

It is my conviction that progress in our scientific work must begin with the elimination of bias. In the realm of logic, we have one powerful means at our disposal, namely the research technique of ascertaining, stressing, and making explicit our value premises, tested for significance, relevance, rational compatibility, and feasibility. No social research can be neutral and in that sense simply "factual" and "objective." Valuations determine not only our policy conclusions but all our endeavors to establish the facts, from the approaches chosen to the presentation of our results.

We can, of course, keep unaware of the valuations that

nolens volens are implicit. And this is unfortunately still regular practice in the social sciences. But by not in a rational manner selecting and making explicit the value premises that steer our research, we provide a space of indeterminateness whereby biases can enter the analysis.

By working with specific and explicit value premises, we are not simply "expressing our own biases," as sometimes has been suggested. For a characteristic of biases is, to begin with, that the researcher is not conscious of them and does not have them under his control. Moreover, we should not be permitted to choose the value premises arbitrarily. They have to be tested for relevance, significance, compatibility, and feasibility. Rational policy conclusions can then be inferred from these value premises, and the facts ascertained from the point of view of the same value premises.

As a profession, economists have remained particularly naïve on this methodological issue. From the classical and neo-classical era they have kept to the idea that there are true and objectively valid values that can be known. The so-called welfare theory represents in modern time this fundamental logical fallacy in economic theory, though now mostly carefully hidden in an escapist terminology. Even when not adduced in more concrete problems, it undoubtedly has served to keep economists innocent about the pervasive influence of concealed and ordinarily non-conscious valuations that then lead to biases.

On this problem of the logic of social research, and of the difficulties that also meet the use of the rational research technique of explicit value premises,[5] I shall not here dwell further. I am more concerned with a different although closely related problem, namely the psychological and sociological causal mechanism through which our research is in danger of becoming influenced by other factors than the existing facts of social reality and our endeavors to establish these facts and their interrelations.

My point is that we would be better prepared for a critical scrutiny of our own research endeavors, and could therefore expect more rapid progress in the social sciences, if we were, as a body, a little less ignorant about ourselves and the forces working on our minds when we do research. A minimal demand should be that we become aware of the problem and attain some degree of sophistication about the personal and social conditioning of our research activity. But rightly, the problem of how research becomes irrationally conditioned is important enough for demanding that systematic empirical research on a large scale should be devoted to investigating this important part of social reality.

Even without that type of psychological and sociological study, biases can be detected in the path I have tried to follow. Since biases come into play in a space of indeterminateness provided by the researcher's failure to recognize, define, and spell out explicitly his value premises, and as he thus draws inferences with one set of premises missing, immanent criticism in theoretical terms can establish their existence and their general character. This is what I am trying to do in this book also, particularly in Chapters 5 and 6 on the problems of underdeveloped countries. One can take this a step further by then raising the detective's standard question: *cui bono?* But this type of theoretical scrutiny can state the problems only for the intensive sociological and psychological studies I find warranted over the whole field of social research.

I had been living with this problem of the "objectivity" of social science, or, more specifically, economics all my working life, long before I came to grips with the development problems of underdeveloped countries. Undoubtedly, however, the forces at work on our minds, which cause irrationality if not faced and controlled, are exceptionally strong and insidious in that field of study.

My opinions on the methodological problems of economic research have not been derived from philosophy, which unfortunately now most often remains aloof from these problems—much more so than a hundred and more years ago, when scholars like Adam Smith and Bentham and later John Stuart Mill, Sidgwick, and many others were prominent both as professional philosophers and as economists. My views have emerged from my struggle with the various economic problems I chose to deal with.

When, in my youth, I studied the political element in the development of economic theory along the classical and neo-classical line, I found the whole structure of this theory, as it had evolved over the generations, to be determined by the need of the economists to protect themselves from their own radical premises as inherited from the era of Enlightenment.[6] That this was an effect mainly of the dominant social and political forces in society, I took for granted, without being able to carry out a deeper study, which would have revealed the mechanism of causation, which I am pleading for today.

When later I came to grips with the Negro problem in the United States, the biases in the scientific literature as well as in popular conceptions became a main theme of my work.[7] So conditioned was I by my earlier work that it was natural, when still later I came to study the conditions in underdeveloped countries, for me to be on the alert for the problem of biases. I shall come back to this in Chapters 5 and 6.

3. Personality Traits

Let me attempt to sketch briefly the nature of the forces influencing research that I feel are irrational. My thoughts on this matter must be in the form of conjectural reasoning based on impressions gathered during my working life. At most, I can hope that my observations may be of some use as plausible hypotheses for scientific study in the psychological and sociological terms I am asking for.

I should first admit that in my own encounters with the problem of biases in economic research, the personality traits of the individual researcher, as determined by his inherited constitution and life experiences, faded into the periphery, simply because I had neither the time nor the competence to go deep into that determinant. The more systematic and incisive study of the problem of biases for which I am pleading should certainly not work under this restriction.

Those students who have played a decisive role in the development of economic thinking—Adam Smith, Ricardo, List, Marx, John Stuart Mill, Marshall, Wicksell, Veblen, and Keynes, to mention only a few—have all been strikingly idiosyncratic, and it would be hard to believe that their personality traits did not set their mark on the direction and character of their contributions. I see here a large field for intensive psychological research, which must, however, situate the individual author in the social setting where he lived and worked.

In my own studies of the problem of the conditioning of economic research, I have mainly felt constrained to deal with the more "social" forces at work on the researchers' minds: tradition for one thing, but, even more decisively, the interests and prejudices dominating their environment.

4. The Force of Tradition

I think it can be said that the impact of tradition, represented by a vast background of literature, is particularly strong in economics.[8] This gives a flavor of methodological conservatism to the work of the economists insofar as the general structure of their thinking is concerned, while within that structure there has always remained space for considerable innovation and even controversy between different authors and schools of thought.

Now and then an individual student breaks away from the beaten path. But in general, his revolt is less radical than it appears at the time. This is true even of the great heretics in economics like Marx. I shall not pursue this thought here, but I would point out in passing that Marx not only took over the theory of "real value" from Ricardo but that, much more generally than is commonly recognized, he remained, like all the economists of his generation (and largely today), under the spell of the natural law philosophy, of which utilitarianism is only a branch (Chapter 15, Section 3).[9]

Keynes certainly enjoyed posing as a rebel,[10] much more so than Wicksell, who decades earlier had anticipated Keynes's main deviation from established economic theory, and who was always eager to root his new ideas in thoughts which, after laborious study, he had found expressed somewhere in the great literature, in part from the beginning of the nineteenth century.

After a break, which, as I said, is ordinarily only partial, the force of tradition may become tied into a new orthodoxy. In the new furrow, other students will set their cutting blades—developing, adding, amending, modifying. This is the picture we get when we take a broad view of what happens in the development of economics and, I shall assume, the social sciences generally.

This relative dearth of radical originality in the pursuit of our sciences can be studied, and is studied, when we trace their development. There are ingrained thoughtways and preconceptions that imply a factor of inertia which by itself is not rational. But there are other more material interests involved that support the force of tradition.

As I hinted in Chapter 1, Section 7, there are rewards for economists who do not deviate too much from the legacy, but show skill in working within the set pattern and demonstrating an ability to enrich, amend, and develop the thoughts contained in that tradition. This is what gives status among colleagues and, in particular, what opens up teaching and research positions in our universities.

Steering away more radically from what are commonly accepted views incurs risks, particularly for the young, from whom we should perhaps expect fresh departures. If, then, following the normal pattern, these young students write their maiden works along traditional lines, they have themselves already come to have a vested interest in adhering to the approaches of the establishment. Only occasionally does clearly unconventional research behavior encounter success and in the end become accepted—at which point, as I have said, it might even give rise to a new line of orthodoxy.

Increasingly, there are also rewards to be reaped from outside the academic world. This is a fairly new situation. It is now often forgotten how much more insulated were the lives and work of economists a little more than a generation ago. We were almost exclusively confined to the teaching profession, trained to become competent to train a new batch of students. The only departure from this narrow line was when some of us reached out to try to teach the general public by writing books and articles for popular consumption.

The state interventions in economic life called for during World War I were mainly handled by politicians, administrators, and lawyers. It was during the Great Depression that economists were first brought in to plan and even to administer public policies, and it was only then that businesses and organizations found out that they could have economists as consultants or even as regular employees.

Economists who have part- or full-time jobs—and incomes —outside the universities now probably constitute the majority of our profession. This new institutional situation has in all probability strengthened the forces operating for methodological conservatism. What is ordinarily demanded is that they be "safe," "sane" economists, having or on the way to acquiring prestige, and usually not the adventurous ones fighting for recognition of new ideas. Adherence to accepted terminology—often containing systematic biases—gets an added value, not only of convenience but of a pretense of strict professionalism when dealing with laymen, whether businessmen or politicians.

And many young economists must feel a need to hold back opinions and remain uncommitted in order not to spoil their opportunities. Usually, their employers ask that they come out with their views only on selected questions and then at the right time.

In the field of economic research on underdeveloped countries, which, since World War II, has been recruiting a rapidly increasing number of economists, a mighty establishment has been growing up, not limited to universities but including all sorts of government agencies and those of intergovernmental organizations. As I shall point out in Chapter 5, a broad conformism in approaches, coupled with ingenuity in minor matters, is of material interest for becoming affiliated with this establishment as experts or consultants.

When trying to understand the extraordinary adherence to tradition in economics, we should also note the great shrinkage of the ordinary economist's training, interests, and knowledge that has occurred since World War I. Until then, practically nobody began his career as an economist. He was either a man of practical affairs like Ricardo, who turned to economics at a mature age, or he had a previous training as a mathematician, historian, philosopher, lawyer, and so on. Usually he had been led to economic studies by his interest in social issues.

The result is that a student begins his study of economics at an earlier age and having only the most fragmentary insights into the society he is studying. He may so be able to become professor of economics and perhaps in time a leading economist, preserving that insufficient basis of knowledge. That this is apt to make him narrowminded and uncritical is obvious. By knowing so little about the real world, and even about what other social sciences have found out about that world, he can live more undisturbed by doubts in his and his colleagues' model world. In the same way, the ordinary economist's increasingly common lack of interest in, and knowledge of, the historical development of his own science also helps to narrow his perspective.

It is also my impression that many establishment economists do not read newspapers with care, particularly not papers from countries other than their own. Often they neither read many books nor follow with any regularity journals outside their special field. In the intensive study of their behavior as researchers, their reading habits should certainly not be overlooked, nor should the scope of their social contacts. The various problems and the tentative hypotheses hinted at in this section are of course important also for the influencing forces discussed in preceding and following sections.

5. Interests and Prejudices

But most important are, of course, the forces in society at large that put pressure on economists to so direct their work that they come to conclusions in line with dominant interests and prejudices. When those interests remain fairly unchanged for a period of time, they then gain support from, and give support to, those forces of tradition I have already pointed to.

When I speak of the influence on the development of economics exerted by dominant interests in society, I do not imply that those interests are themselves rationally conceived. That is the reason why I add to "interests" the word "prejudices." If I had space, I could give a long list of cases, in which the interests to those who perceive them are misunderstood and, moreover, are shortsighted.

Nor do I not take into account the existence at all times of competing schools of thought. Mostly, though not always, they represent different types of adjustment to different dominant interests and prejudices and are usually not fundamentally so dissimilar as is often claimed. Greater dissimilarities, at least for a time, occur in periods of transition, when there are big changes in the field of felt interests and in the power of those holding to them. The so-called Keynesian revolution was, as I pointed out in Chapter 1, Sections 2 and 3, of this type.

But occasionally the pressure of these dominant interests and prejudices will have a negative effect upon a student and spur resentment and opposition. Thus Marx's writings must be explained chiefly as a rebellion against these forces, the background of which constitutes a fascinating personality problem. But this is, at the same time, part of the explanation why the main development in economic science did not follow Marx's lead, leaving the "Marxian" school to survive as an institutionally disfavored and isolated branch of learning.

The so-called Keynesian revolution in economics, mainly an Anglo-American phenomenon, was in my opinion not of this negative character. It was rather positively conditioned by the constellation of policy interests that became important due to the unfortunate economic development in Britain during the Twenties and the Great Depression in the United States during the Thirties, together with the gradually maturing changes in the organization of the labor market, giving increasing influence to the workers, and the generally changed political power structure, which, in Britain, had gradually materialized in the widening of suffrage.

In Chapters 1 and 2, I gave some glimpse of how interests and prejudices have steered economic research approaches in developed countries. In Chapters 5 and 6, I shall discuss the problem in relation to the literature on underdeveloped countries and their development problem.

6. A Final Note

What I have said up to now has merely been an attempt to hint at the problem of the influences working on the minds of the researchers and to spell out a few broad hypotheses for the more systematic and incisive study I am pleading for. Finally, let me say a few words on the co-operation among our disciplines that would seem called for if we are to handle properly a problem like that of the biases in economic research. On the one hand, I have laid bare the shortcomings of economic research in this field and broadly hinted at those interests in society, some of them shortsighted and irrational, that can explain them, but I admit I have not gone deeply into the social psychology and sociology of the biases I have in mind.

On the other hand, I see equally clearly that the psychologists and sociologists will need knowledge of economic issues and the way they have been dealt with in order to apply their insights more specifically. This indicates that what is needed is interdisciplinary research. But the mere recognition of the existence of the problem by my colleagues in these other fields, the outlining of its general character in more definite terms, and, perhaps, an excursion into one specific field of economics (why not the problem of underdeveloped countries?) would be immensely useful. And this is why I have dared to lecture sociologists today on the problem of biases, as seen by an institutional economist.

Chapter 5

THE WORLD
POVERTY PROBLEM[1]

It is the author's firm conviction that progress in the social sciences can be achieved only by continual and searching criticism of approaches and methods. The quality and relevance of the swelling volume of research on the under-developed countries after World War II have suffered seriously from the lack of such criticism. This is, in particular, true of the valiant efforts of economists to tackle the problems of planning for development of these countries.

1. Pre-war Unawareness

Like the nuclear armament race, the pollution of soil, water, and air, and the rapid spread of the use of harmful drugs, the abject poverty of that great majority of the world's population who live in underdeveloped countries now unfolds itself in the wake of World War II as a threatening new problem. But while the first three of these stupendous dangers for the well-being of mankind reflect real trends of change in conditions and human actions, the fourth danger is not new; only our awareness of it is new.

Economic and social conditions in the non-Communist underdeveloped countries are not fundamentally different today from what they were in the colonial time before the war. Then, as now, there was a huge income gap between developed and underdeveloped regions. And even at that time, the gap was continuously widening, as indeed it had been for a century and more, without any great concern being expressed about it. The only major change that has occurred in those "backward regions" since the war has been the recent acceleration in the rate of population increase. But our awareness of the problem of world poverty preceded this change, and, even more, our knowledge of it, which did not come much earlier than with the censuses around 1960.

In the pre-war period, very little research was directed toward study of the economic conditions of the masses of people living in underdeveloped regions. And the research which was carried out was not aimed at making us aware of their poverty and misery. Still less did it raise the practical problem of how to improve conditions by planned policy intervention to engender development.

Cultural anthropologists, sent out from the Western centers of learning and working with the indulgence of colonial and indigenous holders of power, focused interest on the way people lived. With few exceptions, their approach was static, and changes were originally dealt with as "disturbances" of established social relations. They were, indeed, sympathetic to the peoples they studied, and they reacted to European ethnocentricism by attempting to ascribe purpose to the social organization of even the most primitive peoples. All cultures were seen as valuable; this was their ethos. But this inclination, and generally the static approach which corresponded to it, tended to draw attention away from the poverty problem.

More astonishing was the lack of interest shown by most economists of that era. Poverty falls in our field of study: all the traditions of our profession, inherited and preserved for two centuries, should have led us to inquire into the policy problem of what could be done about it as well. For generations and in all our competing sects, we economists have viewed problems from a policy angle. Had we devoted more interest to the "backward regions," we could not have avoided raising the issue of the poverty there as a policy problem.

Under the pre-war colonial and quasi-colonial power system which controlled these regions and the relations between them and the developed countries, there was little demand for such an approach to their conditions. Economic research was foredoomed largely to be issueless. And economists, even more than other social scientists, have always been sensitive to what was practical and politically opportune. The fact that we mostly avoided research on conditions in the backward regions reflected the lack of political importance given to such research in colonial times.

We may note in passing that even the highly idealistic Charter of the United Nations, drawn up as late as toward the end of the war—though it promised that the new world organization should "promote social progress and better standards of life in larger freedom"—did not focus on the plight of the underdeveloped regions and made no special provision for promoting their development.

2. The Great Awakening

All this has now radically changed.[2] Today the poverty of underdeveloped countries is a problem of which everyone who is at all alert has been made aware. We have been living through one of history's most abrupt reversals of political climate in the world. The social sciences, and in the first hand economics, have as usual responded to this political change. In a second round of circular causation with cumulative effects, scientific research itself has then contributed to the rising awareness of the world poverty problem.

A large part of our research resources is today employed in the study of underdeveloped countries. The tide is still rising, and we economists are riding the crest of the wave. As always, we are mainly responsible for giving a dynamic slant to all this new research by raising the issues of development and planning for development.

In the same way as the unawareness of these problems and the paucity and static character of pre-war research were interrelated, and dependent on the world political situation at that time, so now this new awareness and the swelling flood of research in this field have been the result of huge changes in that political situation. The tremendous redirection of research, particularly in economics, has not been an autonomous or spontaneous development of our sciences. It is a mistake to believe that we have concluded from our research that we should venture into this new field. It is not we who have blazed the way to new perspectives. The cue to the reorientation of our work has, as always, come from the sphere of politics.

Responding to that cue, we have then turned to research on issues that have become politically important. Theories are launched, data are collected, and the literature on the "new" problem expands. By its cumulative results, this research activity, which reflects political strivings of the time, may eventually contribute to make these strivings more rational. So it is now, and so it has always been.

The political changes on the international scene that have effected this redirection of our research work and generally raised the public awareness of the problem of world poverty, are clearly before our eyes and can be identified.

First, we have the rapid dissolution of the colonial power structure which, beginning with the decolonization of the

British dependencies in South Asia, has swept the globe
like a hurricane, creating a great number of new, politically
independent countries, which are all underdeveloped. In
Latin America, political independence was won long ago,
but these countries have joined in the decolonization movement by demanding "real" and, particularly, economic
independence as well, meaning a greater measure of control over their own economies.

Second, the released demands for development in the
now politically independent underdeveloped countries
themselves are raised by the alert elite groups there who
think, speak, and act on behalf of their countries, even
though they do not arouse much response among the
masses.

Third, international tensions, culminating in the cold
war, have created a competitive situation where not only
the foreign policy but also internal affairs of underdeveloped countries are of political concern to the developed
countries, particularly the two antagonistic superpowers
and their political and military allies.

The United Nations and its specialized agencies have
been made into sounding boards for the underdeveloped
countries' demands for aid from, and commercial considerations of, the developed countries. Underdeveloped countries did not carry much weight in the councils when the
United Nations system of intergovernmental organizations
was planned and set up, and their particular interests were,
as previously mentioned, not brought into focus. As a direct
effect of the decolonization movement, the United Nations
membership has, since then, risen from the original 51 to
131. The great majority in all these organizations is now
made up of the governments of underdeveloped countries.
The structure of this system has been adjusted to handle
the issues of development of underdeveloped countries.

While, on the whole, the effectiveness of the United
Nations and the affiliated organizations has tended to de-

teriorate even in recent years, particularly in the field of security and more generally all issues in which the developed countries feel they have an important stake, this whole system of intergovernmental organizations has more and more become a series of agencies for discussing, analyzing, and promoting development in underdeveloped countries.

Their secretariats produce statistics and studies aimed at ascertaining, analyzing, demonstrating, and publicizing the pertinent elements of world poverty. This is part of the process through which awareness of the world poverty problem has been engendered in the postwar period. Thus, when it suddenly became politically important, an age-old problem abruptly came to figure as a "new" problem and, as a result, the object of large-scale research and worldwide debate.

3. The Opportunism of Knowledge

A basic fact that is systematically neglected by almost all participants in the debate on the world poverty problem, whether they are speaking as scientists or men of public affairs, is that all knowledge, like all ignorance, tends to deviate from truth in an opportunistic direction—if it is not critically scrutinized with that fact in view.[3] We can all feel satisfied that there is now a general awareness of the poverty problem in underdeveloped countries. This is an advance toward a realistic conception of the world we are all living in. But if our conception of that problem is opportunistically distorted, that becomes damaging to our efforts to react rationally to the problem, i.e., to plan policy actions wisely.

Our views—from the popular to the most sophisticated theories presented with scientific pretensions—tend to be influenced by interests as commonly, though often mistakenly, perceived by the dominant groups in the societies where we are living. They therefore come to deviate from truth in a direction opportune to these interests. This is, indeed, commonly taken for granted when we look back at an earlier period in history. We say about an author or statesman that, of course, he was "a product of the age in which he lived."

But in our own intellectual endeavors, we are ordinarily unaware of such influences—as, indeed, was true of people in every earlier epoch of history. A disturbing fact is that social scientists, and economists in particular, are usually naïve in this respect and do not even consider the possibility that they may be so influenced. This is why I have urged intensive work in the sociology and social psychology of sciences and of scientists (Chapter 4).

We believe—as did our predecessors, and with equal firmness—that we are simply factual and rational, that we base our findings on observations of reality and, when drawing our inferences, that we follow the logical and mathematical rules for reasoning. In attempting to make us critical of our own views, a backward look is helpful.

4. The Colonial Theory

In retrospect it is clear that, in the long colonial era, remaining unaware of the problem of poverty in the underdeveloped regions and being satisfied by the paucity and lack of policy direction of research on their social and economic conditions, were opportune reactions in those developed countries which ruled the colonies or, as in Latin America, exerted a dominant influence, as was the case in all developed countries. It is equally clear that the popular as well as more sophisticated beliefs of that era, while contriving a broad explanation for their backwardness, were plainly apologetic.

These beliefs were fashioned so as to relieve the colonial powers, and developed nations generally, of moral and political responsibility for their poverty and lack of development. They were intended to prove that these vexatious conditions were natural and impossible to change, so that, on the whole, nothing could be done about them.

It was taken as established by experience that peoples in backward regions were so constituted that they reacted differently from people of European stock. Their tendency toward idleness and inefficiency, and their reluctance to venture into new enterprise and often even to seek wage employment, were seen as expressions of their lack of ambition, limited economic horizons, survival-mindedness, carefree disposition, and preference for a leisurely life.

In more sophisticated writings, these mental traits were seen to be rooted in the entire system of social relations, upheld by attitudes and institutions, and fortified also by religious taboos and other prescriptions rooted in superstitious beliefs. In the pre-war literature, these attitudinal and institutional conditions were taken to form a static system rather beyond any large-scale changes induced by policy measures, which might instead create "disturbances." On this score, the anthropologists' static bias was a convenient support.

Particularly in the discussion of economic matters, climate was given a dominant role in explaining low productivity and, in particular, low levels of labor input and efficiency of work. Also, the idea that people in these regions were hereditarily less well endowed than Europeans was never far below the surface, even if it was somewhat suppressed in later decades of the colonial era. Often those two immutable factors were related to each other by the hypothesis that the racial inferiority of peoples in these regions might have been caused by the fact that they have lived for countless generations in an adverse climate.

Occasionally it was noted that malnutrition and generally inferior levels of living lowered stamina and thereby affected willingness and ability to work, and to work hard. But since productivity was so extremely low, and since there were all these other powerful and unchangeable causes preventing higher labor input and efficiency, combatting underdevelopment and poverty by raising incomes and levels of living became an unrealistic policy.

Altogether, these elements of a theory of poverty in backward regions, which in various blends were present in practically all expressions of views on these problems, were clearly made to order for people in the developed countries, who wanted to preserve their superior status and privileged positions in relation to the "backward regions" and their indigenous peoples, but did not want to take much responsibility for improving their lot. Still less were they prepared to incur sacrifices for that purpose.

If there is any doubt whether it is correct to characterize this colonial theory as biased under the influence of opportunistic interests, one need only consider the sudden and complete repudiation of this theory—indeed, forgetting that it had existed—when the world political situation, and then also the interests which pressed for rationalization, changed so radically after the war.

5. The Indigenous Protest

The colonial theory was not flattering to the indigenous peoples of the backward regions. To the upper strata of alert and educated persons among them it was felt to be condescending and humiliating. At the same time, after the war and the wave of decolonization, it was discouraging for any efforts toward development in "the underdeveloped countries," as they were now beginning to be called. In a sense, this had been its purpose. Its function had been apologetic and defensive, explaining away the lack of development under the colonial regimes.

It is understandable that this colonial theory gave rise to an indigenous protest.[4] Indeed, the protest antedated to some extent the downfall of the colonial power system in those colonies where there had been a liberation movement. After political independence had been won, the intellectuals in the new countries were released from the inhibitions many of them had felt as office-holders and, more generally, as belonging to a privileged class in a foreign-controlled dependency. The protests against the colonial theory could then ring out clearly and, indeed, became the official creed, shared, as we shall point out, by both radicals and conservatives in the former colonies.

It is important to discuss the intellectual content of this protest, which established it as a new theory. The colonial theory had alleged the existence of certain peculiarities in the indigenous peoples and in the conditions under the influence of which they lived and worked, including the structure of their societies. It was on that basis that the colonial powers and developed countries generally could reject responsibility for their poverty and lack of development. The indigenous protest simply denied the existence of such differences between developed and underdeveloped countries.

Although it had earlier been largely suppressed, the racial inferiority doctrine was, on good grounds, suspected of living surreptitiously and was condemned as "racialism." Differences in climate were simply disregarded, as were the alleged differences in social structure, attitudes, and institutions. What were recognized were only differences in "culture," and it was implied that they were not obstacles to development.

This position was shared equally by those intellectuals who identified themselves with the Western world and those more aggressive anti-Western nationalists. Both groups had to insist that the development problem was essentially the same in underdeveloped as it had been in the now developed countries. From this assertion they concluded that underdevelopment had to be blamed on the colonial regimes. Expressed more or less emphatically, this protest theory became an essential part of the basic doctrine of the new states. In those countries, particularly in Latin America, which had been politically independent long before the war, the doctrine tended to be similar, except that it was directed more against foreign economic domination and the political influence based on it or complementary to it.

6. The Adjustment of Thinking in the Developed Countries

Those who shape and express public opinion in the developed countries—including politicians, officials, journalists, writers of popular tracts, and social scientists—proved receptive to the protest ideology in the underdeveloped countries.

For one thing, in the Western tradition, we all feel sympathy for the underdog. Particularly as long as it did not cost us much, we could feel hopeful for the underdeveloped countries. Indeed, independence implied that people in the former metropolitan countries were now relieved of their inhibitions stemming from having to carry the responsibility for ruling these peoples and having to explain to themselves and others why they were so poor and why their conditions were not becoming better—exactly the situation that had given rise to the apologetic and defensive colonial theory. When these dependent peoples were abruptly thrown on their own, there was every reason to sit back, wish them well, and share in their hopes.

The experience of ideological competition with the Communists, intensified in the cold war ensuing at the same time, contributed to this sudden conversion in the Western world. Ever since the time of Marx, Communists had condemned colonialism, and they now used their influence, not least in the United Nations, to spur decolonization. They had never shared in what we called the colonial theory but had blamed the poverty in the backward regions on colonial exploitation.

They could agree wholeheartedly with the indigenous protest and even express the opinion that the former colonial powers and, indeed, all developed countries had a debt to repay. But aside from these ideological tenets, which were indeed genuinely held and in line with their traditional thinking, they had, of course, in the ascending cold war all opportunistic interests for backing up the protest ideology. For the Western countries, the easiest way to take the air out of Communist propaganda in the underdeveloped countries was to give up the colonial theory as rapidly and completely as possible and accept a new theory cleansed of all the offensive elements in the old one.

7. Diplomacy in Research and Its Opportunistic Causes

This new theory will be set out below. At this stage in our argument, it should be asserted only that even research tended to become "diplomatic," forbearing, and generally over-optimistic, bypassing facts that raised awkward problems, concealing them in unduly technical terminology, or treating them in an excusing and "understanding" way. While the "white man's burden" in colonial times had been to rule those who supposedly could not rule themselves, it now became a felt need to be diplomatic in research as well as public debate.

This tendency toward bias involved even terminology.[5]

In colonial times a common expression had been the static one: "backward regions." It reflected the fact that most of them were not countries, and it also gave no support to the idea that things could be changed. After decolonization, the term became the dynamic expression "underdeveloped countries." This expressed a recognition of their present state of underdevelopment. As it was used, it also implied the valuations that this is undesirable, that they should plan for development and that, indeed, they should be helped to succeed in doing so by the developed countries.

In the new political circumstances, that term was soon felt not to be polite enough. By a common conspiracy guided by diplomatic considerations, it was changed to various euphemistic expressions. One such is "developing countries," which for many years has been given official sanction in all documents emanating from the United Nations. This term is, of course, illogical, since, by means of a loaded terminology, it begs the question whether a country is developing or not. Moreover, it does not express the thought that is really pressing for expression: that a country is underdeveloped, that it wants to develop, and that it should be planning to develop.

Such politeness may seem to be unimportant. But it is important to note, because it indicates the deeper bias in the scientific approach to the problems of underdeveloped countries, which I shall characterize and critically analyze below.

8. *The Opportunistic Interests*

In addition to these remarks on how, in a general way, the changed political situation in the world led to this diplomatic and over-optimistic approach, it should be pointed out how this new approach more directly served opportunistic interests. Part of the change, once awareness of the

world poverty problem was created, was that people in developed countries were brought to recognize—though still
only in general and noncommittal terms—that they should
aid the underdeveloped countries in their development
efforts. If the over-optimistic approach were realistic, effective aid could be cheaper.

In the underdeveloped countries, both conservatives and
radicals had opportunistic reasons to adhere to this over-
optimistic approach. If it were realistic, the privileged
classes could hope to achieve development without giving
up their privileges. They would not, for one thing, have
to submit to radical domestic reforms, which will be discussed in the next chapter as necessary for rapid and sustained development. It was, indeed, natural that they, and
conservative persons generally, should want to hear as little
as possible about all that had been thrown out of the win-
dow in the new theory, substituting for the colonial theory:
climate, social structure, attitudes, and institutions, and the
adverse productivity consequences of the very low levels of
living of the poor masses.

The radicals, for their part, are naturally inclined to hope
for rapid and effective development as a result of planning.
It should also be recalled here that Marx had assumed that
the effects of industrialization and of investments generally
—in the final instance, Marx's changes in the "modes of
production"—would spread quickly to other sectors of the
economy and also determine the whole "superstructure"
of culture, social structure, and attitudes and institutions.
In fact, "Marxism" was in this respect a prelude to the over-
optimistic postwar theory of economic development which
will be discussed below.

It should at this point be recalled that in underdeveloped
countries most intellectuals had been under "Marxist" influence, many more than those who are now in the Communist fold, and also that Western economists, usually without referring to the source and often not being aware of it,

widely accepted Marx's over-optimistic views on the rapid "spread effects" of economic changes—and many other elements of "Marxism" as well. We should not be surprised to find that the Communist approach in regard to the basic concepts and the theoretical development models used was often not different from the Western ones.

And so the pendulum of bias had swung from one extreme to the other.

9. The Role of the Economists

By all our traditions, ambitions, and working habits, we economists were destined to dominate the rapidly rising tide of research on the postwar problems of underdeveloped countries. This was in sharp contrast to the conspicuously minor role we had played in the previous colonial era, and for similar reasons.

Economists are accustomed and trained to lay a dynamic policy perspective on problems and also to seek out for study such problems where that approach is called for by the dominant political forces. In principle, we are planners, even those of us whose planning prescriptions conclude by advising nonintervention. And we do not shy away from constructing theoretical macro-models, applicable for whole countries and the entire world—exactly what was required when backward regions became politically independent countries and faced, as a primary concern, the problem of planning for development.

Unfortunately, our profession also happened to have at hand a body of theory that, when applied to underdeveloped countries, perfectly answered to the post-colonial system of opportunistic bias, the origin and character of which were described above. It had been developed to fit conditions in the developed countries and to serve the political life of those countries by discussing their short-term and

long-term policy issues in a realistic and rational fashion.
We had, indeed, been so successful that our concept and
theoretical constructions had permeated and stamped not
only the thoughtways but even the language of public
debate. Even taking into full account all the critical points
I raise against the establishment theory, I am of course willing to concede that this theory better fitted the problems
in developed countries than it could those of the underdeveloped countries.

It was perfectly natural, indeed, that economists, when
suddenly feeling called to undertake massive research on
conditions in underdeveloped countries, came to rely upon
the theoretical tools they had perfected and made such
good use of in the developed countries. It could not be expected that economists in the underdeveloped countries
would take another approach. Besides the opportunistic
interests working on the minds of both the conservative and
the radical intellectuals referred to above, most of them had
either been trained at Western universities or by teachers
who had acquired their training in the West, and all of
them were exposed to the great economic literature in the
Western tradition. Familiarity with, and ability to work in
accordance with, the concepts and theoretical models that
have evolved in that tradition were apt to give status in
their native countries as well as abroad.

10. The Unrealistic Assumptions

With all the variances between different authors and
schools of thought, the whole body of economic theory had
certain important common assumptions, which simply did
not fit conditions in underdeveloped countries. It so happened that many of these assumptions implied abstraction
from most of the elements in the colonial theory, against
which the indigenous protest had been raised, gathering

general support in both developed and underdeveloped countries, as has already been pointed out.

Generally speaking, this new approach abstracted from most of the conditions that are not only peculiar to the underdeveloped countries but are largely responsible for their underdevelopment and for the particular difficulties they meet when attempting to develop. It therefore served the earlier mentioned postwar biases toward diplomacy and over-optimism by leaving out of account much that was awkward, difficult, and undesirable in these countries.

Thus climatic conditions[6] have never been very important for economic development in the developed countries, which are all situated in the temperate zones. But underdeveloped countries happen to be in the tropical and subtropical zones. It is a fact that all successful industrialization and economic development has taken place in the temperate zones. In colonial times, this was not taken as an accident of history. As already mentioned, climatic conditions were then given an important role in explaining underdevelopment in the backward regions. In the postwar economic literature, they were, on the contrary, either entirely ignored or casually dismissed as being of no importance.

From the point of view of making scientific study realistic and relevant, this is, of course, unwarranted. Even if little research has been carried out in this field, it is clear that, generally speaking, the extremes of heat and humidity in most underdeveloped countries contribute to a deterioration of soil and many kinds of material goods. They bear a partial responsibility for the low yield of certain crops, forests, and animals. Not only do they cause discomfort to workers, but they also impair health by favoring the existence, multiplication, and spread of various micro-organisms which give rise to parasitic and infectious diseases. In these and other ways, climatic conditions decrease the participation in, and duration of, work and its efficiency.

Overcoming these unfavorable effects—and occasionally turning some of them to advantage, which, in regard to agriculture in several countries, is quite possible—requires expenditures, often of an investment type. Since capital and all other real cost elements, such as effective administrative action, put demands on scarce resources in underdeveloped countries, climatic conditions often impose serious obstacles to development which must be overcome by planned policy measures. To abstract from climatic conditions in the study of underdeveloped countries represents, therefore, a serious bias.

In a crude way, the colonial theory also laid stress on various aspects of the social organization, institutions, and attitudes in underdeveloped countries. By the static assumption that these conditions were practically immutable, and not responsive to any induced or spontaneous changes, the colonial theory was undoubtedly biased in a pessimistic direction. But when, after the war, economists began to study the underdeveloped countries' planning problems in purely "economic" terms, completely ignoring these "noneconomic" factors, this was a contrary and, as we shall find, most serious bias in the optimistic direction.

In economists' studies of developed countries, from which they derived their concepts, models, and consequently their principal assumptions and research approaches, such an abstraction was, to an extent, more warranted. The social setting in these countries and, in particular, their institutions and attitudes are usually already highly rationalized in the sense that they do not block development impulses. Or they can be assumed to adjust rapidly in this direction.[7] But this cannot be assumed in a realistic study of underdeveloped countries that have been stagnant for a long time.

Again, as pointed out above, the colonial theory reckoned with productivity consequences of the extremely low level of income and living of the masses of people in the backward regions, although they saw little hope of raising these levels. The relatively higher levels of living and income in developed countries and their social security measures make it possible to consider nutrition and, more generally, levels of living merely from the point of view of people's welfare interests, as they are largely unrelated to their willingness and ability to work and their efficiency when working. In Western growth models, consumption is therefore usually left out as a factor determining productivity.

This simplification is, however, not permissible when analyzing the problems of underdevelopment, development, and planning for development in underdeveloped countries.[8] Incomes and levels of living do have effects on productivity. The situation is complex, since some consumption items—for instance, food and educational facilities—are more important for productivity than other items, which implies that even consumption and production for consumption must be directed in planning for development.

Here again, the colonial theory was biased in a pessimistic direction, as the possibility of raising the levels of the masses was not envisaged. The postwar theory, as represented by the total omission of consumption as a factor in the growth models, became biased instead in an optimistic direction, as it is implicit in those models that the extremely inferior levels of major items of consumption among the masses of people do not impose resistance to the growth of production in underdeveloped countries. This was accentuated by the common and unqualified stress on the need for increased savings, even on the part of these masses.

In one respect, the assumptions taken over from the economists' body of theories for the developed countries did work for rationality and realism and against bias. Ever since its origin in the era of Enlightenment, economic thinking has kept extraordinarily free from speculation about hereditary differences in regard to intelligence and other aptitudes between groups of people. In that respect, the economists have been on the side of the angels, for there is no scientific foundation for such speculation.

As already noted, the doctrine of racial inferiority was already on its way out in the later decades of the colonial era or lived a surreptitious life in people's privately held thoughts. That it could not possibly find a place in the writings of economists may have further contributed to its more complete disappearance after the war.

11. Differences in Initial Conditions

The distortion caused by the uncritical transference of the basic assumptions of economic analysis of developed countries led to the view that differences in the level of development have only a "dimensional," not a "qualitative," character.[9] More specifically, it was assumed that there is merely a "time lag" between developed and underdeveloped countries.

This thesis was put forward by Marx, who wrote in the preface to *Das Kapital:* "The country that is more developed industrially only shows, to the less developed, the image of its own future." Particularly in the United States, it has been popularized in simplified theories of "stages of growth," usually without accounting for their origin in old-fashioned "Marxism," and occasionally presented as an "anti-Marxist" conception. This formula of a one-dimensional development process is, in essence, only a consolidated expression of the uncritical application of the basic assumptions of the growth models worked out for, and used in, developed countries. It therefore gives a teleological slant of optimism to the study of conditions in underdeveloped countries.

Within the general framework of such an over-optimistic approach, it was natural that views tended to become distorted in the same direction, even in regard to conditions in the underdeveloped countries that, by themselves, should not be conceptually difficult to include in an "economic" theory.[10] This would, indeed, apply to climatic conditions, although, by tradition and for good reasons in regard to developed countries, they have been disregarded in economic analysis.

In the same way, it can easily be seen that economists, at least until recently, have not attached enough importance to population density and, in particular, the increasingly rapid population increase in underdeveloped countries. As a matter of fact, people mostly live in crowded circumstances, and there is "overpopulation" even in those countries that have large land reserves and an abundance of other natural resources. Spreading out population would, however, often demand, in addition to large investments and effective administrative exertions, domestic institutional reforms, especially in regard to land ownership and tenancy, and a political climate hospitable to such reforms. Going deeper into such matters is not in the tradition of Western economic theory.

Outside the traditional economic approach was also, even more generally, proper consideration of politics and political development. The now developed countries started out, well before industrialization, as fairly consolidated nation-states, able to pursue national policies. The underdeveloped countries, and not only the larger number of them that have only recently become independent, have to plan for bringing about and speeding up development while still striving to become consolidated as states and nations, effectively pursuing planned policies.

In regard to international trade, being a latecomer in the small developed world of the nineteenth century was not a disadvantage—often quite the opposite. Now, when huge backward regions try to emerge from political and economic dependency, they cannot simply repeat in the field of trade the development process of the developed countries. They also lack easy access to capital from abroad at low rates of interest, which the then developing countries had (in Sweden around 3 per cent and sometimes less).

The export prospects look dim for most underdeveloped countries. For industrial development, they have generally had to rely on investing in industries for import substitution. This is a development which cannot be planned too well, as the primary cause is usually exchange difficulties, bringing about import restrictions that tend to give highest protection to less necessary production.[11] This leads automatically to an often sky-high protection of such production and makes possible the growth of high-cost industries. Although, of course, these phenomena have been analyzed, it is not unfair to reproach economists with generally tending to underestimate the inhibitions and obstacles facing underdeveloped countries in their attempts to turn trade into an "engine of growth," as it was, and still is, in developed countries today. The highly successful development in a few smaller countries is the exception, not the rule.

It is commonly assumed that, in one respect at least, underdeveloped countries should today have an advantage over the present developed countries when they started out, since there exists a much more highly developed technology, which they can make use of without having the burden of inventing it. Even taking into account the need to adjust technology to the different factor proportions and other conditions in underdeveloped countries, there would be a net advantage. This is, however, a static view.

The rapid and steadily accelerating scientific and technological advance in the developed countries has had, and is now having, an impact on the underdeveloped countries' economies which, on balance and with some exceptions, is detrimental to their prospects for development.[12] In the developed countries, we shall continue to raise agricultural productivity and probably also protect our own farmers, make savings in the use of raw materials, and develop substitute products for traditional imports from underdeveloped countries. Scientific and technological advance in developed countries, and not only the present high level, is also partly responsible for the difficulty underdeveloped countries have in breaking through by increasing their production and export of industrial goods. All this is well known and commented upon in the specialized fields; however, the cumulative adverse effect on development in underdeveloped countries of scientific and technological advance is usually not accounted for in the development literature.

More generally, and contrary to a common misconception, change was not rapid in the countries which are developed today. In underdeveloped countries, there is now not time for the gradual transition experienced by the developed countries. The onslaught of the need for modernization, accentuated by the population explosion, leads to a situation where elements of modernism are sprinkled throughout a society in which many conditions have remained almost the same for centuries. As Jawaharlal Nehru said for India: "We have atomic energy, and we also use cow dung."

To take the view that spurts of modernism are important "growing points" is to assume a number of things: not only that the hampering effects of the population explosion at home and of the ever more rapid technological advance in the developed countries can be overcome, but also, more specifically, that the "spread effects" within the underdeveloped countries can be made to operate more effectively than most of them have done up to the present time.[13] This, in turn, would presuppose, among other things, determined policies initiated to effectively influence attitudes and institutions directly. But these "non-economic" factors were traditionally kept outside economic analysis and the planning of policies made on the basis of this analysis in "economic" terms. In regard to force and rapidity of the spread effects, economists have often innocently followed the lead of Marx.

These reminders are apt to become characterized as "pessimistic," which is natural in the intellectual milieu of "optimism" created by the postwar approach—dominated by economists trained in theories which may be more or less adequate to conditions in developed countries, but which were highly prejudicial in the study of them in underdeveloped countries. Both "optimism" and "pessimism" are, however, nothing but biases, from which scientific analysis should free itself in order to become, instead, realistic.

When a realistic study of the conditions in underdeveloped countries engenders a more sober view of the prospect for development, this should not lead to defeatism. Instead, it should motivate increased, and in many respects more radical, efforts: speedier and more effective large-scale domestic reforms in the underdeveloped countries and greater concern and more substantial sacrifices in developed countries. A realistic view of the world poverty problem must rightly demand a courage and determination that can never be inspired by opportunistic optimism.

The most serious moral criticism of the optimistic bias in the analysis of the development problem in underdeveloped countries conveyed by the postwar approach in economic research is that it supported complacency in the underdeveloped countries and lack of solicitude in the developed countries. This approach to the policy problems corresponded precisely to the shortsighted interests in both underdeveloped and developed countries, which, as we have pointed out, made that kind of bias opportune in both types of countries.

12. The Proper Use of Models

Every scientific approach must be simplifying. This is particularly necessary on that macro-level where conditions pertinent to planning for the development of an entire country are being studied. But it is not permitted to abstract from conditions that are crucially important in the society under study. An analysis in "economic" terms, abstracting from the existing social organization, that is, predominantly institutions and attitudes (but, as we noted, many other things too), may reach conclusions that are valid for developed countries but not for underdeveloped countries.[14]

The important point to stress is that such an analysis is not simply superficial, but also distorts and prejudices our view in a particular direction. That is why the thought implicit in much of the theorizing about underdeveloped countries—that it is a methodologically permissible procedure in research to establish first an "economic" theory, reserving the possibility of later adding considerations of the "non-economic" factors—is misleading. The theory must work with concepts that are adequate to reality in underdeveloped countries from the beginning, i.e., in the very approach to the problems. It is not advisable to throw the yeast into the oven after the bread has been baked.

Indeed, it is not even possible to define clearly what should be meant by "economic" problems or "economic" factors in underdeveloped countries without plunging deeply into the "non-economic" determinants that are so important there. From a scientific point of view, the only demarcation that is logically tenable when building our models is between relevant and less relevant factors.

13. Criticism of the Economic Models and the Use of Statistics

The growth models implied in conventional economic analysis of the development problems in underdeveloped countries—in terms of demand, supply, and prices, employment, unemployment, savings, investment, gross national product or income—were based on certain general assumptions that are unwarranted. One is that it is possible to reason in terms of aggregates for an entire underdeveloped country. In turn, this assumes, among other things, the prevalence of markets—and fairly effective markets at that. A third assumption is that it is realistic to exclude consumption from a growth model. And there are even other unrealistic assumptions.

This might be the place to insert a few remarks on the economists' use of statistics in the analysis of underdeveloped countries. In the beginning, the very fact that our knowledge about conditions in these countries was so extremely scant encouraged, or at least did not discourage, a careless use of the Western models. This was particularly true for those many economists who were content to construct models in the air and to insert Greek characters when data were missing.

When data were then obtained, they did not disturb economists working with the Western models, as these data were assembled by utilizing the conceptual categories implied in those models. The resulting mountains of figures have, therefore, either no meaning at all for analyzing economic reality in underdeveloped countries or an entirely different meaning from that imparted to them. The inadequacy of the conceptual categories utilized contributed, at the same time, to the extraordinary deficiencies of these statistics as, on the level of primary observations, it implied trying to ascertain things that did not exist or, in any case, could not be subsumed under these categories.

Thus the gross national product, or income, and its growth, were permitted to play a most important role in all discussion of development in underdeveloped countries. Even in developed countries, we are becoming aware that these concepts are flimsy (see Chapter 10). They take no consideration of distribution. Pollution and resource depletion are usually not accounted for. There is lack of clarity about what is supposed to be growing—whether it is real growth in any sense or merely accounting for costs caused by various developments, some of which are undesirable. The absolute or relative uselessness of conspicuous private or public consumption and investment is not taken into account. In underdeveloped countries, the absence of effective markets over a wide field of their economies and many other conceptual difficulties, peculiar to these countries, are additional. Partly because of all that, but partly also because of extreme weaknesses in the operation of the statistical services, the figures so confidently quoted in the literature on national product or income must be deemed almost valueless for most underdeveloped countries (Chapter 10, Section 7).[15]

For similar reasons, the same holds true of the figures quoted for other "economic" concepts in the macro-models —for instance, the figures for savings. Quite aside from the general weakness in the primary observations and the virtual impossibility of accounting properly for direct investments in agriculture and many other parts of the economy, the clear conceptual distinction in developed countries between two parts of an individual's income—that part which is consumed and that which is saved—has no counterpart in underdeveloped countries, where consumption and, in particular, some types of consumption to a different degree, are akin to direct investment.[16]

Statistics on international trade and capital movements should be more reliable. The concepts are clear-cut. And since political boundaries are crossed, this provides a double check on accuracy. In spite of large-scale smuggling in some underdeveloped countries, underdeclaration of exported merchandise in order to acquire foreign exchange outside the national controls, and undeclared capital flights, these statistics should be more reliable than most others.

But unemployment defined as an aggregate of workers, skilled in their trade, seeking but not finding employment at the prevailing wages in a market they know, is a concept which fits conditions in underdeveloped countries only for a very minor part of their labor force and even for them very imperfectly.[17] The term "underemployment," invented to fit conditions there better—implying, as it does, that there is a part of the labor force that could be "skimmed off" without decreasing production—has, when critically scrutinized, no definite meaning at all. The reality of actual and very apparent under-utilization of the labor force in underdeveloped countries has to be studied in purely behavioral terms, which relate to observable facts—which people work at all; for what periods during the day, week, month, and year they work; and with what intensity and effectiveness. Other concepts that have frequently been used, though they are plainly inadequate to reality, are, for instance, "accountancy prices"[18] and a number of constructs in the analysis of the economic effects of changes in the population field.[19]

The exemplification cannot be extended, or analyzed, in the context of this brief chapter. Let me merely assert that, when beginning massive research on conditions in underdeveloped countries along the lines of their theoretical models taken over from the analysis of the problems of developed countries, economists have commonly showed great carelessness in their use of statistics. The articles and books are punctuated by figures, many of them not worth the paper they are printed on. In confronting the development problems of underdeveloped countries, economists have in this respect commonly been tempted to operate on a lower level of carefulness and responsibility than we are accustomed to reckon with from their work on developed countries. It does not, for example, compare with the practices of the demographers, who have kept to their fine tradition of giving importance to scrutinizing the concepts they use and to accounting properly for the uncertainty of the data they present.

A basic cause is undoubtedly their approach, implying an overstraining of their theoretical models when uncritically applying them to underdeveloped countries. From what has already been said, it was to be expected that this use, or rather misuse, of grossly defective statistics generally implied giving passage to the optimistic bias. One flagrant example, a little outside the main concepts, is the use of figures for school enrollment. These figures are extremely unreliable in themselves, but they are, moreover, rather commonly used as if they measured what we are really interested in, namely whether children attend school, which they often do not (see Chapter 6, Section 7). The statistics on literacy are likewise very weakly founded and usually exaggerated.

14. The Master Model

The archetype of the theoretical growth model, which in the beginning dominated the literature, and which has continued to determine the very structure of the plans, is the one in which aggregate output is related to physical investment by the capital/output ratio. Designed originally as a theoretical tool in dealing with the problems of economic stagnation and instability in developed countries, this one-factor model was applied to the utterly different development problems of underdeveloped countries.

From what has been said above it is clear that this model, when used for analysis and planning in underdeveloped countries, implied on a gross scale an unwarranted abstraction from other relevant relationships, misplaced aggregation even in regard to the factors highlighted in the model, and an illegitimate isolation from other changes, induced or spontaneous.[20] It should be added that these critical points were equally valid when the model was broken up into separate models for two or more sectors in an economy, if, as was usual, the main approach was maintained.

The capital/output approach gained popularity among economists after the war because of several studies in Western countries that purported to show a close relationship between physical investment and economic growth. In fact, for a time the capital/output ratio came to be regarded as akin to the constants that have made it possible to advance knowledge of the physical universe by purely abstract mathematical reasoning. The application of the model for analysis of the development problems of underdeveloped countries was undoubtedly also opportune, because of the commonly shared and, as we shall find, not in itself entirely unrealistic view that the main "assistance" developed countries could render to the development efforts of the underdeveloped countries was to make more capital available.

In recent years, however, more intensive studies of economic growth in some highly developed Western countries have revealed that only a part of it could be explained by the amount of investment in physical capital. While estimates of the unexplained residual vary widely, they generally support the view that even in developed countries it is considerably bigger than that part of economic growth that can be explained by capital investment.

This important negative finding demolished, even in regard to developed countries, the foundation of the model cast in terms of physical investment alone and threw the door wide open to speculation about other operative factors in development: education, health, research, technology, organization, management, administration, and so on. Interest was focused mainly, however, on education. At least the more elaborate models all reduced what came to be called "investment in man" to the one factor: education.

The importance of education for development is, of course, nothing new, but had been appreciated by the classical and neo-classical economists from Adam Smith on. When in recent years it was announced as a discovery by some economists, the explanation is simply that it had been forgotten by members of our profession, particularly since World War II, when in their development models they began to think merely in "economic" terms and, more specifically, in terms of physical investment.

More striking, however, is the conservatism in basic approach of even this newest school of economists. They restrict themselves, in fact, merely to widening the abstract concept of investment in the capital/output model to include, besides physical investment, also "investment in man," usually understood as investment in the educational sector. Otherwise this model, so basic to the postwar approach, was left unchanged and as sovereign as before. We have thus arrived at a situation where the greater number of economists and planners continue to think almost exclusively in terms of physical investment, while some of them insist on including also education as investment in man.[21]

None, however, has ever attempted to ascertain or calculate returns on these latter investments for underdeveloped countries. But the approach is invalid for deeper reasons than the total absence of any other quantities than input. Adam Smith and Marshall would never have thought of theorizing along this line. Marshall even warned against treating education in terms of input and output. It can only conceal the real problems of the role of education in development. They are all related to the content and direction of education and its impact on attitudes and also institutions, in particular those of economic and social stratification, and the repercussions of these factors on education. As I shall show further in Chapter 6, Section 7, much education in underdeveloped countries has negative effects on development, and where the effects are positive they have no simple relation to the input, however it is accounted for.

Before leaving the master model, it should be noted that it is in accordance with that model that plans are still regularly presented, discussed, and later evaluated as financial plans, most often, in fact, as fiscal plans for public investment.[22] Since most of the policy measures needed for engendering development—besides physical investments— whether they are of the short-term operational type or imply more permanent alterations in social organization and attitudinal or institutional structures, have at most only the most incidental relation to costs and returns in financial terms and even less to a fiscal budget, this permits presenting the appearance of a plan without much real planning.

This is a large topic and one that must, in the present context, be covered by only a few general remarks. Of course, a fiscal budget is needed for orderly conduct and control of public expenditure and public administration. But that type of "planning" cannot serve as a rational coordination of, or even as a basis for, real planning, which should encompass induced changes in all sorts of economic and social conditions carried out in a coordinated fashion.

15. Trends

Even when the flimsy figures for gross national product or income have often indicated successful development— "more rapid than ever in the now developed countries," it is often asserted—there were many other signs apt to dampen the over-optimism caused by the opportunistic biases accounted for above and nurtured by the economists' rash approach, which excluded consideration of factors in the underdeveloped countries that make development so much more difficult. Partly because economists could not remain entirely unaware of this, they have generally become ever more eager to make the most generous reservations and qualifications—indeed to emphasize that, in the last instance, development is a "human problem" and that development must aim at "changing man."

Having thus made their bow to what they have become accustomed to calling the "non-economic" factors, all too many of them thereafter proceeded, however, as if those factors did not exist. Not even the most empty abstract model-building, without any real attempt to relate it to observable facts, is missing. High respect is even today paid to mathematical "sophistication" without much scrutiny of the concepts employed and the assumptions implied. An appearance of precision and rigor is created by gross simplifications, but there is a basic logical confusion in this way of thinking that is hidden by a common lack of clarity in regard to definitions of concepts and assumptions and scrutiny of their adequacy to reality.

Meanwhile, the more empirically inclined economists increasingly attempt to attain realism. By enlarging their vistas, they seek to encompass more and more of what was excluded from the simplified economic models. It should readily be admitted that in recent years the literature has been giving us more and more factual information about reality in the underdeveloped countries. As the models representing the scientific approach are found to lack realism, the idea is spreading that we "do not yet have a theory of development."

As already mentioned, however, the use of statistics made by even the empirically inclined economists lays itself open to severe criticism. Even when they have been made aware of the fact that, for underdeveloped countries, concepts like the national output or income, savings, or unemployment are inadequate to grasp reality in underdeveloped countries, they nevertheless continue uncritically to use these terms and also the statistics collected and aggregated under these categories, as if they were proper categories. And in spite of the fact, for instance, that it has been demonstrated that the figures for aid and assistance from the developed countries have been grossly falsified in an opportunistic fashion (see Chapter 7, Section 13), this criticism is ignored, and the figures are still often quoted and used as a basis for analysis.

And when the general point is made, as in this article, that an opportunistic bias has been permeating not only public debate but also the approaches applied in scientific economic analysis of the development problems in underdeveloped countries, this is met by blunt silence. The thought that economists, like other human beings, if they are not very careful in scrutinizing their thinking, are influenced by the tradition in which they are working and the inclinations prevalent in the society of which they are part, is taboo to the ordinary economist and excluded by incurable blindness from the conception he has of his work.

Meanwhile, the thousands of economists working on development problems have become an establishment with vested interests. These are shared by the great majority of all those involved in this field, politically and practically or as experts and consultants to governments and the various intergovernmental organizations. To these more material vested interests (including jobs and a chance to travel) should be added the inertia and conservatism of scientific thinking in economics, whenever the question is one of the structure of theories and not only of the specific arrangements within the general framework of this structure, which to most students give enough space for originality and even some controversy.

Nevertheless, the very fact that many researchers are now wrestling with the development problems of under-developed countries will, in ten or fifteen years' time, necessitate a change of scientific approach in the direction of institutional economics, taking due account of all the relevant "non-economic" factors. It is already on its way; we are in a transitional period.

In the very last few years the increase of interest in the importance of the "non-economic" factors has, indeed, led to United Nations resolutions and conferences for an "inte-grated" or "unified" approach in planning for development, which must of course make the author of this book happy. There is still, however, much confusion. But a development is on the way that in the end will be as radical as that from the colonial theory to the postwar approach. All honest re-search has an inbuilt, self-cleansing capacity.

The main responsibility for research pertinent to the problems of development and planning for the underdevel-oped countries will continue to rest on the economists. Even when those factors that have been largely excluded by the economists' theoretical approach are being broached by writers in the behavioral sciences or by persons working on practical problems such as community development, agricultural extension, or family planning, these analytical attempts of a different type mostly live a life apart, in special books and articles or in separate chapters in the plans, never really integrated into those plans. Seldom, and never effectively, do they challenge the economists' theories and their implicit assumptions. In any case, no alternative macro-theory and macro-plan are ever presented.

I have no doubt that economists will continue to play first fiddle in this field of study. We need to retain our tradition of taking the broader perspective of a macro-plan for an entire country but at the same time of keeping our eyes open for all the "non-economic" factors that are so crucially important to development problems, particularly in underdeveloped countries: the social structure and the political forces, broadly, attitudes and institutions, and also the productivity consequences of levels of living where those are very low. To avoid the arbitrariness that opens the door for bias, and to escape empty metaphysical exercises like those of "welfare economics," we must also equip ourselves more systematically with the research technique of working with explicit value premises, realistically tested for relevance, significance, rational compatibility, and feasibility.

Chapter 6

THE NEED FOR RADICAL
DOMESTIC REFORMS[1]

1. From a Different Angle

CHAPTER 5 was focused on the world poverty problem from
the viewpoint of how it has been approached in public
debate and in economic research. In this chapter, an attempt will be made to state positively some of the main
facts relative to the underdeveloped countries' actual situation and, in particular, to characterize the types of
policies that must be applied in order to engender rapid
and sustained development. It is in the nature of things
that the text must be condensed, consisting only, in fact,
of an assortment of *obiter dicta*, the evidence for which
has to be sought elsewhere. And even though the selection
of domestic reforms needed for development has been
made according to their importance for this purpose, there
are big gaps left. The stress will be laid on those types of
policies that tend to be disregarded in conventional economic analysis.

Every conscientious writer in the field has felt urged to
stress the great differences between the underdeveloped
countries and, indeed, districts of one country. When the
author labored over a comprehensive study of South Asia,
he made it a strict rule to stress throughout that his generalizations and inferences related only to that very large
region, which he had studied more intensively. But when he

later elaborated his policy conclusions and then tried to look a little closer at conditions in other underdeveloped regions as well, in order to reach policy conclusions for the whole of what is called the third world, he was surprised to find these conditions, and, in particular, the need for specific domestic reforms, much more similar than he expected. This will be stressed as we now attempt to view the world poverty problem from the angle of the planned policy measures needed in order to fulfill the quest for development.

2. Inequality

In spite of the radical premises for their theories that they inherited from the philosophers of natural law and utilitarianism, economists in all generations from the classics on have in general shown an inclination to assume that there is a conflict between egalitarian reforms and economic growth, in the sense that the price of a somewhat lower growth rate has to be paid for these reforms. This bias has been broken only in very recent times and in the most advanced welfare states. This conventional view was consistently argued in speculative terms (see Chapter 1, Section 4, and Chapter 3, Section 4).

When, after World War II, economists hastily came to direct their research interests to the development problems of underdeveloped countries, a preconception almost self-evident to most of them was that these extremely poor countries could not afford to think in terms of social justice and to pay the price for egalitarian reforms. As an American economist explained in a highly extolling book on the economic development of Pakistan under the tight upper-class regime headed by former President Ayub Khan:

A conflict exists . . . between the aims of growth and equality . . . the inequalities in income contribute to the growth of the economy. . . .

The author in question represents a group of economists who had for a long time tutored the planners in Pakistan. The book was published in 1967, immediately before Ayub's oligarchic rule over Pakistan was beginning to break down under the pressure, not simply of great and growing inequality between regions and classes of people, but of gross and unabashed corruption, which apparently had not been noticed by the economists and in any case had not been seen as detrimental to development.

There are a number of general reasons why in under-developed countries, contrary to the preconception of a conflict between the two goals of economic growth and greater economic equality, the latter is rather a condition for rapid and sustained growth.[2]

First, large masses of people in underdeveloped countries suffer from undernourishment, malnutrition, and other serious defects in their levels of living, in particular lack of elementary health and educational facilities, extremely bad housing conditions and sanitation. This impairs their pre-paredness and ability to work and to work intensively. It holds down production and implies that measures to raise income levels for the masses of people would raise produc-tivity. In the opposite direction, the forced savings on the part of these masses, brought about by inflation and the habitually high regressive taxation in underdeveloped coun-tries, may make possible some more physical investments, but at the same time it holds down or can even decrease labor input and labor efficiency.

Second, social inequality is tied to economic inequality in mutual relationship, each being both cause and effect of the other. Since social inequality, by decreasing mobility and free competition in the widest sense of the term, is undoubtedly detrimental to development, it is clear also that even through this causal link greater economic equality would lead to higher productivity.

Third, the usual argument that economic inequality, by

enriching an upper class that is able to save more of its income, has even less relevance in most underdeveloped countries, where landlords and other rich people are known to squander their incomes in conspicuous consumption, conspicuous investments, and sometimes (not only in Latin America) in flights of capital. Because of extreme deficiencies in the assessment and collection of taxes, inequality of incomes and wealth cannot contribute to public savings either.

Fourth, all underdeveloped countries have to strive for national consolidation. Inequality, particularly when it is on the increase, is a serious obstacle to such strivings.

Fifth, the experience that continued social reforms have been productive in the most advanced welfare states, with their much higher levels of living and already accomplished greater equality (Chapter 3, Section 4), should, *a fortiori*, apply to these very poor and inegalitarian countries. In these countries, well-planned and well-coordinated egalitarian reforms at the same time, from a national point of view, are regularly the most profitable investment that can be made, even though their gestation period might be considerable.

The real significance of these general reasons for egalitarian reforms, even from the point of view of engendering economic development, is revealed only when the issue is brought down to earth and discussed in relation to the need for specific reforms, as I intend to do below.

3. A Strange Paradox

We face a strange paradox in regard to the quest for greater equality in underdeveloped countries. On the one hand, the policy declarations in all underdeveloped countries stress the need for greater equality and, in particular, for raising the levels of living of the masses. On the other hand, economic as well as social inequality is not only very gross and harsh in most of these countries, but seems generally to be increasing. Policy measures declared to be taken in the interests of the poor are mostly either not implemented, or turn out in practice to favor the not-so-poor. Whatever development there has been has mostly enriched only the top strata, the urban "middle class," including all the "educated," what in South Asia are called the "rural elite," and sometimes also the organized workers in large-scale industry and transportation, leaving the swelling masses in the rural and urban slums about where they were —or sometimes worse off.

This cannot be unrelated to the fact that almost all underdeveloped countries are ruled by varying constellations of people in the upper class, taken in this wider sense. This is true even in countries such as India, where free discussion and other civil liberties are guaranteed, and with a system of government built upon universal suffrage. But it is usually even more the rule in the many underdeveloped countries under a more authoritarian rule, even when the rhetoric of the leaders claims "radical" and egalitarian policies.

The masses are generally not informed enough to be aware of their interests; still less are they organized to stand up for them in an effective way. When they break out of inarticulateness and passivity, they are too often driven by religious or ethnic fanaticism, combined with impulses to steal land and household property from each other. That type of "rebellion" is not only useless, but stands as an inhibition to rational and organized mass action in order to defend real and common interests.

Because of these tendencies, egalitarian reforms were then not initiated or, if initiated and even legislated, were either not implemented or were distorted. The upper classes are, however, in a serious ideological dilemma, and their moral position is weak. They were the harbingers of the modernization ideals from the West and from the Communist countries, among which ideals the egalitarian ones held a prominent place. To a large extent, they still often hold to them in their hearts. But, in the absence of determined and organized pressure from below, they have permitted their own interests, often shortsightedly perceived, to block egalitarian reforms.

The Seventies, designated by the General Assembly of the United Nations as the Second Development Decade, may well see increasing under-utilization of the labor force in growing rural and urban slums, and accentuated inequality and misery for ever larger numbers of people. Whether such a development will, by itself, increase the pressure from below is uncertain.

One factor that seems apt to consolidate the masses into rebellion is when a country like Vietnam, large parts of Africa, or even countries in Latin America can experience nationalism by being confronted with foreign forces. Compared with other modernization ideals, that particular type of nationalism seems more easily communicable to the masses. And under such circumstances, the radicals among the educated "middle class" can act as promoters and organizers.

On the other hand, the efficiency of modern weaponry and the increasing reliance on the military for governing a country may effectively hold down rebellions from below. This is not certain, however. A military dictatorship may initiate egalitarian reforms.

Generally speaking, any forecast of the political development in underdeveloped countries is complete speculation. The point stressed here is merely that, until now, most underdeveloped countries have harbored an inner conflict between a declared policy goal of egalitarian reform and an actual development toward preserving and even increasing inequality.

4. Industry and Agriculture

It was natural that industrialization became, from the beginning, a primary goal of the development efforts of underdeveloped countries.[3] It was even rationally motivated.
Indeed, for countries like India and Pakistan, it is not
possible to conceive that they will be able to retain even
the present low levels of living, still less to raise them, if
at the end of this century a much larger proportion of their
labor force, then double the size, is not employed in industry. With few exceptions, this holds true for most underdeveloped countries.

But what was not seen—and is often not seen even
today—is that, for the near future, the growth of modern
industry will not create much new employment in most
underdeveloped countries.[4] This is because of the low level
from which industrialization starts and the tendency of
modern industry not to be labor-intensive. In fact, because
of the "backwash effects" of squeezing out crafts and traditional industry generally, the growth of modern industry
might for a time actually decrease the total demand for
labor. This is particularly important since, whatever is
happening in regard to the spread of birth control among
the masses, the labor force will be increasing by 2 to 3 per
cent per annum, and in some countries even more, until the
end of this century or even longer.

If for no other reason, the trend toward attaching greater
importance to agriculture is well warranted. This does not
often involve a question of "priorities" in regard to the
disposal of resources. First, most of what is needed for
increasing agricultural yields (besides labor) is locally
available and in any case does not require much foreign
exchange, as is the case with industrialization. Often it is
not even a question of a change in the use of resources but
only of social organization (see below). Second, industriali-

zation may be directed toward serving agricultural advance by producing fertilizers, tools, and other implements for increasing agricultural production.

5. Land Reform

With few exceptions—principally plantations, which, like mining, should more properly be reckoned as industry— yields in agriculture are mostly very low in underdeveloped countries. This is related to the fact that agriculture is not— as is commonly assumed because of the very large part of the labor force tied to agriculture—intensive. It is, indeed, extensive. Labor utilization is extremely low, because of the very low input of the labor force and very low labor intensity.[5]

The low yields and the fact that almost every improvement in production techniques that is not merely labor saving is bound to increase the demand for labor of which there is a plentiful supply should give cause for some optimism in regard to the possibilities of increasing agricultural productivity. There are many inhibitions and obstacles in the way of doing so, but the main difficulties are undoubtedly rooted in the systems of land ownership and tenancy. They differ widely in the various countries and districts, but have one thing in common: they limit the opportunities and incentives for cultivators to work, and to work hard and efficiently.

The land reform that is needed could take various forms, depending on the conditions in the various countries and districts within countries. A more egalitarian redistribution among the cultivators, including the laborers and other landless groups, is one possibility. Cooperative farming is another. Municipal or state ownership is a third. It is even possible that in some countries a reformed type of capitalist farming could have an important role to play, but it would have to be purged of the pre-capitalistic practices of absentee land ownership and sharecropping, and give special protection to the workers. What is commonly needed is the creation of a new relationship between man and land that gives opportunities and creates incentives for man to work more, and more effectively, and to invest whatever he can to improve the land—starting with his own labor.

Land reform has long been on the political agenda in practically all underdeveloped countries. And almost everywhere governments have made a sham of it. When legislated, it has been a mini-reform, and, even then, has not been carried out effectively. In general, the interests of the landless laborers have been totally neglected. Secondary reforms—community development, agricultural extension, credit and other cooperatives—have had an easier passage. But in the absence of effective land reform, they have tended to assist the upper strata in the villages and thus actually increase inequality.

The recent availability of high-yielding varieties of grain is by itself a most important innovation. But it cannot possibly be a substitute for land reform. On the contrary, in the absence of land reform, it tends yet again to increase inequality. It draws into agriculture a new group of capitalist entrepreneurs that can afford to buy irrigated land, fertilizers, and other aids for intensive agriculture. It is they who then become favored by the various credits and subsidies—and their profits are largely untaxed. Their impact will become most serious when they convert to labor-saving equipment. This will then speed up the exodus to the slums of the cities. There the migrants will become displaced rural people and swell the open occupations, where labor is just as under-utilized as in agriculture.

But the general euphoria surrounding the discussion of the green revolution undoubtedly contributed to giving an excuse to researchers as well as politicians to let the need for land reform fade from their thoughts.

6. Population Policy

In practically all underdeveloped countries, populations are increasing at an unprecedented rate.[6] As already hinted at, the blunt fact is that no increase in the use of birth control among the masses, if it could be brought about, would have much effect on the growth of the labor force for a long time ahead. The new age cohorts that will be entering the labor force for decades to come are already born, or will soon be born.

This will steadily increase the difficulties in agriculture, which employs the greater part of the population and which is still guilty of a vast under-utilization of the labor force. The effect on economic and social stratification is to make it even more inegalitarian than it already is. Farmers who own some land will more often be reduced to share-croppers or landless laborers, while small farm units will in general tend to become still smaller. And again the stream of refugees from agriculture to urban slums will tend to swell.

On the other hand, the widespread use of birth control would have an immediate and favorable effect on the age distribution of the population. There would be fewer children to support. In many direct and indirect ways, a higher level of living would then result in an increase in labor productivity. In a next generation, both the reproduction potentialities and the rate of increase of the labor force would be lowered. But this could happen only by bringing down fertility now. For these reasons, all underdeveloped countries have the strongest interest in spreading birth control as soon and as effectively as possible.

In the now developed countries, both Western and Communist, birth control had to spread by "private enterprise" in individual families—in fact, through "subversive activity," since it was contrary to public policy, which used all the forces of organized society to stop it, including the church, the administration, the schools, the medical profession, and legislation. The underdeveloped countries, on the other hand, can make birth control public policy. Another advantage is that, while birth control in the developed countries did not depend much upon contraceptive techniques, the underdeveloped countries can teach these techniques and, in fact, have at their disposal an improved birth control technology which is still rapidly improving.

Nevertheless, the task of spreading birth control among the masses and asking millions of couples to change their most intimate sexual behavior is immensely difficult. And this must occur in populations that are very poor, illiterate or semi-illiterate, often with impaired health and vigor, and mostly living in traditional and stagnant communities with an inegalitarian and rigid social and economic structure, all of which breeds fatalism and apathy. It can truly be said that what underdeveloped countries are in dire need of accomplishing is something as unprecedented in the world as was the rapid fall in mortality due to the new medical technology made available after World War II, and the ensuing population explosion itself.

First, a government must, against strong prejudice and many widely spread false and opportunistic beliefs, make a firm decision to take action by instituting a vigorous public policy to implement birth control. Second, they must build up an administrative apparatus for the purpose, reaching out to the individual families in the villages and the city slums. They must employ a large staff of medical and paramedical personnel when such staff is extremely scarce and badly needed for many curative and preventive duties.

It is, indeed, not difficult to explain why family planning up till now has not been very successful—except in some of the smaller countries, which are usually not on the lowest economic level, where development has been faster and where the masses have been given a sense of social and economic dynamism; in the Asian regions they have often been under the cultural and political influence of China and Japan with their traditions of social discipline. But there is no alternative. Failure would everywhere be a serious blow to the hopes for development, and in many large countries it would be simply calamitous.

7. Educational Reform

The inegalitarian and rigid social and economic stratification in underdeveloped countries, which is depriving the masses of real opportunities to rise out of abject poverty, is above all based on two institutional structures: the structure of landownership and tenancy, and the educational system.[7] Even in the developed countries, education tends continuously to favor the upper class, thus contributing to a class-ranking which becomes partly hereditary, although in general diminishingly so as a result of reform activity stretching back over generations. In underdeveloped countries, however, this educational mechanism for preventing social and economic mobility continues virtually unbraked.

Following World War II and the Great Awakening, leaders in many underdeveloped countries demanded a radical reform of the educational system. In the main, that is exactly what has not happened, however. The school system has been allowed to follow a conservative laissez-faire line, passing a swelling stream of pupils through the established channels, without any interference except to try to enlarge those channels where the pressure in society was greatest. And the effective demand for education comes from the educated and articulate upper strata that everywhere have retained most of the political power in the local, provincial, and national governments.

One revolutionary idea was, however, widely accepted

and never contradicted: the abolition of illiteracy. This was a rational policy choice. Literacy is needed for acquiring higher skills in all occupations, including agriculture; it is essential for fostering more rational attitudes in all human relations; it cannot be put on a par with any of the other fine aims of popular education, as it is primarily an instrument whereby the other skills and aptitudes can be acquired. Any attempt to create an integrated nation with extensive participation by the people assumes a more widespread literacy. It is self-evident that an approach toward effective political democracy would have the same prerequisite.

But although, in general, literacy was adopted as a goal, actual implementational policies have not followed suit. For one thing, in non-Communist countries adult education has been almost scandalously neglected, and there must be adult education if general literacy is to be achieved within a reasonably short time span. Even more basically, it is needed to help make the school education of children effective. All the information we have suggests that children of illiterate parents tend to fall behind in scholastic achievement, become repeaters and dropouts, and that even those who stay on in school more easily lapse back into illiteracy.

The literacy goal became translated into a program merely for rapidly enlarging the enrollment of children in primary schools. Although the declared purpose was to give priority to the increase of elementary schools, what has actually happened almost everywhere is that secondary schooling has been rising much faster and tertiary schooling still more rapidly. This has happened in spite of the fact that secondary schooling seems to be some three to five times more expensive than primary schooling, and schooling at the tertiary level five to seven times more expensive than at the secondary level. This trend seems to be particularly accentuated in the poorest countries with the lowest levels of literacy.

Primary schools have, on the whole, been kept to a very inferior standard in regard to equipment and the quality of teachers. Again, this is particularly true in the poorest countries and the poorest regions of countries. As mentioned in the last chapter, the enrollment figures, particularly in the poorest countries and regions, are entirely unreliable because of the prevalence of irregular attendance, repeating, and dropping out. This represents a huge waste of resources. If expenditures were expressed in terms of costs per child who successfully completes primary school, the cost per pupil would be very much greater than is commonly accounted for. Unfortunately, the cost per pupil so calculated would be particularly high in the poorest countries and the poorest districts. The wastage is greatest where it can least be afforded.

Despite all efforts to make secondary and tertiary schools practical, technical, and job-directed, the results have mostly been only marginal. The bulk of them have remained "academic," "literary," and general. Teachers are of poor quality in these schools, too, and are often classified as "untrained."

Behind these various developments lie common causes. The winning of political independence did not work great changes in the peoples or their societies. The educational establishment is part of the larger institutional system, which includes the social and economic stratification, the distribution of property, and the power system. Those whose opinions and actions had some weight in these countries did not want radical reforms of the educational system. This system embodies strong vested interests on the part of the administrators, the teachers, the students and, above all, the families in the powerful upper strata who do not want to undermine the bolstering of their position provided by the inherited school system. Even radical students who demonstrate and protest at their universities have usually no inclination to go out in the villages and the city slums to teach and to organize the poor, as their counterparts in Russia did long before the Communist revolution.

The fact that a more practical and vocational orientation of the secondary schools would often require participation in manual work as part of the routine makes such schools less popular than the traditional ones. Generally, what is sought is the kind of status conferred by a degree, reflecting the system of valuations in largely stagnant inegalitarian societies, and some preparation for desk jobs. The whole school system is thus fashioned in a way that is anti-developmental. It consistently results in pressures to swell the administrative personnel, particularly in the lower brackets, and nevertheless in an increase in the number of "educated unemployed," who are simply miseducated not to want to soil their hands with manual work.

The radical reforms that are needed are, first, stress on adult education. The universities should be engaged in the effort. This, incidentally, would benefit both the students and the teachers by bringing them nearer to the acute problems of their countries and thus giving more purpose and meaning to both their studies and their lives.

The high priority of primary schooling should be carried out in practice, but even the expansion on the primary level should not be so fast as to permit a continuation of the low quality level of these schools, as now often happens. The enormous wastage of irregular attendance, repetition, and dropping out could then be combatted more effectively. The competence and status of teachers should be raised. The institutions for teacher-training should be made into "power plants" that generate moral and intellectual energy among students to prepare the people for development.

The expansion of tertiary and, in most underdeveloped countries, even secondary schooling should be halted or even reversed for some time. This would make it possible to raise quality standards and, in particular, to increase sub-

stantially, at the same time, the number of those schools
that give technical, vocational, and professional training—
providing, instead of generalists, more and better trained
teachers, agricultural extension workers, medical and paramedical personnel, to point out only a few of the fields
where more trained personnel are urgently needed.

8. Greater Social Discipline

All the underdeveloped countries are, though in varying
degrees, "soft states."[8] There are deficiencies in their legislation, providing loopholes, and in particular, in law observance and enforcement leading to widespread arbitrariness. Public officials on all levels disregard rules and
directives which they should follow. Often they act in
collusion with powerful persons and groups of persons
whose conduct they should regulate. This all acts as an
impediment to policy-making and policy implementation,
weakening and distorting efforts to plan for development.

The laxity and licentiousness in a state can be, and are,
exploited for unjust enrichment by persons who have economic, social, and political power. But in a soft state there
will be a much wider spread of a general inclination to
resist public controls in all strata. This failure to fulfill
duties in a state has apparently little to do with its form of
government. A country under authoritarian rule, such as
Thailand or Indonesia, as well as many countries in Latin
America or Africa, can be as soft as India or Ceylon with a
functioning parliamentary system and a government dependent on regular elections—or, in fact, mostly even softer.

In any one of the underdeveloped countries this pattern
of its state has to be explained in terms of its history,
which has set its mark on the various forms and shapes that
have developed in the appearance of its softness. But in
spite of big differences in regard to historical development,

all underdeveloped countries today show a remarkable similarity in the main features of softness in their states. Almost nowhere can a definite and rapid evolution of a more effective state be discerned today. This is serious. It is everywhere evident that without more social discipline development efforts are being frustrated.

Corruption is a significant element in the life of a soft state, crucially important in itself as well as in its generally demoralizing effects on all social, economic, and political relations. It is not only extraordinarily widespread in all underdeveloped countries, but seems mostly to be on the increase, nurtured by almost every change that occurs.

Corruption is highly detrimental. It introduces an element of irrationality in all planning and plan fulfillment. As the method of exploiting a position of public responsibility for private gain is the threat of obstruction and delay, it impedes the processes of decision-making and execution on all levels. It increases the need for controls to check the dishonest officials, while it makes the honest officials reluctant to take decisions on their own. In both respects it tends to make administration cumbersome and slow.

Corruption, and the widespread knowledge of corruption in the population, counteract the strivings for national consolidation. In particular, they decrease the respect for, and allegiance to, the government. Indeed, they endanger political stability. It is a fact that, wherever a political regime has crumbled, a major and often a decisive cause has been the prevalence of misconduct among politicians and administrators, and the concomitant spread of unlawful practices among businessmen and the general public. A common pattern is, however, that any new regime soon becomes equally corrupt, or more so.

One important causal factor in promoting corruption in underdeveloped countries is the practice of Western business firms of bribing politicians and officials in order to get a deal through and to run their enterprises without too many obstacles. Undoubtedly, this is damaging, not only to the development interests of the underdeveloped countries, but also to the long-term interests of Western businesses and Western countries.

Western businesses are already stigmatized in the eyes of many intellectuals in underdeveloped countries as being associated with exploitation, colonialism, and imperialism. The observation that they undermine the integrity of politicians and higher administrators is now added to these sources of resentment. In addition, gaining advantage by bribery constitutes an obvious means of unfair competition, which the business community in all Western countries has been eager to have stopped at home by legislation.

When corrupt practices in underdeveloped countries have systematically been shoved under the carpet, this is a strange example of the shortsightedness of Western capitalism and Western governments. Bribing officials in their own states is ordinarily a serious crime, but not when it is done abroad. When practiced in underdeveloped countries, it is even condoned by letting the bribes be counted for tax exemption, as for ordinary business expenditure. And the problem is never publicly discussed, either in the parliaments or in the businessmen's own organizations, national or international. I know of no Western country that does not have this blot on its escutcheon.

But, quite aside from Western interests, which are obviously on the side of enforcing honest practices, the abstention by Western business firms from bribing their way into the economic life of underdeveloped countries would be a very substantial "assistance" to those countries in their attempts to overcome the disabilities that make them soft states.

9. Common Traits

These conditions in underdeveloped countries, and the suggested radical reforms, have one trait in common. They concern crucial aspects of inequality of opportunity, and the reforms are all intended to work toward creating greater equality. The underlying thesis is that bringing about greater justice by wisely planned egalitarian reforms, exemplified above for several main fields, would also enhance the possibilities for growth and development. Indeed, domestic reforms along these lines are a by far more important requisite for their rapid and sustained development than any favors obtained from abroad.

But these things all concern "non-economic" factors and are therefore easily excluded from development analysis along the economists' conventional approach. It is not unfair to state that in the literature on planning for development, land reform as a condition for raising productivity in agriculture has generally either been disregarded entirely or dealt with in a superficial and prejudiced way. Recently, the green revolution has rather commonly been permitted to let the issue of land reform be overshadowed altogether.

The more recent contribution by some economists, who have raised education as an important issue in development, was hedged into dealing with it as "investment in man" in aggregate input/output terms. As was pointed out in Chapter 5, Section 14, this blurred people's vision and prevented them from grasping the real and very serious problems in that field, which all concern who is taught and what is taught.

In regard to corruption and, more generally, the reality of the soft state, economists have kept themselves in a strange state of forced innocence about these facts of life. The matter is usually not even mentioned in most economic literature. A few economists—usually Americans, because

other Western or indigenous economists have preferred to
remain more completely silent on this issue in their writings
—even put the erroneous thought into print that bribery is
harmless, or even that it may serve as a lubricant in a
cumbersome administration, while the truth is that corruption is a major reason for administration becoming cumbersome and less efficient.

All these reforms must be carried out by governments in
the underdeveloped countries themselves. And when economists, following out their systematic abstraction from attitudes and institutions and neglecting to include consumption in their growth models, shy away from dealing with
the immensely important problems for development dealt
with in this chapter, this implies gross and systematic
biases, satisfying the opportunistic interests of the ruling
upper strata everywhere in underdeveloped countries who
stand against reforms. That these interests mostly are short-
sightedly perceived, even from the point of view of these
strata, does not make the approach less biased.

10. Other Shortcomings

There are many other systematic shortcomings in the
policies and planning of policies in the underdeveloped
countries which are not directly related to the equality
issue. The reason for stressing in this chapter the egalitarian
reforms that are needed for reaching greater social justice,
but are at the same time of crucial importance for engendering rapid and sustained economic growth, has been
that, at least until very recently, they have largely been
left out of the economic literature on planning for development in these countries, or have been dealt with in a
superficial and prejudiced way.

Many of these other shortcomings in economic planning
are, however, indirectly related to the equality issue, as

they very generally tend to reinforce the trend of increasing inequality. Most of these countries try to encourage industrial investment and enterprise by direct subsidies, cheap rates of foreign exchange, and protection from foreign competition by import restrictions, low prices for services and goods from the public sector, and low effective taxation of profits. Generally speaking, these policies favor big enterprises and rich people. The various services, as well as all sorts of credits and subsidies, rendered to agriculturists likewise tend to support those who are relatively better off, whatever has been said to the contrary in motivating these policies.

Generally speaking, all these measures to encourage investment and enterprise have been applied so strongly that at the same time negative controls have to be applied in order to preserve balance[9]—like driving a car with the accelerator pressed to the floor but the brakes on. Many of the positive controls—for instance, the awarding of foreign exchange or licenses to import—but also most of the others are applied in ways that imply discretionary administrative decisions, while price policies and other nondiscriminatory policy measures are less often used. The same is even more true of the countervailing negative controls.

The widespread existence of conflicting controls thus implies that more controls are needed and also that a larger part of the controls become of a discretionary type than would otherwise be necessary. This is particularly unfortunate from a development point of view, as one of the most serious bottlenecks in underdeveloped countries is the lack of administrators with competence and integrity.

The point to be stressed in the present context is that this situation, where so often slips of paper are coming to be worth money, increases the temptations to bribe and to take bribes. When, in almost all underdeveloped countries, corruption is so widespread, tends to be on the increase, and also tends to take very similar forms, independent of differing historical backgrounds, an important part of the explanation is the trend toward discriminatory controls and the reluctance to use price policies and other nondiscriminatory policy measures.

11. The Neo-colonial Mechanism

The egalitarian reforms dealt with in the preceding sections are all in line with cherished ideals in developed Western countries. With individual variations of timing and accomplishments, they all have now become democratic welfare states. These types of reforms have become part of their economic, social, and political history—those in education, for instance, for a century and more, but with a rapid acceleration in recent decades.

Rationally, it should be strongly in line with Western ideals to support the liberal forces in underdeveloped countries that are now fighting for domestic reforms. There is hardly a single member of the legislative assembly in any Western country who would not welcome an underdeveloped country's taking effective action for land reform, spreading birth control among the masses, democratizing its educational system, enforcing more social discipline, and taking vigorous measures against corruption.

In 1965, Congress inscribed in the United States Foreign Assistance Act the so-called Title IX, which instructs the Agency for International Development to use its influence to assure maximum participation in the task of economic development on the part of the people of developing countries, through the encouragement of democratic private and local governmental institutions in the interest of "sustained economic and social progress." No congressional decision, however, has been left more toothless and without tangible results. Very generally, the influence exerted by developed

Western countries has worked to support reaction in these countries. Why is this so?

In the worldwide colonial power system as it functioned until after World War II, there was a built-in mechanism that almost automatically led the colonial power to ally itself with the privileged groups. To support its reign, the colonial government would thus feel an interest in upholding or even strengthening the inegalitarian social and economic structure in a colony. There is no doubt that a similar mechanism has been in operation since the disappearance of colonialism and that now, as before, it also has its counterpart in those underdeveloped countries that were politically independent, primarily in Latin America. This is the main justification for the use of the term "neo-colonialism."

It is understandable that business interests in the West would be more willing to invest in an underdeveloped country where the reins were tightly held by an oligarchic regime bent upon preserving the social, economic, and political *status quo.* It was also natural that they preferred to deal with the rich and powerful there. Indeed, they had to. That this, in turn, strengthened these people in their own countries is equally self-evident. They are, however, exactly the groups who raise the resistance to domestic reforms or see to it that they become ineffective or even distorted. The governments in developed countries felt inclined to take into account the interests of their business firms operating in underdeveloped countries. In their aid policies the governments, like business firms, also had to deal with the groups in power.

I have stressed this development as an almost automatic process when very rich countries have economic relations with very poor ones. Events would tend to take this course rather independently of any but very firm policy decisions on the part of the developed Western countries. This process was, however, given an extra impetus by the cold war, which had its beginning and further development *pari passu* with the process of decolonization. The United States, which took upon itself the responsibility of leader of the "free world," used national policy to keep that mechanism well oiled, especially during the long Dulles-McCarthy era, when anti-Communism was the determining factor in its foreign policy. Financial and unilateral aid was, and still is, very firmly awarded to utterly reactionary regimes.

All in all, it must be concluded that the developed Western countries have not used their influence in under-developed countries to spur them to develop their societies in line with Western liberal ideals. Rather, on balance, they have supported economic, social, and political reaction of sometimes the most sinister character. When economists shunned analysis of the importance of radical domestic reforms for development in underdeveloped countries, this bias not only pleased the ruling oligarchies in these countries but also suited the policies actually pursued by the developed countries.

12. Trade and Capital Movements

The inherited theory of international trade was never worked out to explain the reality of underdevelopment and the need for development in the poor countries.[10] While international inequality has been steadily increasing for a century or more, this imposing structure of abstract reasoning was directed rather toward showing that international trade initiates a tendency toward a gradual equalization of factor returns among different countries. This tendency, however, can operate only under assumptions that are grossly unrealistic.

The fact is, contrary to established economic theory, that unhampered international trade—and capital movements—will generally tend to breed inequality and will do so the more strongly when great inequalities are already established. By what I call circular causation with cumulative effects, a country which is greatly superior in productivity will tend to become more superior, while a country on an inferior level will tend to be kept at that level or even to deteriorate further, as long as matters are left to the free unfolding of the market forces.

Leaving the inadequate theory aside, we here face another built-in mechanism, operating automatically to the disadvantage of the underdeveloped countries. As in the case of aid, it has become strengthened by the policies of developed countries. Their commercial policies generally discriminate against the export interests of underdeveloped countries in many various ways.[11]

Following independence, underdeveloped countries had the opportunity to break this vicious circle by purposefully planning their own commercial policies. Even if their planning and its implementation are above par, they can still influence only their own underdeveloped economy, which does not take them very far. Such an economy is very dependent on the rest of the world and, in particular, on the market conditions and the policies of developed countries, which dominate world commerce and finance.

They must, therefore, press for changed policies on the part of the developed countries and obtain not only their abstention from discriminatory commercial policies but their finding means of positively promoting the export interests of underdeveloped countries. The whole structure of the economies and the international trade of these countries has become so warped and "unbalanced" as a result of the unhampered play of the market forces for generations, aided by the narrowly selfish policies of developed countries, that nothing less would be really effective. This is what the great movement of the underdeveloped countries that led to UNCTAD is all about.

A major part of the explanation why great results have not as yet been achieved is the widespread maintenance in developed countries of shortsighted commercial policies that are injurious for the underdeveloped countries. The industries where the latter countries could compete—resource-based and labor-intensive—are usually not the industries which it is in the developed countries' long-term interest to promote or even to preserve at home. They are usually low-wage industries. Rational planning in developed countries should regularly attempt to keep labor resources scarce and to move them to high-productivity industries. A similar criticism can be made of the developed countries' agricultural protection—of sugar production, for instance. The blame should ordinarily not be put on the "capitalist system." On these points, it is the people, represented by trade unions and other interest organizations, more often than "big business," who are reactionary and who lack vision.

13. Aid and the Juggling of Statistics

The development of underdeveloped countries depends first of all upon what these countries themselves do to engender it. This generally accepted view stands out even more importantly when, as is done in this chapter, the crucial role of egalitarian domestic reforms is recognized and duly accounted for. Nevertheless, considering the desperately difficult position in which these countries find themselves, not only more commercial considerations but also financial assistance could play a significant role.[12]

Leaving aside for the moment to what countries aid is going, its purposes, and the political conditions under which it is bestowed, aid as measured in real terms has been decreasing globally in the last decade. It has never been allowed to imply sacrifices for people in developed countries. Increasingly, loans have been substituted for grants, and both types of beneficent capital transference have been tied to exports from the "donor countries." The political interests of those countries have continuously been allowed to play a major role.

In this situation, aid statistics, as published by the developed countries, have been juggled. The figures as presented usually have not even taken account of rising prices, which, of course, would never happen in regard to national products or wages in any of the developed countries. By lumping together loans and grants, the aid element in capital transfers has been exaggerated. Tying both loans and grants to exports favors some private industries at home, but restricts the aid-receiving countries' freedom of choice and often considerably increases costs. The United States has taken the lead in decreasing its aid to underdeveloped countries and in juggling the statistics.

Added to this is the politics of aid-giving. Between a quarter and a third of what is accounted for as foreign aid is simply part of the United States' military involvement in Indochina—going to those parts of South Vietnam it controls and a few satellite countries in the region helping it in that war.

Making an honest account of what can be classified as genuine aid would, for the United States, reduce the official figures by more than half, perhaps by two thirds, perhaps even more. In the figures presented by most other developed countries, there is also a lot of misrepresentation, although generally less so. This has importance in that it shows the United States' share in global aid-giving as being even more falsified.

These twisted figures are then uncritically accepted and presented in annual reports by the Development Assistance

Committee (DAC) of the Organization for Economic Co-operation and Development (OECD), which includes practically all of the developed non-Communist countries.

Besides these "public flows," DAC also presents statistics for "net private flows," which are a very mixed bag of business transactions, ranging from direct investments to short-term and often expensive export credits that never would be reckoned as aid or assistance when made between developed countries. No intensive analysis is carried out, for instance indicating the share of direct investments that in a very few spots on the map of the underdeveloped world goes into the extraction of oil and other minerals in brisk demand and that, even there, can have few development effects compared to investments in manufacturing industry.

Moreover, as profits, interest payments, payments for licenses, and so on are not included in the "back flows," and neither is the capital sent out by residents of underdeveloped countries, these figures do not give a true picture of what actually happens in the financial field. It is generally accepted, for instance, that in Latin America the back flows, including those not accounted for in the DAC statistics, are much bigger than public and private inflows as defined by DAC.

But when DAC's figures for the public and private flows —after what is called an "aid review" by officials of the member countries—are computed and published, they are then widely accepted as measuring "development assistance" or simply "development aid." This mutation occurs in scholarly as well as popular and political writings and pronouncements.

Pertinent to the problems discussed in this chapter is the fact that the economic profession on the whole has not effectively criticized these manipulations of the data. It all works in the interest of the developed countries, which want their efforts to aid underdeveloped countries to figure higher than they are. The experts of underdeveloped countries acquiesce in this deceptive practice, by opting for the view that "you don't look a gift horse in the mouth."

Now that the defects of the DAC statistics have been revealed, I have been informed that the DAC Secretariat will gradually try to rectify its statistics—as much and as rapidly as the vested interests of the member governments will permit.

14. Aid and Motivation

Even though economists have mostly been less than careful in regard to the definition of aid to underdeveloped countries, and accepted and used statistics in an uncritical way, as a group they have generally been in favor of aid and increased aid in the whole postwar era. Indeed, much of the economic literature on the development of underdeveloped countries has the character of pleas to the peoples and governments in developed countries to be prepared to do more to aid underdeveloped countries.

They have then had to show motivations for aid-giving by developed countries, and have followed a pattern that is common to all who have argued for aid—that aid is also in the interest of developed countries. I criticized this motivation in Chapter 3, Section 7, showing that it is based on unproved rationalizations, not upon true knowledge (see also Chapter 9, Sections 3 and 4). I also gave reasons why the faltering in recent years of the willingness to give aid must be explained principally by the fact that people in developed countries do not believe in, and are not moved by, the pretended self-serving interests of developed countries.

More generally, the discovery that aid—of the type and magnitude actually awarded—cannot be seen to have promoted democracy, peace, and development, not to speak of the false baits of gratitude and political sympathy—has tended to breed cynicism and even a biased pessimism about the development prospects of underdeveloped countries (quite the opposite of the biased over-optimism that initially characterized the approach, commented upon in the last chapter).

On the other hand, it is equally obvious that in the few, mostly smaller, developed countries where aid has been increasing and is accounted for in a more correct way, these arguments in terms of self-interest have been given less weight or have been totally absent. Aid has had to be argued far more simply as motivated by human solidarity with, and compassion for, the needy. And I state my firm conviction as an economist having studied these problems, that this is the only motivation that holds, and it is this we must stress if we want to reverse the global trend toward decreasing aid to underdeveloped countries.

It is unrealistic and self-defeating to distrust the moral forces in a nation. As an American writer rightly observes, when the American public appears "massively indifferent to the aid program," the explanation may be that "its humanitarian and fundamental decency have not been properly appealed to."

Before leaving this problem of the motivation for aid to underdeveloped countries, a crucial relationship to the internal development in these countries should be stressed. As long as they show great and increasing inequalities, as long as they are ruled by rich oligarchies, as long as corruption is widespread and increasing, it will continue to be difficult to argue for aid in terms of solidarity and compassion. The man in the street will ask: Why don't they tax their own rich and reform their own countries before they come to us with the begging bowl?

This points to the necessity for setting moral and political conditions for aid, if we want to increase it substantially. No aid can be neutral. Preference should be given to underdeveloped countries which are trying to carry out reform.

If aid is given to other countries, it should be given in such a way that it promotes internal equality.

These rules are set out here, not only because they are in the interest of rapid and steady development in underdeveloped countries, as has been argued above, but also because the moral valuation basis for aid will otherwise not be solid. A main reason why popular support in developed countries has been decreasing is that, up till now, aid has on balance not been properly directed, but given instead to prop up reactionary regimes.

15. Concluding Observations

Pointing to the brief period during which the idea that developed countries should feel concern for development in underdeveloped countries has had any reality, I expressed at the end of Chapter 3 a guarded optimism in the slightly longer run. Until well after World War II, the colonial power system had served as a protective shield for consciences in Western developed countries. There was, in particular, no political basis for feeling any degree of collective responsibility on the part of the peoples there for what happened in underdeveloped countries. When we have criticized the policies in regard to trade and aid, we should remind ourselves how very new the idea is of such a collective responsibility on the part of developed countries. Perhaps, for this reason, we should not feel disheartened about the prospect of those international relations gradually developing in line with the valuations that have given the developed countries their still rapidly evolving domestic welfare states.

Nor is there reason to mistrust the future progress of economic science in the many areas where this and the preceding chapter have found it so seriously wanting. Again we have to recall that scientific interest in the development problems of underdeveloped countries is still a very recent thing—almost entirely a postwar phenomenon. As we continue to wrestle with these problems and are compelled to check out hypotheses and findings against actual facts, a new, truly institutional approach will gradually establish itself. As in all scientific progress, new perspectives will open up through controversy and through more careful investigation of the facts.

Rectification of the present situation in regard to both theoretical speculation and empirical research is needed for three reasons. It is needed because what is presented in our literature as facts and interrelations between facts should be true. This is a general requirement of our scientific endeavor. It is also urgently needed if we are to succeed in impressing upon the peoples of developed countries the necessity of exerting themselves, and even undertaking sacrifices, in order to help underdeveloped countries to develop. Last but not least, it is needed to give the support that true knowledge can give to the liberal forces in underdeveloped countries which, against heavy odds, are struggling for domestic reforms.

Chapter 7

HOW SCIENTIFIC ARE
THE SOCIAL SCIENCES?[1]

---

1. Gordon Allport

I FEEL HONORED to have been invited to be the first Gordon
Allport Memorial Lecturer at Harvard. I am not a psychologist in any sense of the word. I was personally never close
to Gordon Allport, although we once met here at Harvard
in the late Thirties and found ourselves in heartfelt agreement on how we wished the social sciences to develop.

Since then, our scientific endeavors have, of course, been
made in different spheres. I have remained an economist,
though more and more definitely oriented in an institutional
direction. Gordon Allport had, throughout his working life,
remained faithful to his original vocation as a psychologist,
combining his fundamental interest in the problems of the
personality of individuals with an urge to reach out toward
a social psychology. Allport lived through periods when he
was considered a rebel against what was generally conceived of as the established course of psychological study.
But he also witnessed the acceptance after some time of
specific lines of research—though he was not always credited with having been the one who had opened them up.

Whenever in my working life I happened to come across
a book or article by Allport, I felt the sympathy of the like-
minded. I say this to explain why I felt I could not possibly

decline when I was invited to give this lecture. If you will
excuse me for a brief digression from the topic of my lecture tonight, I would like to give a personal testimony explaining why I felt this sympathy.

First, and most important, Gordon Allport never isolated
social problems from moral valuations. He began his teaching here at Harvard as an instructor in social ethics and he
ended it as the first Richard Clarke Cabot Professor of
Social Ethics. He was, if not the initiator, nevertheless one
of the most prominent leaders of the Society for the Psychological Study of Social Issues. He thus followed out
what another great American scholar, John Dewey, once
proclaimed:

> Anything that obscures the fundamental moral nature of
> the social problems is harmful. . . . Any doctrine that elim-
> inates or even obscures the function of choice of values
> and enlistment of desires and emotions in behalf of those
> chosen, weakens personal responsibility for judgment
> and for action.

Not only in economics but also more generally in the
social sciences this question of moral valuations has too
often been forgotten. To reason as if people were not concerned with what is right and what is wrong, and as if they
were not all struggling with their consciences, has been
supposed to make social research particularly "hard-boiled."
To Allport, this was simply unrealistic.

Another trait of Gordon Allport as a student of human
beings and their society was his clear recognition that there
is an element of the *a priori* in all research, even though
the endeavor must always be to confront it with, and adjust
it to, the facts. Facts do not organize themselves into systematic knowledge, except from a point of view. This point
of view amounts to a theory—theory being understood in
the only meaning it can have: a logically consistent system
of questions to the social reality we are studying.

Another of the main characteristics of Gordon Allport's scholarship was that he remained within two great traditions, both of which we inherited almost from the era of Enlightenment but which have tended recently to be neglected.

First, the researcher should never complicate his presentation more than is strictly needed for fullest clarity and incisiveness. Allport never mistook the unnecessary elaboration of a strange terminology, or the exercise in diagrams and mathematical equations where the missing data are represented by Greek characters, as, by themselves, significant contributions to scientifically relevant knowledge.

Second, the student, however engaged he might be in his research, should be prepared to take time off to speak plainly to the general public. This was in earlier generations felt to be a duty of every learned person, and adhered to not least by the greatest and most originally creative in our line of work. Now it has in our profession too often become an ambition of false scientism that we should speak only to each other and keep the public out.

The reason why I was tempted to make these introductory remarks on Gordon Allport as a student in his field was the deep sympathy I have felt with the direction of his work. I wanted to use this opportunity to express it.

When I was then brooding over what topic to choose for this Memorial Lecture, I was naturally seeking one that would have interested Gordon Allport, were he now among us, and I finally decided upon "How Scientific Are the Social Sciences?" Our working lives have, as I said, taken us into different spheres, and I would not assume that Allport would have agreed in all respects with what I shall say—which is, of course, founded upon my own particular research experiences. But I feel certain that the problem as a problem is one he had himself lived with, as I have.

2. The Boundary Between Natural and Social Sciences

The question raised by the title of my lecture contains a comparison with the natural sciences, which I shall conceive of as including medicine. There is, to be sure, a broad borderland between the social and natural sciences. Thus psychiatry is mainly, though not altogether, in the field of social science. Also, almost all branches of medicine have to reckon with social conditions and processes that interplay with physiological ones in diagnoses and prognoses as well as therapy.

Some problems in experimental psychology are clearly of the natural science variety, even if they have to be combined with quite different types of insights in order to be at all complete in explaining a psychological problem in personality terms. In the same way, economic analysis and planning have to integrate elements of knowledge from almost all the natural sciences, for instance climatology or soil chemistry, and also a number of special technologies.

From these border problems and, generally, the interrelationships between social and natural sciences, I abstract in what follows. I intend to reason in terms of pure types of social and natural sciences.

3. Why Does Social Science Seem Slow?

There is a general understanding, that to us social scientists must be disturbing, namely that in our field of study progress is very much slower than in the natural sciences. It is the discoveries and inventions within the natural sciences that are thrusting radical changes upon our societies, while what we are producing in the social sciences, until now, has been much less consequential. To this is related a creeping anxiety about a dangerous hiatus inherent in this contrast.

While man's power over nature is fast increasing, his control over himself and his society is lagging far behind.

Part of this problem has to do with the greater difficulties we social scientists meet when trying to have our knowledge applied. To that problem of the relative ineffectiveness of "social engineering" I shall return at the end of my lecture. But the more fundamental problem is whether advance in the social sciences is slower than in the natural sciences, and the adjacent problem of why this is so, if it is so.

One possible explanatory hypothesis would be that, in recent decades, a smaller proportion of a nation's superlatively gifted young people have been entering the social sciences, while a larger proportion entered the natural sciences. In the social sciences we would then not attract our due share of the small minority in every generation who are endowed with that rare combination of mental and physical stamina, willfulness, adventurousness, and high intelligence that can engender radical departures from conventional approaches and produce great discoveries and inventions.

In the social sciences we should suffer from a relatively lower intake of geniuses. The rapid, and acceleratingly rapid, advances of natural sciences in our time and their very apparent practical importance must lend them prestige and glamour, and would also often enhance the prospects of great immaterial and material rewards to those who feel themselves highly capable and who trust in their intuitive apprehension and their luck. I do believe that the hypothesis is plausible enough to warrant more conclusive studies about the selection process which determines the recruitment of students to the various sciences. This is, in the first instance, a challenge to the psychologists.

The hunch I have reached by scientifically uncontrolled induction from unassorted experiences, gathered while living and working as an economist with many contacts with colleagues both in the social and the natural sciences, is that there might perhaps be something in that hypothesis. But even were it true to some extent, it can certainly not be a major cause why advance in the social sciences seems to be slower than in the natural sciences.

4. Our Problems Are More Difficult

The crucial fact is rather that the problems we are dealing with are truly much more difficult to master than those in the natural sciences. And the specific character of the greater difficulties we meet is, at the same time, such that our findings appear, and also are, less "scientific," measured by standards applicable in the natural sciences.

In explaining our lagging, it is sometimes pointed out that in the social sciences we are usually not permitted to make experiments. Astronomy is, however, even more completely denied the opportunity to experiment with the universe than we with our fellow human beings. Moreover, medical research has to work with similar inhibitions in this regard.

The really important difference between us and our natural science colleagues is illustrated by the fact that we never reach down to constants like the speed of light and of sound in a particular medium, or the specific weights of atoms and molecules. We have nothing corresponding to the universally valid measurements of energy, voltage, amperes, and so on. The regularities we find do not have the firm, general, and lasting validity of "laws of nature."

If we economists, for instance, establish by observation the income or price elasticity for, say, sugar, our findings are valid for only a specific group of consumers in a single community or region at a particular time—not to mention the fact that the concept elasticity itself loses what I call adequacy to reality, and thereby analytical usefulness, in underdeveloped countries that have no, or very imperfect, "markets," in the sense given to this term by the economists.

For a short while, a few years ago, some economists thought that the relation between capital investment and growth of production in a country, the so-called capital/output ratio, almost approached being a constant of the natural science type. But [as I pointed out in Chapter 5, Section 14] closer studies soon revealed that capital investment could not even be considered the major cause of economic growth. And we have not yet come even near to determining the characteristics and quantitative importance of the various elements that make up the as yet unspecified residual, which thus remains a "residual of ignorance." We know one thing, however: they will be shifting in time and for different countries.

The explanation of this fundamental dissimilarity between social and natural sciences—that we social scientists never arrive at constants and generally valid laws of nature —is that our study of facts and relationships between facts in the social field concerns much more complex and also shifting and fluid matters than facts and relationships in our physical universe. In that sense, natural scientists undoubtedly face problems that are simpler and in regard to which definite knowledge is attainable, knowledge that is timeless and universally valid and can thus be generalized.

What all social sciences are dealing with is, in the last instance, human behavior. And human behavior is not constant like the movement of celestial bodies or molecules. It is dependent upon, and determined by, the complex of living conditions, the institutions, in which people exist, and by their attitudes, as those have been molded by, at the same time as they are reacting against, those living conditions and institutions.

These phenomena differ widely from place to place and from group to group. Nor are they stable in time. Instead they manifest different and changing combinations of changeability and rigidity. Indeed, even at a particular point of time and in a specific situation, they are difficult even to define, observe, and measure as facts.

5. Importance of Language in the Social Sciences

One indication, or symptom, of this crucial dissimilarity between social and natural sciences is the significance of language in our field of study. The impact of a contribution in the social sciences, on our colleagues as well as on the general public, is, as we all know, very much dependent upon the skill of presentation, which is much less the case in the natural sciences.

Sometimes, however, there is a throwback. When many of John Kenneth Galbraith's more pedestrian colleagues decline fully to recognize the contributions to knowledge he has made, it is partly because of the extraordinary literary qualities of his writings. On the other hand, the relative lack of clarity and conciseness another otherwise great writer, Maynard Keynes, often chose for presenting his views, particularly in his main work, *The General Theory of Employment, Interest, and Money,* has lured other economists into performing difficult exercises in exegesis and demonstrating originality in following out various lines of thought only vaguely and confusedly presented in the original text.

Another indication of this difference, founded upon the greater importance of language in the social sciences, is the role in our type of work of particular expressions which, in compressed form, have come to stand for complex, though sometimes vaguely perceived, ideas or theories about social reality. In my own field of economic science I have myself experienced such an elevation to significance of a term I have used: in the "theoretical" phase of my working life, for instance, *"ex ante"* and *"ex post,"* and "circular causation with cumulative effects"; and in the later "institutional" phase, the characterization of the racial problem in the United States as a "dilemma"; or still later, when I came to work on the problems of underdeveloped countries, words like "spread effects" and "backlash effects," the "soft state," and many others.

I am referring to my own experience, but I am, of course, not alone in my experience of words I have used becoming laden with meaning and significance, and then being used as shorthand characterizations of specific types of causal relationships. I do not believe that anywhere in the natural sciences has a need been felt for investing particular wordings with that type of extraordinary importance.

6. Economics as a Special Case

Paradoxically, the one social science that traditionally keeps itself furthest from any attempt to reach down to ultimate determinants of the behavior studied, viz. economic science, seems to come closest to natural science. This is probably also what the majority of establishment economists actually believe, though I think mistakenly. The likeness refers to form of analysis and, particularly, of presentation, but hardly to substance.

Indeed, because of the highly abstract level on which economic theory now mostly moves, economics is sometimes excluded from what is called the "behavioral sciences." Economists use, for instance, a concept "market," which has no resemblance to a real market. And on the basis of this abstraction they carry out their analysis in terms of aggregates (like "supply" and "demand," "input" and "output") or averages (like levels of "wages" or "incomes").

Economic theory has in that sense always been extraordinarily abstract, ever since the time of the physiocrats, Adam Smith, and Ricardo. Exactly what this type of abstraction means is not even attempting to dig deeper under the observable facts of human behavior, which are then dealt with in a very summary fashion. It implies, therefore, that certain abstract assumptions about living conditions, institutions, and attitudes are laid as a basis for the analysis, either implying that they stand unchanged, or that they adjust automatically in a specific way to occurring changes in regard to the aggregate or average magnitudes used in the economic analysis.

These assumptions, however, are commonly not made too explicit. As, moreover, the very concepts used are defined in relation to these implicit abstract assumptions, serious questions can be raised about the adequacy to reality of that type of economic theory and its relevance for policy and planning.

The traditional way of explaining away these fundamental difficulties has been, and is today, to state that we economists deal only with what are called "economic factors." This, however, is begging the question. First, even to define what "economic factors" are implies a scrutiny of all factors, including what economists call "non-economic" factors. That scrutiny is ordinarily not made as a preparation for defining the concepts used.

Second, the isolation of one part of social reality by demarcating it as "economic" is logically not feasible. In reality, there are no "economic," "sociological," or "psychological" problems, but just problems, and they are all complex. The only concept which need not be defined and cannot be defined is economics. From that concept, inferences about reality can never be drawn.

Logically, the only distinction that is scientifically valid is the one between more relevant factors and less relevant ones. And proofs are regularly not rendered that the so-called "economic factors," as accounted for by aggregates and averages, are always the relevant ones.

Most of the great economists in the classical and neo-classical line from Adam Smith to Alfred Marshall were vaguely aware that this was a mistaken approach. As they were prepared to include in their analyses what they saw as relevant elements of living conditions, institutions, and attitudes, they were, indeed, almost all "institutional economists" long before that term was invented.

7. Simplified Models with Mathematical Dressing

In recent decades, however, there has been a strenuous, even strained, effort by the majority of my economist colleagues to emulate what they conceive of as the methods of the natural scientists by constructing utterly simplified models, often given mathematical dressing. This type of model-building has recently been rapidly spreading through the other social sciences, too, where the researchers then apparently seek to emulate the economists.

It should be clear, however, that this adoption of a form, which the natural scientists, in more simple, pointed questions, can use for analysis and presentation, does not really make the social sciences more scientific, if that form is not adequate to social reality and, therefore, not adequate for the analysis of it. It is on the basis of having reached down to the bottom of the reality they are studying, signified by the existence of constants, that it has been possible for the natural scientists often to make fundamental discoveries at their desks by simply applying mathematical reasoning to ascertained facts and relationships.

Fashion changes in a cyclical way in our field of study. These changes should, indeed, be equally worthy of analysis by the historians and theorists of the evolution of sciences as is the business cycle, which has been studied for generations by us economists. As I mentioned in Chapter 1, Section 3, my first visit to the United States at the end of the Twenties coincided with the flourishing of what was called the "new economics," which was then the institutional school in line with Veblen, Commons, and Mitchell. Since then, the pendulum has swung over to abstract model-building, not only in the United States but also in the rest of the world. As I also suggested, I foresee, however, that ten or fifteen years from now, the institutional approach will again be in vogue. The recent attempts to emulate the methods, or rather the form, of the simpler natural sciences will be recognized largely as a temporary aberration from realistic truth-seeking.

My reason for venturing this forecast is that the study of social facts and relationships really must concern much more complex, variable, and fluid matters than those represented by parameters and variables in highly abstract models, where behavior, accounted for only in terms of aggregates and averages, is left unexplained.

8. Further Remarks on Model Thinking

I have nothing, *per se*, against models. All scientific research must be generalizing and thus simplifying. It is important only that the selection of factors to be included should be done according to the criterion of relevance. Nor am I adverse to the use of mathematics, if it can contribute to the increase of knowledge. When, in *Asian Drama*, Appendix 2, on "The Mechanism of Underdevelopment and Development and a Sketch of an Elementary Theory of Planning for Development," I tried to spell out in simplified form the model applied in that book, I actually came up with an illustration in the form of a set of algebraic equations and a huge diagram. But as we are far removed from having even approximate quantitative information on the coefficients of interrelations between changes in all the different factors in the social system of circular causation with cumulative effects, which I tried to outline—that type of knowledge is quite incomplete even in developed countries—I abstained from using them. To me it would have been pretentious, and conducive to the mistaken view that it would have added anything to the knowledge I was trying to convey in the text.

When the builders of abstract economic models characterize their approach as "quantitative," even when they have no quantities at their disposal—or only grossly deficient ones—in contradistinction to the institutional approach, which they are inclined to call "qualitative," this is, of course, a misnomer. Quantifying knowledge is a self-evident aim of research, and the institutional economist, as the more censorious researcher, is apt to press harder for empirical data. If he often has fewer figures to present than the conventional economists, particularly in regard to underdeveloped countries, this is because he is more critical in ascertaining them.

My third point is an admission. In spite of the very common absence of a thorough scrutiny of the underlying abstract assumptions and of the concepts used, it is a fact that econometric models even of the macro-type, referring to an entire country, often do reach relevant conclusions and are more useful than they were when Alfred Marshall denounced that method as unrealistic. In developed countries the statistical material is now very much more complete and reliable. And the "non-economic" factors are apparently often less important in the analysis, as they either are adjusted to, or will rapidly become adjusted to, letting the economic impulses through.

To what extent, and how, this is true is a problem that should rightly be made the object of research, which then would have to be of the institutional type. This is the more necessary as the validity of that type of assumption cannot, even in the highly developed countries, be taken for granted. That there is what in the United States is called "structural unemployment" in the rural and urban slums, was for a long time observed only by social workers and sociologists, while economists tended, until a few years ago, to deny its existence. And even in a country like Sweden, where there are no slums and where the process of rationalization of living conditions, institutions, and attitudes has generally gone further than in the United States, it has, for instance, been demonstrated that mobility in the labor market, and still more the prices of labor, is less exclusively and simply dominated by demand and supply in the labor market than economic model-thinking is sometimes forced to assume.

In any case, as I pointed out in Chapter 5, when, after the avalanche of decolonization in the wake of World War II, the economic analysis of underdeveloped countries started out by simply applying Western models, it went seriously wrong. The abstraction in the common growth models applied in planning from modes and levels of living, political forces, institutions, attitudes, and levels of consumption was in regard to these countries definitely unwarranted. After working for many years on the development problems in South Asia, I find to my dismay that it must be deemed very much open to doubt whether the assistance to planning afforded by the economic profession has always helped more than it has confused and hurt these unfortunate new nations (Chapter 5).

At the end of this critical section of my lecture I would, however, like to add that, like Gordon Allport's, my own attitude is catholic, in a sense eclectic. And I am certainly hopeful in regard to the advance on our research front. There is, as I have already said, a self-healing capacity in scientific research which by necessity emerges when it is vigorously pursued.

At bottom, I am inclined to appreciate all honest research, relying upon the expectation that, as the years pass, our scientific approaches will, through controversy, become rectified and ever more relevant to the explanation of social reality.

9. Valuations in Social Research

Another cause of greater difficulties in social research, besides the fact that we do not arrive at generally and timelessly valid knowledge, is related to the role of valuations in our research.

It is true that, in principle, all scientific work has to be based on value premises. There is no view without a viewpoint, no answers except to questions. In the viewpoint applied and the questions raised, valuations are involved.

In the field of natural phenomena, the value premises are simple, evident, and so mostly *a priori*. Basic research can branch off in every direction where knowledge can be advanced. Applied research has the simple criterion of profitability or, as in medical technology, the prolongation of life and, prior to that, the prevention and cure of disease. At most, the direction of basic and applied research on which money and research personnel are spent can be questioned from the valuation angle. To this I shall return. But if the direction toward specific fields of inquiry is given, research can go straight on with the one determining aim of increasing our knowledge.

This is not so in the field of social sciences, where valuations are immensely diversified and anything but self-evident. In order to avoid biases in research and to make it "objective" in the only sense this term can have in the social sciences, we need to select and make explicit specific value premises, tested for their feasibility, logical consistency, relevance, and significance in the society we are studying.

This is needed not only to determine the broad direction

of our research, as in the natural sciences. As a matter of fact, valuations enter into research from the start to the finish: determining the approach, the definition of the concepts used and thus the facts observed, the way of drawing inferences, and even the manner of presenting the conclusions reached. Explicit value premises are thus logically required, not only to draw meaningful and correct practical and political (i.e. technological) conclusions, but also in order to ascertain relevant facts and factual relationships. We are otherwise drawing inferences with one set of premises missing.

I here touch on a main methodological problem of the social sciences. Without being able in this book to give the full reasons, I have to restrict myself to the assertion that there can never be, and has never been, a "disinterested" research in the social field, as there can be in the natural sciences. Valuations are, in fact, determining our work even if we manage to be unaware of it. And this is true, however much the researcher is subjectively convinced that he is simply observing, recording and analyzing facts.

10. Hidden Valuations

The teleological philosophies of natural right and utilitarianism, from which all the social sciences branched off more than two hundred years ago, actually asserted that the valuations could themselves be objective in the sense that they can be known as valid. This was indeed the metaphysical element in these philosophies.

Conventional economists have not broken away from this legacy of false thinking, even though they are more reluctant than an earlier generation to account for how they are thinking. It also, of course, dominates popular thinking everywhere, which does not distinguish between beliefs about reality and valuations about how it ought to be.

What economists and also other social scientists have commonly done is to conceal the valuations that underlie their analytical structures—and, indeed, the very terminology they use—so deeply that they can happily remain unaware of them in their researches and trust that the latter are merely factual. Very generally, social scientists are unsophisticated "positivists."

Among the social scientists, the economists have, by their so-called "welfare theory," provided themselves with a vast and elaborate cover for their escape from the responsibility to state, simply and straightforwardly, their value premises in concrete terms—a "monumentally unsuccessful exercise . . . which has preoccupied a whole generation of economists [indeed, several generations] with a dead end, to the almost total neglect of the major problems of our age," to quote an angry statement by Kenneth E. Boulding, speaking as president of the American Economic Association, but nevertheless behaving as the rebel he is.

It grows like a malignant tumor. Hundreds of books and articles are produced every year on "welfare economics," even though the whole approach was proved to be misdirected four decades ago.[2] If the approach is not entirely meaningless, it has a meaning only in terms of forlorn hedonistic associational psychology and utilitarian moral philosophy. I have always wondered why psychologists and philosophers leave economists alone and undisturbed in this futile exercise. This is part of the isolation of the several traditional social science disciplines and subdisciplines within them complained about earlier in this book.

The trend toward narrow "professionalism" in contemporary established economists in regard to training, reading, and, indeed, awareness of everything outside the limited field where they are working, which I commented upon in Chapter 4, Section 4, protects them from being disturbed by much knowledge about modern psychology and philosophy. And the relative neglect of the history of economics, which I also mentioned as part of their "professionalism," helps them even to have an exaggerated belief in the newness of their own contributions and often even protects them from grasping that what they are attempting is normative economic theory.

Those great economists who originally developed the hedonistic and utilitarian welfare theory—among them Jevons, Sidgwick, and Edgeworth—could work with conviction and in clear terms, since they knew what they were doing. They were not apt to skip over the basic psychological and philosophical assumptions involved in welfare theory. The contemporary welfare theorists mostly miss the historical perspective they should gain by intensive study of their predecessors and, at the same time, the awareness they could gain by such studies of where the basic difficulties are buried.

Few attempts have been made to study, empirically and in terms of modern psychology, people's behavior as income earners, consumers, and investors. What few attempts there have been to carry out realistic psychological research about economic behavior, free from the assumptions of the old and new welfare theory, have been completely disregarded in establishment economics. The deeper reason for this neglect is, of course, that the results of such research cannot possibly be integrated into the conceptual framework of welfare theory of the inherited and still dominant type.

We should note in passing that the recent flourishing of welfare economics is closely related to the growing predilection for hyper-abstract theoretical models. Among the implicit and not sufficiently scrutinized assumptions of these models, and sometimes even in their explicit structures, the objectified welfare conception almost always plays a role. An institutional approach cannot so easily escape the human valuations that are at the same time objects of research and premises in research.

11. A Dearth of Undisputed Truth

These main difficulties of social research and the escapist ways through which we have tried to bypass them are not unrelated to the fact that so relatively little ranks in our findings as undisputed truth. In regard to almost all problems there are schools of thought with somewhat different gospels, from among which politicians and public can choose according to their predilections.

It has even become a popular myth that economists never agree. In recent years, for instance, the bewildered American public has followed the spectacle of a fight between two schools of establishment economists, differing as to the role and importance of the quantity of money in regard to internal economic balance. If people are usually not so disturbed by blatant disagreements among other social scientists, it is probably because they care less about what they are saying.

When, two generations ago, Knut Wicksell, now belatedly recognized as the great economist of his time, gave his inaugural lecture as professor of economics at Lund University in 1904, he began by stating that economics, "like theology and for approximately the same reasons," had failed to arrive at commonly accepted results. It is true, he pointed out, that advance in all sciences proceeds through controversy. But in the natural sciences such warfare has a definite outcome.

Theories are refuted, hypotheses become obsolete, the frontiers of knowledge are pushed forward. "The Copernican idea of the universe, the Newtonian system, the theory of blood circulation, and the phlogiston theory in chemistry once found both adherents and opponents. . . . Nowadays these theories are either universally believed or disbelieved —provided, in the latter instance, that they have not simply been forgotten." In economics, on the contrary, all doctrines persist. He gave examples, and, in somewhat modified forms, since conditions and problems have altered, they are all present today.

Wicksell, as a faithful believer in hedonistic psychology and utilitarian moral philosophy, saw the explanation of this unfortunate situation in economics in the fact that we had not yet succeeded in measuring "utility"—what in a carefully concealed form is the basic concept also of the modern welfare theory. That one day we shall succeed in doing so he did not question. And it should be conceded that if that were possible, we would have advanced to the same situation as the natural sciences. We would then have constants and absolute measurements and be able to solve all political problems in terms of maximization of welfare.

But this is exactly what we shall never be able to do, because there is in the very concepts of utility and welfare an inescapable logical defect that economists of all generations have encountered, namely that there is no simple yardstick for people's "pleasures" and "pains." The only way of defending "objectivity" in research is to work with explicit and, where possible, alternative, specific value premises.

Another great economist in the past, Karl Menger, once pointed out, however, that in a sense and to an extent the gifted student is superior to his methods. Our situation in the social sciences would otherwise be much worse than it actually is. In fact, we see all around us important findings of particularly great practical importance being reached by researchers whose fundamental notions of methodology are confused and faulty.

One of Wicksell's own contributions was, as I pointed out

in Chapter 1, Section 2, his early formulation, at the beginning of this century, of the theoretical approach we now refer to as Keynes's. Much more generally, our knowledge of social facts and relationships is advancing, though not as rapidly as we could wish or as would be possible with greater clarity on the methodological issues.

12. The Unity of Bias in a Society

The disturbing fact that research in the social sciences does not, as it advances, regularly result in a new and commonly accepted knowledge, but that room is left for schools of competing thought, is related to the two other facts I have already dwelt upon: one, that our research is much more crucially dependent upon value premises than is research in the natural sciences; and, two, that social scientists have nevertheless always tried to present their findings as factual and independent of valuations. They have concealed the valuations that have actually determined their approaches, observations, and analysis.

As these hidden valuations are not openly declared, they can be held general and vague, and there is then room for arbitrariness (see Chapter 4, Section 2). It is within this field of indeterminateness that differences of basic concepts and models, and, therefore, observations and inferences, become possible. And it is by utilizing this arbitrariness that contending schools can maintain their existence to an extent unknown in the simpler natural sciences.

Even more important is, however, the relative unity of bias prevailing in a particular society at a particular time— creating the general conformity of an establishment, as I pointed out in Chapter 1, Section 1. This conformity regularly reflects the influence of dominant, though often mistaken, interests (see Chapter 4, Section 5). When value premises are not explicitly stated, such scrutiny has to be immanent in nature, seeking to reveal the concealed valuations that have been operating.

I became aware of this in my youth, when I studied what I called the political element in the development of economic theory along the classical and neo-classical line. When later I came to grips with the Negro problem in the United States, the biases in scientific literature as well as in popular conceptions became a major theme of my work. When still later I came to study the conditions in underdeveloped countries, I found the literature heavily biased in a diplomatic and, to begin with, over-optimistic direction. In Chapters 5 and 6 I demonstrated how these biases have distorted our analysis of the development problems of these countries and the interests and prejudices in developed and underdeveloped countries that have encouraged this biased analysis.

13. Translating Research into Action

I promised to touch upon another difference between social and natural sciences, namely, the much greater difficulties encountered in applying the former. Not only is undisputed knowledge in the social field harder to acquire and establish, its translation into action is a much more cumbersome and uncertain undertaking.

Whether it is a question of new products, new processes to produce a product, improvements in military weaponry, or advances in medical technology, an invention—often made possible by basic research—is almost sure to become rapidly applied. The evaluation of an invention in terms of costs and returns by private enterprises or by the states is simple and, in a sense, objective. Application therefore follows relatively easily and almost automatically.

Our discoveries and inventions in the social field must

generally be applied by the collectivities, i.e., in the first place, the state and subordinated communities. They must become public policies, accepted by those who have the power to determine action or inaction by these collectivities. Ordinarily, these people—from the elected or appointed officials down to the members of the electorates—have their preconceived ideas. No less ordinarily, these ideas are founded upon what they feel to be their interests. These may be shortsightedly or even erroneously conceived, aside from the fact that they do not necessarily, or even commonly, coincide with what would emerge as the public interest of the citizenry, if they were all alert and rational.

There are what we call vested interests and prejudices. And those responsible for public policy have not the same respect for the social engineers as everybody has for technical engineers and medical doctors. They, in fact, all have their own social theories. And the fact that, as I have pointed out, social scientists so often disagree among themselves—and still more commonly abstain from drawing policy conclusions—increases the self-assurance of the policy-makers and provides them, in addition, with the freedom to select and quote authority to support their own particular preconceptions.

14. Natural Sciences and the Threat of Disaster

I could elaborate much further, particularly on the practical question of how we social scientists could increase the effectiveness of social engineering and, more especially, how greater methodological clarity could also enhance the political importance of our findings.

But let me finally touch upon the anxiety natural scientists and technologists—and, indeed, all of us—now feel about the advances in natural sciences and the uncontrolled technological application of new knowledge leading to disaster. This problem has become acute in regard to the pollution of air, water and soil and the depletion of natural resources following industrial progress and, of course, to the even more threatening armaments race, which develops by the automatism of the competitive application of new discoveries and inventions in the field of weaponry.

The point I want to make in this context is the very limited competence the natural scientists can have in regard to these destiny-laden political problems. The only thing they can do—besides going on strike and trying to break up the "government-industrial-academic complex," if I might slightly change President Eisenhower's description —is to specify and explain the pending calamities which they see evolving and then to complain about the absence of effective social engineering which would redirect and control the dangerous *laissez-faire* that operates in the application of their research results.

As to the means of accomplishing the induced change of the political processes that is needed to avert the threatening course of events, and the difficulties that must meet such attempts at social engineering, the natural scientists can have no better judgment than any layman who tries to inform himself. The responsibility lies wholly with us social scientists and social engineers.

15. Summary

I have come to the end of my attempt to answer the question I raised in my title. I have had to deal with it in very general terms, and I have drawn on my own research experiences as an economist. I believe, however, that our problems are so basically similar in all the social sciences that my conclusions can be generalized and illustrated from other fields of social research as well.

It is fruitless to expect that the social sciences will ever formulate the type of universal and unchangeable relationships between facts that are accessible to researchers in the simpler natural sciences. We are dealing with the behavior of human beings, each of whom has a soul, and is influenced by his living conditions in the widest sense of the word. These vary widely and change all the time, as does also their relationship to behavior.

To emulate the form but not the substance of research in natural sciences is no solution to our methodological problems. Too often an analysis which is paraded as particularly "strict" and "rigorous" is, when critically scrutinized, found to be not only empty but grossly mistaken, lacking in both adequacy to reality and logical consistency.

In our very different field, the social sciences, we have to fight against the tendencies to bias. The means to do this are, first, to be aware of the ubiquitous danger and, second, to avail ourselves of the means that logic places at our disposal, that is, to use the technique of explicit value premises. The fact that this is needed in social research automatically delineates the gulf between our research and the simpler research of natural scientists.

If we are aware of the gulf, and are prepared to take the consequences of the difference, we are, however, certainly entitled to look upon our work as scientific—in the sense that we are seeking true knowledge about man and his society.

Chapter 8

TWISTED TERMINOLOGY AND BIASED IDEAS[1]

THE TENDENCY of all knowledge, like all ignorance, to deviate from truth in an opportunistic direction becomes reflected in twisted terminology.

1. *The "United Nations"*

The very name of the system of intergovernmental organizations represented by the "United Nations" is logically fallacious. Indeed, the very first words of its Charter, where the subjects enacting it are said to be "We the peoples of the United Nations," is a pious falsehood. The members of the United Nations and of all the composite organizations within that system are not peoples or nations, but governments of states.

The General Assembly or plenary session of the delegates of an intergovernmental organization is thus not in any real sense equal to the legislative assembly of a state. The delegates are not elected by a constituency of voters, as in a democratic state. As there is no supra-state world government, it is still less similar to that type of semblance to a legislative assembly as is often created by authoritarian governments, with members appointed or chosen in some way other than universal suffrage by free ballot. The delegates represent nations only indirectly, if at all.

It should be added that the large and rapid increase of member states since the enacting of the Charter, and the trend of political development in the third world of underdeveloped countries and also in some semi-developed countries such as Greece and Turkey, have very much increased the proportion of such governments upon whose policies the broad masses of people in their state, and very often even the majority of their educated and alert upper strata, have little or no influence. Their legitimation for membership in the United Nations is not that they can truly be said to represent nations, but that they control a territory recognized as a state.

Even if, for practical reasons, no more adequate term can now be substituted for the "United Nations," this qualification should constantly be borne in mind. Indeed, the adjective "international" contained in the official names of many organizations, and generally used to characterize relationships or problems stretching over the boundaries between the states, is mostly a misnomer. In any case, the term "international organizations" should strictly speaking be replaced by the term "intergovernmental organizations."

2. Terminology Does Matter

Terminology, and the meaning given to terms, do matter. They represent, if not subjected to continual scrutiny, temptations and opportunities for the logical gliding of our thinking in unrealistic directions.

There is thus an opportunistic tendency in all of us to want to believe that the United Nations, and all the intergovernmental organizations within its system, form a suprastate or, at least, the beginning of it, that it has goals and implements collectively formulated policies as does the government of an individual state.

The hierarchical constitutional structure of the organizations within the system contributes to give a semblance of realism to this analogy with a state. Some are subordinated to others, and this constitutional structure resembles the political and administrative setup of an individual state with its provinces and functional agencies. But as they are all made up of delegates of governments, and as those to a subordinate organization are often not only more competent in a particular field but higher placed in the state administration, it is clear that the interrelations between organizations on different levels are often more of a cumbersome formality than a power reality.

The fact that we have become accustomed to talking about members of the secretariats as "international civil servants" again implies a false analogy to the officials acting on behalf of, and on the authority of, the government of a state. There is no government of the world.

Even leaving aside the chapters in the Charter of the United Nations on the Security Council and the International Court of Justice, which were deliberately given extensive supra-state functions, the verbiage of the Charter and the founding constitutional documents of all the organizations in the system tend to lead our thoughts even more firmly in that direction.

The organizations were equipped with far-reaching "principles and purposes," containing promises with regard to their future activity that have often not been fulfilled to any large extent. These pronouncements, however, have been constantly quoted. They have also been complemented by a great number of resolutions, often unanimously adopted by the representatives of the governments making up the organizations.

The organizations, moreover, are designated certain "functions" and "powers," which encourage the idea of their being political entities in their own right. This is strengthened in turn by the importance given to voting and the reluctance to stress the restrictions of what a "decision" reached by voting can accomplish.

These excessive, though often vague, pretensions in the constitutional documents to the intergovernmental organizations in the United Nations system being something more than, and something above, the member states, lie like a mist over all discussions of these organizations. It is this otherworldly concept of what the United Nations is that is grist to both the optimists and the pessimists. The influence of language is great, and not only on the thinking of the multitude of common people, politicians, and journalists—these ideas even invade scholarly writings.

That government delegates as well as spokesmen for the secretariats—and not only their publicity services—are all selling these vague ideas of the United Nations playing a supra-state role is apparent. In the establishing of these illusory concepts of what the intergovernmental organizations are, the terms "action" and "decision," for instance, have become popular in secretariat documents as well as in speeches by government delegates. This eccentric way of speaking occurs almost in inverse proportion to the amount of opportunity afforded to the organizations by the participant governments to register substantive agreements reached among them that could in any real sense be considered action or decision by the organization.

Everything, then, becomes garbed in a bizarre, make-believe verbosity, usually, again, in inverse proportion to the importance of what goes on within an organization. And government delegates are as guilty of this as the secretariats. This is what often makes documents emanating from intergovernmental organizations such strange, often indecipherable literature to discerning persons. Although often diplomatic and innocuous, the semantic peculiarities of this literature undoubtedly contribute to upholding the fictitious belief that the organization is something which, ordinarily, it is not—a body above the national government that acts in pursuance of goals set by collectively formulated policy.

3. Reality

The United Nations and the intergovernmental organizations within its system certainly are a political reality, but this reality is different from what all these words imply and the formal structure given them in the constitutions. In our time, and as far ahead as we can think, they are ordinarily no more and no less than agreed matrices for the multilateral pursuit of the national policies of the participant governments—in fact, instruments created for the diplomacy of a number of disparate individual states. This does not necessarily imply that the intergovernmental organizations cannot be important. Everything depends on the will of governments, working under internal and external influences of all sorts, to reach agreement on substantive issues and to implement them.

On substantive as well as procedural questions, governments often act in blocs, and weaker, dependent governments are influenced by pressures from stronger ones. Particularly in more recent years, when membership of the intergovernmental organizations has been swollen by the admission of so many newly liberated former colonies, there have also been some successful pressures in the opposite direction, i.e., exerted by the many weaker governments on the few stronger ones.

In neither case does this constitute an exception to the rule that intergovernmental organizations basically and essentially are matrices for the multilateral pursuit of the governments' diplomacy. When governments act in blocs and/or let themselves be influenced by pressures, it is because, for one reason or another, that is in line with their policies.

In this context I shall not pursue the analysis further but refer to my forthcoming volume, *Toward a Critical Appraisal of the United Nations.*

4. The Pitfalls of Language

Quite commonly, the vocabulary making up the language we speak and write is illogical or invested with unwarranted associations. That the meaning of the commonly used term "values" is not only unclear but invested with misconceptions was noted in Chapter 3, Section 1. We can hardly avoid using the word "country" as a synonym for the less loaded term "state." But in so doing, we become tempted to assume that "countries" are more similar in a number of respects than they really are—for instance, in regard to national consolidation and particularly citizens' participation in, and power over, their governments.

Our perception of a specific difference between countries on which the discussion is focused—for instance, their relative economic levels—is then in danger of not taking into account other existing differences that may be important and related to the former difference and that therefore really matter. It should be clear to the discerning economist that the discussion of "country planning," which has now been laid as a basic consideration for economic aid awarded by United Nations Development Program (UNDP) and enthusiastically acclaimed in both underdeveloped and friendly developed countries, gives rise to quite illusory ideas concerning how policies are decided upon and planning made and implemented in most underdeveloped countries.

The direction of this loading of our terminology can broadly be characterized as "diplomatic." In Chapter 5,

Section 7, I noted a particularly flagrant example of such diplomacy through tendentious terminology: the use of the term "developing country" to characterize a state on a very low economic level. As also mentioned, this plainly illogical term has for many years received official sanction, and is now used in all statements and documents issued by the organizations within the United Nations system, and also by everybody speaking for a government even outside these organizations. In the economics profession, too, it has unfortunately become customary to use this term, or some other euphemistic expression, implying the same diplomatically biased tendency.

How the initial and still rather prevalent approach to the problems of underdeveloped countries, applying concepts and models used in the analysis in developed countries, leads to misconceptions was a main theme in Chapter 5. That, in particular, many of the terms and concepts utilized, when applying that approach, are grossly inadequate to reality in underdeveloped countries—for instance, "unemployment" and "underemployment"—was noted in Chapter 5, Section 12. These concepts, and the spurious statistics compiled by their application, are continually used by most economists with utmost carelessness.

"Bilateral aid" is, of course, a linguistic monstrosity, a self-contradiction in terms, the more so as it is certainly not meant to account for the sometimes rather sinister self-interests of an aid-giving country like the United States or, indeed, any policy action taken by the aided country in return for the gift. It is simply a diplomatic gesture, rather like the term "partnership," used in the United States to characterize relations with other countries, even when unilateral policies predominate and when pressures are exerted.

The term "free world," used to characterize all states that have in common the negative quality of not belonging to the Communist bloc, regardless of whether they stand for freedom in any real sense, is another example of twisted terminology. And it is a sad fact that even professional economists, particularly in the United States, for a long time commonly used it. Another example of plainly propagandist terminology, still prevalent in scholarly writings, is to call all the subregional organizations in Western Europe simply "European."

5. Conclusions

That we are here dealing merely with a slipshod use of language without material importance is not true. I repeat: Terminology does matter. It often swings the thoughts; when illogical and false, it reveals a disposition toward biases; and it indicates the direction of that disposition.

To keep concepts and terms clean, disinfected, logical, and adequate to reality is a primary behest to the scientist. In this slippery field only the utmost purism can be accepted.

It is apparent that economists as well as other social scientists have in recent decades dangerously lowered their scientific sights and work standards. An outstanding cause of this regrettable development is international tension and, in particular, the cold war. In regard to conditions in underdeveloped countries, the initial and still prevalent application of approaches used in the study of developed countries is a major cause (Chapter 5, Section 9). As also pointed out in that context, this unwarranted approach goes hand in hand with an opportunistic and diplomatic bias.

Diplomacy has its legitimate place in politics, and I have at various times in my life filled national or international positions, where I had reasons to keep my tongue in my cheek and be diplomatic, at least by being silent—though experience has taught me that even in politics it usually pays off to be plain and outspoken. In any case, diplomacy has no place whatsoever in scientific research. I long ago made it a rule to express myself in absolutely the same terms, whether I am talking in Washington, D.C., Moscow, New Delhi, Rio de Janeiro, or Stockholm.

When diplomacy comes to influence the writings of economists, another explanation is undoubtedly that, as I pointed out in Chapter 6, Section 4, economists are now, more than ever before, working for, and sometimes within, national and international administrative and political agencies as well as private businesses and non-official organizations. To the code of ethics, which I believe we should be interested in formulating or at least always bear in our hearts, belongs the rule that, whenever we become involved practically in this way, we should never compromise with our duty to speak the language of strict science.

Many of the errors in terminology pointed out above, when they are not founded on ignorance, are thus, to me, unethical. Ignorance does exist, for instance about the "labor market" in underdeveloped countries, which permits economists to use the concepts "unemployment" and "underemployment" and gives rise to the spurious statistics collected and analyzed in these categories. This happens even, as we know, when these methods have been criticized, which then is ignored without attempts to disprove the criticism.

Thus ignorance, like knowledge, can be opportunistic and so becomes subject to ethical judgment. It was not necessary and must therefore have been chosen.

Chapter 9

POLITICS AND ECONOMICS IN INTERNATIONAL RELATIONS[1]

FOR ONE HUNDRED YEARS prior to World War I and right up till today, there has been a tendency to stress economic factors in international relations. That trade and economic relations generally worked for peace was an important corollary to the free trade doctrine and, indeed, this assumption was part of, or at least, very much strengthened, that doctrine. Liberal economic theory from the classical writers on was, in this respect, not different from what in recent decades became the "Marxist" tradition, as represented by the official doctrine of the Communist countries and expounded in general terms by their statesmen and scholars. In particular, it is glibly assumed in both camps that trade in an important way works for peaceful relations, even politically. This thesis has, as a general proposition, now become generally acclaimed.

1. The Importance of Politics

Drawing conclusions from my practical and political experience as Executive Secretary of the United Nations

Economic Commission for Europe (ECE) during the first
ten years since the inception of that organization in 1947,
which had its work focused on trade, particularly East-
West trade, and also from my professional studies before
and after that time, I would, of course, not deny that there
is an element of reason in this conventional view. But that
element is a very small and heavily conditioned one. I
believe that the much more important causal relationships
go in the opposite direction, so that a low level of trade and
financial relations is the result of political conditions and
is an indication that these political conditions are not favorable for either peace or trade.

As I have often had occasion to stress, politics is sovereign. There is, for instance, no political dividing line established between states, even one that in the most unnatural
way puts barriers in the way of trade and other economic
relations, which does not in time tend to become "natural,"
in the sense that the economies on both sides adjust to the
political conditions so created.

Big cities such as Berlin or Jerusalem can be brutally
divided by a political line, demarcated by a wall or a zone
of no-man's land. Or new national boundaries, that from an
economic point of view are "unnatural," can be created,
such as those between India and Pakistan after partition,
almost extinguishing long-established trade and financial
links. The adjustments called forth by the political fiat are
normally such as to create the conditions for the perma-
nency of the broken trade and financial links, thus making
the "unnatural" "natural," or at least "more natural."

While political forces can strangle economic relations
almost instantaneously, it will usually be a difficult and
time-consuming process to change back to normal relations.
Even should a new political situation permit it, a full restoration of the *status quo* in economic relations might never
occur, for the adjustments of the economies to the lower
level of trade and financial relations are bound to have

changed resource allocations in the direction of self-suf-
ficiency. And when long-established connections have been
broken, they are not easily repaired.

In regard to the recent horrible and tragic development
in the political relations between West and East Pakistan,
and the present relations of both of them with India lying
between them, I would first want to stress that what happened after the partition of British India and thereafter continually up till now implied not only inhibitions and obstacles for development and the danger of increased
poverty and misery in the whole region, one of the poorest
in the world. It also implied, from the beginning, grave
dangers for peace, indeed much greater than *apartheid* in
South Africa, though no government found it possible or
worthwhile to place the whole problem on the agenda of
the steadily more politically immobilized Security Council
of the United Nations until open warfare broke out. Even
then, the Council was prevented from dealing with the
problem in a realistic way, and the later resolutions by the
General Assembly of the United Nations were not attuned
to the horrible reality and therefore lacked practical importance. In this chapter, my main point is only, however,
that this very adverse political development was not in any
major way caused by economic conditions or changes. The
line of causation was plainly in the opposite direction.

Speaking here, in the heart of Austria, I cannot refrain
from pointing out that the postwar division of Austria into
zones and the many constraints on the Austrian economy
caused by this split had no economic causes. Also, the State
Treaty which gave Austria back her full political freedom
—with the preparations of which I was at that time somewhat involved as Executive Secretary of the Economic
Commission for Europe—was a political settlement, including important economic clauses that opened the way
for freer and more appropriate commercial relations. It was
not the other way around. It was not that economic relations

and economic policies developed in a way to make possible improved political relations.

2. East-West Trade in Europe

This thesis of the overwhelming importance of political conditions and changes is, in my opinion, crucial to an understanding of the development of East-West economic relations in Europe. We might start with the situation in the interwar period. Both international trade and financial relations between the Soviet Union and the rest of the world—incidentally also with the countries in Central and Eastern Europe which now belong to the Eastern bloc— remained at relatively very low levels.

The explanation is largely the strained political relations with all non-Communist countries beginning at the time of the October Revolution, which frustrated economic relations. And in the Soviet Union, as well as in all other countries, an economic adjustment to these political conditions, making this situation more "natural," had occurred. What-ever foreign trade and financial relations with the outside world there were in the Soviet Union in the interwar era were mainly the result of the type of adjustment to the political realities I have been talking about.

The reason why East-West trade and financial relations remained very low after World War II, and in fact deterio-rated even further, was again political: the steadily inten-sified cold war. A major role in this political development was played by the so-called strategic export embargo policy of the United States, which was also somewhat unwillingly accepted by the West European countries, as well as by most dependent countries in other parts of the world.

A young Swedish economist, Gunnar Adler-Karlsson, at that time working at the Stockholm University Institute for International Economic Studies, and who has devoted a full-scale study to this phase of world history which, for understandable reasons, has not tempted other members of my profession to careful study, called his book *Western Economic Warfare, 1947–1967*.[2] The motivation for this discriminatory interference in trade, which went far outside what could in any sense be called strategic goods, was, on the Western side, plainly political.

In my foreword to that book, I expressed the opinion that this Western policy was not unwelcome to Stalin. During this period, when the Eastern bloc was becoming politically solidified, he undoubtedly found it useful to be able to point out to the satellite countries that, for their development as well as for their defense, they had to rely upon themselves, upon the Soviet Union, and upon each other. He must also have been happy that in this way the United States also prohibited too many and too close contacts between Western government officials and business people and their Eastern-bloc counterparts.

As I see it, the intensification of the cold war during these years developed as a process of circular causation with cumulative effects, indeed by a sort of strange political "cooperation" between the two superpowers, when both parties to the conflict could expect from the other actions spurring on the political conflict.

Stalin's death in 1953 implied, from this point of view, a political change. Another political change on the Western side that began to occur at about the same time was that Marshall aid petered out, while even United States military aid to its West European political allies also decreased. The West European countries used their regained greater political independence to liquidate the very inclusive COCOM embargo list. So far as Europe is concerned, the remaining list of forbidden exports has for many years been more of a nuisance than a serious trade barrier.

As there was at that time on both sides of the iron curtain in Europe an increasing willingness to trade over the political barrier, I was able, in the spring of 1954, to call the first ECE Trade Consultation, where government representatives could meet in the guise of being merely my consultants in the secretariat.[3] Arrangements were made so that they could discuss trade bilaterally as well as multilaterally. Among many of them, relations had at that time been completely or almost completely relinquished. Through these consultations, and the further bilateral negotiations then initiated in the various capitals, East-West trade could fairly rapidly begin to increase substantially, though it nevertheless even now remains at an "unnaturally" low level. (The recent rapprochement between the United States on the one side, and China and the Soviet Union on the other side, is clearly the result of political decisions that also permit increased economic relations.)

Generally, there is clearly a mutual causal relationship between the two types of development. Improved political relations make possible an increase in trade between the countries in the blocs, while the increased trade, to some extent, tends further to lessen political tension. This sort of circular causation with cumulative effects is undoubtedly what we have experienced in recent decades. It agrees, however, with my main hypothesis as explained at the beginning of this chapter, that the development of trade has been more of a response to political change than the reverse.

As far as the present levels of East-West trade in Europe are concerned, there are still important inhibitions and obstacles to overcome, many of them having an institutional character which, under favorable political conditions, could be lessened. But all this will have to be left out of my brief account here.

My only point is to stress the crucial importance of politics for trade and economic relations generally and, at the same time, to deprecate the widely spread, diffuse idea that the low level of economic relations stands as a major cause of international political tension, with the corollary thesis that simply raising these levels is a practical way to obliterate, or at least substantially alleviate, these political tensions.

Trade, if it is permitted to develop between two countries or two blocs, will certainly not only be economically advantageous for both sides, but may also tend to have some favorable influences on the further development of political relations. That I should deny this is, of course, out of the question. For long periods of my working life, it has been my main occupation to strive in this direction.

But the influence of economics on politics must be minor in the politically divided world of today. And the resistance to such strivings comes mainly from the political sphere.

3. Relations with Underdeveloped Countries

I shall now select for discussion one more world problem of even wider dimensions than East-West trade in Europe: the problem of development of underdeveloped countries.

I mentioned in Chapter 3, Section 6, how in the early stages of the evolution of the national welfare state in the developed countries there was sometimes an idea that social reforms of the egalitarian type worked for internal peace. The reforms were motivated as a means of keeping the poor more satisfied and were thus supposed to function as a sort of insurance against rebellion on their part. This motivation for social reform disappeared long ago from public discussion in the advanced welfare states. Social reforms are argued in terms of justice.

But in regard to the underdeveloped countries, aid is still commonly motivated as being in the self-interest of the developed countries. Even professional economists and not only popular writers and politicians agree on this point, that underdeveloped countries must be aided in order to preserve peace in the world.

This is an entirely unsupported rationalization of how people who are well off think they would feel and act if they lived in misery and saw no hope for an improvement. Known facts do not provide proof of this rationalization. It is also inherent in this type of glib generalization about human nature that it is supposed to be self-evident and not in need of proof by empirical studies of human behavior.

If any generalization can be made, it would be rather that people get restless and rebellious when they are getting a little better off but not fast enough. In fact, there are some scholarly persons who have constructed models and collected selected evidence to prove this contrary but equally glib theory. They have occasionally presented their theory as valid for racial tension in Detroit or New Jersey, the Sukarno "confrontation" with Malaysia and, in fact, rebellions and wars everywhere. The characteristic of that type of one-factor tension theory is, however, also uncritical speculation avoiding careful study of the empirical facts.

Equally unsupported by serious research is another glib theory, often asserted even by economists in developed countries when seeking a motivation to impress their politicians and the general public about the wisdom of giving aid, namely, that an underdeveloped country would become more "democratic" if it had a little economic progress. To begin with, it is very difficult to say what "democracy" means in largely illiterate countries, where the masses are largely apathetic, not informed about their interests, and still less organized to protect them. But taken in whatever meaning, no empirical substantiation for this theory of "democracy" being dependent on a little economic progress has ever been presented.

The further idea that democracy favors peace, particularly between countries, is quite obviously a false proposition. In the developed countries, where we more generally and more meaningfully can speak about political democracy, we have time and time again seen nations, particularly in the beginning of an armed conflict, become belligerent, sometimes more so than the governments and their establishments. The idealistic view that people as people always stand for peace is unfortunately not true. That underdeveloped nations, different from developed nations, should basically be more peaceful, is not likely, and is certainly not substantiated by research.

4. *"The Revolution of Rising Expectations"*

Supporting the whole category of glib theories about peoples' political reactions to the economic facts of poverty is the common idea of the "revolution of rising expectations," which is sometimes given by economists the apparently more learned name of "demonstration effect." Incidentally, this theory is, in fact, only an extension and amplification of Marx's theory of the political effect of the impoverishment of the workers. To lead to rebellion, actual poverty or its worsening would, according to this modern theory, not be necessary, but merely the lack of realization of expected improvement.

It should be pointed out in Marx's defense that he was careful not to apply his theory to the *Lumpenproletariat*. At all events, no honest empirical research has ever been brought forward to support this theory. It is simply another example of how people who are well off, whether in the developed or the underdeveloped countries, think they would behave if they were very poor.

The "revolution of rising expectations" does, however, exist among the upper class and the so-called middle class of the "educated" in the underdeveloped countries. Representatives of those countries in intergovernmental organizations and other international gatherings, who, for natural reasons, belong to their privileged elite, certainly talk, with full conviction, about such a political reaction to economic progress or lack of it, as it undoubtedly is their own reaction. This is how they feel about themselves and often about their nations.

And since underdeveloped countries, rather independently of whether their actual constitution is founded upon universal suffrage or is more authoritarian, are ruled by shifting alliances of people in the upper strata, the latter's attitudes are important in how their countries behave politically and militarily, at least as states, that is, internationally.

But then two questions remain unanswered:

(1) To what extent do these oligarchies take into consideration only what of economic progress they and perhaps the whole tiny upper and middle class experience, and to what extent does their political behavior also become motivated by whether that progress is shared by the rural and urban masses; and

(2) what particular degree of economic progress is making them satisfied and therefore inclined to becoming peaceful?

The main point I am trying to drive home is that all general and speculative theories about the relation between economic progress of underdeveloped countries and peacefulness are utterly void of true knowledge and of relevance for the problem of peace and war between countries, as well as peace or rebellion within the countries. (See also Chapter 6, Section 3.) And, as pointed out in Chapter 3, Sections 6 and 7, and in Chapter 6, Section 14, aid to underdeveloped countries has to be motivated in quite a different way to be really effective in eliciting it from developed countries.

5. The Responsibility of the Developed Countries for Peace in the Underdeveloped Countries

This should certainly not imply that I do not deem it of the utmost importance to preserve peace within and among underdeveloped countries, nor that I mean that the rich and developed countries should not carry their share of responsibility for reaching that result.

The present world situation is, on the one hand, characterized by a nervous peace among the developed countries themselves, a state of affairs maintained by the balance of terror, as between the two superpowers. A full-scale war between them can no longer be won by one of them in any meaningful sense. In an era of terror weapons and the unhampered armaments race, the other developed countries can certainly not be tempted to risk war, either between one another or still less against the superpowers.

Moreover, the majority among the smaller and weaker developed countries have even been brought to enter into political and military alliances with one or the other of the superpowers. We are all intensely aware that there are elements of horrifying uncertainty in this precarious balance of power, as we are also aware that rapidly rising armaments expenditure is destroying the world economy. But for the time being, there is peace among the developed countries.

There are, on the other hand, everywhere in the underdeveloped world outbreaks of violent rebellion within the countries, and there are also wars, and serious threats of wars, between countries. This particular contrast between rich and poor countries is certainly most ominous and calls for measures to bring peace to that great majority of mankind. Such measures have not been taken. On the contrary, the rich countries, or, more specifically, some of them, have encouraged unrest in the underdeveloped world.

Back in colonial times, the metropolitan countries certainly prevented civil wars within their individual colonies and, with some exceptions, did not involve them in wars among themselves. But they left a legacy of potential conflicts by exploiting ethnic and religious splits and animosities within a colony and, in regard to the relations among what have now become independent countries, rather tended to isolate them from each other by keeping them closely aligned with the so-called mother-country, economically as well as culturally. After World War II, some developed countries, like France and the Netherlands, conducted devastating colonial wars to preserve their dominance.

The United States early supported the French colonial war in Indochina in a massive way. After the defeat of the French, it took over the war and gradually spread its military interventions over the whole of Indochina. In that war, the United States carelessly used means of warfare which the great majority of the members of the United Nations—and many in the United States—consider forbidden by international law and, what is even more significant, which the United States would certainly not use in a war with a developed country. In this case, the United States had to "go it alone," as also often in Latin America, without help from its allies in Europe and supported only by a few satellite countries in the region, among them, in Vietnam, unfortunately Australia and New Zealand.

In economic relations with the underdeveloped countries there are often clear elements of neo-colonialism, as I noted in Chapter 6, Section 11. Most important is the inconsiderate pursuance of political and military strategic interests. The two superpowers—assisted to some extent on the Western side, particularly earlier, by the two European powers traditionally still called great powers, namely France and Great Britain—have spread their network of political and military alliances formed against each other in the underdeveloped regions, particularly in Asia.

This has often decreased the possibility of economic and other cooperation there. They have used their so-called bilateral aid to build up systems of what are, in fact, satellite underdeveloped countries. They have encouraged them to use their scant resources on the procurement of armaments, and have also given weapons as military aid or sold them at reduced prices. Even the many under-developed countries who want and pretend non-alliance and neutrality in the great conflicts between blocs of developed countries have often become heavily dependent on aid of both types.

6. Pawns in the Cold War

In the postwar era, the underdeveloped countries have thus been used as pawns in the cold war. It can today be said that a main part of the burden of that world conflict was visited on the underdeveloped countries. It is true that it could more safely—for the superpowers and their allies among developed countries—be permitted to become hot war in the underdeveloped region. While the superpowers dare not go to war with each other, and while the other developed countries also feel compelling reasons not to break the peace, it was apparently deemed less dangerous to permit, or even to encourage, wars in the underdeveloped world.

Thus the conflict in West Asia, which, from the colonial era, we have become accustomed to call the Middle East, has almost taken on the character of a war by proxy on the part of the two superpowers—with Britain and France playing a more doubtful and less easily discernible role. A main common interest of the developed world in cushioning this conflict is now the self-interest of preventing it from leading to a disastrous head-on collision between the two superpowers.

The Stockholm International Peace Research Institute (SIPRI), a completely independent research organization on whose board I am chairman, has published a 900-page study on the provision of armaments by developed countries to underdeveloped countries and also analyzed how this traffic serves the hegemonic interests of the superpowers in particular.[4] It provides a sobering and thought-provoking piece of reading.

But even without any deeper investigation and documentation, we all know that the deeply tragic civil war in Nigeria was fought by weapons given or sold by Great Britain and the Soviet Union to one side and by France, less openly, to the other. The large-scale butchery in East Pakistan was similarly carried out by weaponry given or sold by developed countries all over the world—on a small scale acquired even from Sweden, I am distressed to say, although that country does not give away any weapons and has a much more restrictive legislation on arms sale than other countries. How the two parties in the Middle East conflict are furnished with weapons from the Soviet Union and the United States (and, intermittently, also by Britain and France) we have been able to read about in the daily press.

It was that type of war that the United Nations Security Council was created to prevent and to stop. That it should be feasible was demonstrated when India and Pakistan went to war with each other in 1965. A forced settlement was then possible, because the two superpowers for once did find a common interest in stopping it.

7. Conclusions

I have not been able to more than hint at an analysis of how wars are possible and how they are caused in the underdeveloped world. If I am at all correct in my judgment, it is clear that the causes are political and not economic, and that there are no economic measures which can contribute much to solving the problem of safeguarding peace within and among the underdeveloped countries. Negatively, it can be argued, however, that if we could proclaim the rule and get it respected, that aid should not be misused by developed countries in a way that encourages and makes possible civil wars and other wars in underdeveloped regions, that would certainly be in the interest of peace.

But such a changed aid policy would assume a political change in the way the superpowers and their allies now use the underdeveloped countries as pawns in their own political conflicts. And if such a political change were possible, many more political measures of even greater importance for peace-keeping would also be possible—mainly those rules for intergovernment action envisaged in the chapters of the Charter of the United Nations dealing with the functioning of the Security Council, which are now largely obsolete, because the governments do not permit the Council to function as it was supposed to function.

Chapter 10

"GROWTH" AND "DEVELOPMENT"[1]

1. Prelude to a Growth Theory

THE EMERGENCE and triumph, about a hundred years ago, of the theory of marginal utility and its embodiment in the static equilibrium conception marked an end to the interest the classical authors—and, of course, Marx—had shown in the long-term problems of growth and development. The focus was put on problems about static efficiency and static allocation of resources, relative to given consumer preferences as expressed by aggregate demand. When, later on, a dynamic theory was developed, change was dealt with as a short-term problem, increasingly focused on the regularities of economic interrelationships from month to month and year to year discussed in the flourishing business cycle theory.

One of the earliest writers in the neo-classical line who refocused attention on long-term growth was Gustav Cassel. In the first chapter of his *Theoretische Sozialökonomie*,[2] delivered in manuscript in 1914 but not published until 1918, he developed his theory of the *"gleichmässig fortschreitende Wirtschaft."* In reality, his theoretically construed long-term growth was understood to be broken, and then conditioned, by the short-term changes, which

Cassel dealt with in the fourth part of his work, devoted to business fluctuations.[3]

In relation to growth, Cassel presented for the first time, as far as I know, what after World War II became known as the capital/output model.[4] This and other similar models, which appeared in great varieties after World War II, were worked out as tools for dealing with growth but more specifically stagnation and instability in Britain and other developed countries. For a time, and often even now, they were utilized, however, for studying the very different long-term problem of planning for growth, particularly in underdeveloped countries, as I noted in Chapter 5, Section 14.

The most important impetus for refocusing the interest of economists on the long-term problems of growth and development was, however, without doubt the importance given to the concept of gross national product, of which national income is an affiliation. By breaking up the GNP into its constituent parts and seeking their causal determinants and the causal interrelations among them all, it is no exaggeration to say that a new theory emerged, rather different from the neo-classical equilibrium theory and also transgressing the theoretical framework of the traditional short-term business cycle theory from earlier time. Comprehensive statistical investigations for various developed countries, often stretching back a century or more, were carried out, aimed at filling the gaps in the concepts utilized in economic theory. Through these efforts, economic growth, defined as an increase in GNP, naturally and necessarily came to the forefront. The Swedish Academy of Sciences in 1971 rewarded Simon Kuznets with the Nobel Prize for Economics for his pioneering work in this very large field.

2. Gross National Product

It is my conviction that the evolution of economic theory will not stop at its present point and that further development will have to take as one of its starting points a critical examination of the central concept of GNP. Although this concept is commonly used by economists without any such scrutiny, there is a creeping awareness that it may be inadequate to reality and to the policy problems rooted in this reality, when dealing with long-term growth and development.

Let me attempt briefly to enumerate the weaknesses of the GNP concept from the viewpoint of seeking realism. I shall concentrate first only on the developed countries, but shall, at the end of this chapter, take up the problem as it manifests itself in underdeveloped countries.

All income elements to be included in the GNP are dependent for their definition on institutional arrangements, which are constantly changing and regularly show differences for different countries. This must make comparisons, in time and still more between countries, hazardous. Added to this is the fact that income elements, which are included, are often defined in an arbitrary way. Still more arbitrary is the inclusion or non-inclusion of income elements.

It is clear, for instance, that the decision not to reckon leisure time as an element of income and consumption is highly arbitrary. (In their collective bargaining, employees have regularly to weigh whether they will press for shorter hours or higher wages.) The non-inclusion of what people produce in goods and services for their own consumption or investment is equally arbitrary. Again, there are changes in time and also differences between countries. The work of housewives—and sometimes husbands—at home constitutes another particularly large income element arbitrarily left out. It has been pointed out that if, without any substantial changes in the interrelations within the family institution, wages were estimated and counted for home work, the GNP would increase very considerably, although differently both in time and for different countries.

While, with these and many other reservations, it should be possible to reckon private incomes (and consumption and investment) with some meaning in terms of market prices, the same is not true for what the citizens get in the form of public consumption. These incomes are simply accounted for in terms of public expenditures for salaries and other costs. This is obviously a very arbitrary way of ascertaining that part of GNP. Their true value depends on what, in the widest sense of the word, may be called the "effectiveness" of public services and indeed on the entire organization of society, which, like the size of the public sector in this specific sense, is changing and also varies for different countries.

And besides these select examples, there are a great number of other income elements which are either not accounted for at all or calculated in an arbitrary way. Those who actually make the primary statistical observations, the often crude estimates implied in their computation, and finally the aggregation into a figure for GNP and its main ingredient elements, are usually aware of this. Sometimes they state their reservations, though seldom very completely. But the figures are then used by economists as well as politicians and journalists, who all take them at their face value, usually showing little interest in the need for reservations.

The professional specialization of two types of researchers, those who produce the figures and those who use them in economic analysis, is a chief explanation of the common misuse of the GNP concept for long-term problems of growth and development. I have often thought that we need more of a confrontation between these two groups of

researchers and that, using the results of such a confrontation, a much more careful analysis should be made of how
these statistics are actually produced, how they should be
produced, and what they mean.

3. Less Commonly Observed Deficiencies

These exemplified types of shortcomings may be characterized as conventional reservations to the conventional
GNP concept. But this is only the beginning of the scientific scrutiny to which this concept and the common manner
of using it should be subjected.

Thus many income items represent expenditures that
have to be incurred to meet undesirable conditions and
developments. Some of them are expenditures and losses
caused to private citizens. Others are public expenditures.
A country without slums does not have the incomes related
to public expenditures for fire and police protection of the
continually growing slums in the United States, to point to
only one example; the slums also cause private losses and
expenditures, which should be subtracted. Again, the higher
level of criminality in the United States causes greater
public and private expenditures and losses. In any international comparison, these types of incomes, caused by higher
expenditures as well as the losses, should rightly be set aside.
If the social order is improving or deteriorating in a country,
similar problems arise of a need for correction of the crude
figures for the times series of GNP as ordinarily calculated.

These remarks are meant only to point to a very large
field of uncertainty and arbitrariness in the definition of
GNP. Attempts to correct the GNP figures in such respects
would open up problems of almost all social conditions and
trends in a country.

Problems of a somewhat similar nature face us in relation
to public and private conspicuous consumption and invest-

ment, defined as expenditures which are not calculated as having a normal return in consumption or production as ordinarily defined. To deal just with public conspicuous consumption, the huge expenditures for the moon flights and for wars and armaments in the United States should not be permitted to count in its GNP, when comparison is made with a country that disdains such a use of its productive resources, or indulges in it to a much smaller extent. Indeed, the GNP figures should not be valid for the considerable and steadily growing minority of liberal congressmen in the United States and their constituencies. More generally, a change of policy upward or downward in this respect should motivate a similar need for correction of the time series of GNP.

Debate over the past few years has made even the general public aware that the GNP figures do not take into rational consideration the problem of environment (Chapter 11). In regard to depletion of resources, this becomes really disturbing when stress is laid on the inordinately great part of the world's resources that are now exploited by a minority of people in the developed countries. This makes it virtually impossible to believe in, and strive for, long-term development in underdeveloped countries without assuming a radical change downward of what we now in developed countries can count as incomes, investment, production, and consumption. Such a policy change, however, is not now within sight, though in future we cannot allow ourselves to be so unconcerned.

Also, in recent years, the general public has been made aware of the rapidly ongoing pollution of air, water, soil, and indeed our own bodies. Of this the statistics on GNP take no account. If we assume that we shall not unwittingly let disaster overcome us, the GNP, as ordinarily accounted for, should be reduced in the same way as in regard to the depletion of resources.

In abstracto, the necessary corrective terms could perhaps be defined as the costs of preserving the *status quo* in the individual states: (1) the costs that would be implied in measures to stop further depletion of resources, or to find substitutes; and (2) the cost of stopping further pollution. But such calculations take no account of the international aspect of these problems, and international considerations, to one extent or other, will become unavoidable. As they, like the simple considerations of national interests, will have to be decided by a political process, the course of which is not charted in advance, all calculations will consequently have to be hypothetical.

Moreover, the actual facts of ongoing depletion and pollution are highly uncertain and to a large extent controversial. We do not therefore have, and cannot within the near future expect to have, the knowledge needed for calculating the costs that rationally should be subtracted from the present crude GNP figures. We know only that their magnitude must be assumed to be very substantial, judging from the few, mostly speculative studies now being made by economists who have become aware of the problem.

The shortcomings referred to in this section have two things in common: they are very grave, and we have no hope of estimating corrective terms for them.

4. The "Quality of Life"

Economists occasionally try to safeguard the traditional GNP concept by saying that it measures only production of goods and services, but that there are other things determining the "quality of life." This latter concept is bluntly unclear and useless as an analytical tool. All the items enumerated in the two preceding sections as excluded or dealt with in an arbitrary way, have also an effect on production of goods and services, and all the items actually accounted for have an obvious importance for the "quality of life," whatever we mean by that.

The term cannot, therefore, be applied as providing a distinction between what is, and what is not, accounted for in the GNP. It only raises in a vague manner problems concerning what people get out of their productive activity and, indeed, the direction of their whole life. The problem is certainly important, but it is not even raised and properly defined by the conventional and grossly arbitrary definition of GNP.

A more learned expression of a similar thought is to rely on the inherited and, in establishment economics, conservatively preserved "welfare theory," pointing out that, in regard to welfare, equal weight should not be given to all kinds of income and expenditures. But the question of the importance for people's welfare cannot possibly be thought to depend on whether an item is properly included in GNP, or left out, or calculated in an arbitrary manner.

This reason is conclusive. But quite apart from this, the modern welfare theory is just as metaphysical as the old one, as I have repeatedly pointed out in earlier chapters, particularly Chapter 7, Section 10, where I also gave a reference. In spite of the escapist terminology, developed right from the beginning of the marginal utility theory, if the welfare theory means anything, it does so only in terms of the hedonistic associational psychology of 100 years ago and in terms of the equally obsolete moral philosophy of utilitarianism.

5. "Development" as Different from "Growth"

A third way of attempting to rescue the GNP concept is to make a distinction between growth and development. It is maintained that GNP measures only growth of production, while development represents another and wider category.

It is true that development must be conceived of as more than the increase in production, always supposing that the latter concept can be properly defined and accounted for. I understand development as the movement upward of the whole social system. In other words, not only production, distribution of the produce, and modes of production are involved, but also levels of livings, institutions, attitudes, and policies.[5] Among all the factors in this social system there are causal interrelations. Even in developed countries, the coefficients of the interactions among the various factors in the social system are largely unknown and, in any case, not available in precise form. For this reason alone, the possibility of working out an index of development in this sense is not within sight.

When I first applied this system analysis in terms of circular causation with cumulative effects to the Negro problem in the United States,[6] I still believed it would be theoretically possible to define "the status of the Negro people" so precisely that it would seem possible to work out an index of its development, though I saw the difficulties of weighing all the factors that would have to be taken into account, particularly as a change in one factor causes changes in the other factors, which in turn cause changes all round, and so on. Now I feel that, even theoretically, there is no rational system of evaluation available. The process of development cannot even be thought of as being represented by one figure, i.e., by an index.

The question remains, however, whether the GNP cannot be defended as measuring the level and change in one important set of factors in the social system, viz., production. Even if we give up the idea that the GNP accounts for what we must understand as development, it could nevertheless be of scientific importance, for the study of the wider problem, to know that particular factor, which could supposedly be ascertained in quantitative terms.

The first reason why the traditional GNP cannot acceptably fill even this less ambitious role is, of course, that it gives an altogether unwarranted precision to the level and growth of production. I refer here to the exemplification in the preceding sections of items excluded from the calculation of GNP or those dealt with in an arbitrary way. The second, and main, reason stems directly from the concept of a social system. All the factors in that system—even production, if it could be properly defined, which it is not in the conventional concept GNP—are interdependent.

The true situation is that we are facing an immensely complicated problem of development in the sense given above as the movement of the social system, in which production is interrelated with, and dependent upon, all other factors. It is difficult to see any point in pressing statistics to produce one single figure for even one of the complex factors—growth of production—when it is once admitted that it is not possible for the wider category—development. It amounts to committing an all too common sin in contemporary economics: unwarranted precision. Such precision becomes, of course, particularly fallacious when one considers the very great and purely statistical imperfections listed in earlier sections.

The very idea that it is possible to characterize the situation of a country and its changes by an index, even for production as a factor of development, is mistaken. In any comparison over time or between countries, to be realistic we have to consider a whole series of different components. Only for a very short time and for closely similar countries can an index say something, and even then only most approximately.

For elements under the level of GNP, we can calculate figures of some meaning. It they are properly defined, there is every reason to use in our analysis of the wider development problem whatever figures we have for production in various fields, consumption of various types and in various social classes, investments of different types, prices and wages, exports and imports, and so on. For large fields, even when narrowed down in this way, we have, however, no figures or only very loose estimates.

6. Distribution

I have not yet touched upon the problem of distribution. The conventional concept of GNP, the economic theory built around it, and the figures as commonly calculated do not take distribution into account. In this respect, economic speculation follows a traditional line.

In Chapter 1, Section 4, I mentioned John Stuart Mill's distinction between production and distribution and the tendency among economists to disregard the problem of distribution, which they also simplified by thinking only in terms of money incomes. They have traditionally assumed, without much attempt at empirical investigation, that there is a price that has to be paid for egalitarian reforms in that they slow down economic growth. Only in recent decades and only in the most advanced welfare states has this inherited assumption of an incompatibility between growth and egalitarian reforms been toned down.

I felt that these brief remarks on the general background of more than a century's economic speculation were necessary before I proceeded to discuss the fact that the GNP concept does not take into account distribution and the interrelationship between production and distribution. The thinking among most contemporary economists apparently follows the old belief that it is possible to establish first what is produced while leaving it to a second and separate consideration how the produce is distributed. The fallacy in that approach is the non-consideration of the interdependence between production and distribution.

Even when that interdependence is not entirely forgotten, the old idea of the antagonism between growth and egalitarian policy measures still lingers. Without being able to go deep into that question here, I do want to point out that there are policy-determined alterations in distribution that enhance the growth of production. Such distributional changes, as well as those that have the opposite result by decreasing the growth of production, by themselves make invalid both comparisons in time of GNP for one country, and still more comparisons in space between different countries following different lines in regard to distribution.

A thesis underlying much that is said in this book about development in developed and underdeveloped countries is that wisely planned social reforms can have the character of "investments," leading not only to greater "justice," but also to higher production. Such "investments" often require considerable time before maturing in the shape of returns, but should not for this reason be forgotten more than other long-term investments.

To illustrate my thesis, I shall again turn to conditions in the United States, a country whose development I have followed more closely than that of other developed countries. As I mentioned in Chapter 1, Section 7, one aspect of the poverty problem in that country is that the labor force growing up in the rural and urban slums has to a large extent become an "underclass," that is, not "in demand," because it is not up to the standards of modern society.

It is generally recognized by knowledgeable students in the United States that the poverty problem must be attacked vigorously and systematically. The reforms needed are huge. Financially, the public expenditures for these reforms will amount to trillions of dollars and, even if the reforms are begun on a large scale in the near future, it will take a generation before the full beneficial effects are realized. The reforms are absolutely necessary if the United States is not going to face great dangers for its stability as an orderly and progressive democracy.

Realistically speaking, the costs of these social reforms represent a "debt to the poor" in the United States, which must be amortized and, in the end, fully paid. In productivity terms, the continued increase of that debt is equal to capital consumption. When, in the calculation of GNP, account is not taken of this huge debt and the totally insufficient way it is as yet accepted and met for the time being, it means an overstatement of the magnitude of GNP and, indeed, of the level at which the country's economy is running. This problem will again be taken up in Chapter 14, Section 8.

A country like Sweden, another country I know fairly well, which had fewer inequalities from the beginning and which now has behind it several decades of accelerated social reforms, should, according to the GNP figures, have a somewhat lower production and income than the United States. Taking into account the latter country's huge conspicuous consumption of various types and, in particular, its debt to the poor, which is not being paid off, this gives an entirely wrong conception of reality. And even in Sweden there are still egalitarian reforms to be carried out, which have the character of social and political necessity. They are all of importance also to the development of production.

7. In Underdeveloped Countries

I have been dealing with the situation in developed countries. In underdeveloped countries, all the critical points raised above are pertinent, some more so than others. (I refer here to Chapters 5 and 6.)[7] Because of the climate in the tropics and subtropical zones, where they are situated, and the population explosion, the pollution problem is, for instance, often more serious. Partly because of the lower levels of income, the problems related to distribution are more pressing. Those Western growth models, abstracting from the productivity consequences of levels of consumption, are particularly apt to lead astray. Without radical egalitarian reforms in regard to landownership and tenancy, education, the stamping out of corruption, and generally enforcing greater social discipline, they have at most slight hopes for sustained development.

Besides these factors, which can be subsumed under the type of critical discussion carried out above for developed countries, there are additional and specific shortcomings in the conventional concept of GNP when applied to underdeveloped countries. Aggregation is less possible, since, among other things, there are no markets, or only very imperfect ones. The statistical services are also very much less efficient. But the inadequacy of their statistics is to a large extent due to the fact that they have been collected, compiled, and analyzed by the use of totally inadequate categories—those taken over from the economic analysis of developed countries, despite the fact that conditions are vastly and systematically different in underdeveloped countries. The result is that the published GNP figures, continually permitted to play a very large role in the literature on the development problems in underdeveloped countries, are particularly unreliable (Chapter 5, Section 12).

Much more generally, economists have shown great carelessness in the use of statistics and have not even pressed effectively for their improvement. The primary need is, in a sense, theoretical: to establish categories for the collection of data that are adequate to reality in underdeveloped countries. Attention needs to be devoted to what economists call "non-economic" factors, which are of much greater importance not only for development but primarily for growth of production than in developed countries. Even more important than in developed countries is the request that the approach chosen should be, in the sense defined, institutional.

The strivings to quantify our knowledge should certainly not be given up, but pushed vigorously. However, most of the figures now uncritically utilized in the attempts to analyze growth and development in underdeveloped countries are not only statistically weak in the ordinary sense, but grossly misconceived. That the now commonly compiled figures for GNP or national income are not worthy of remaining the kingpin of that analysis is certain.

Finally, I must confess that it was only the severe shock I experienced when I went into research about how figures like those for GNP and national income were computed in underdeveloped countries that put me on the path of my generally critical thoughts, briefly accounted for above.[8] I am afraid that without that research experience I might have behaved like my colleagues in general and used these figures at their face value, having only vague feelings that they contained some inaccuracies.

Chapter 11

ECONOMICS OF AN
IMPROVED ENVIRONMENT[1]

THE ANXIETIES now expressed by biologists and other natural scientists working on the world's ecosystem concerning the impending depletion of irreplaceable natural resources (water, energy, some crucial metals, and arable land) and the pollution of our environment (air, water, land, animals and our own bodies) should rightly have important consequences for development planning in developed and underdeveloped countries and primarily for economic theory both on the macro and micro levels.

1. Conditioning Earlier Experiences

Of the two environmental factors, pollution is, on the whole, a quite recent worry. In regard to depletion, there have been several development experiences reaching back more than a century that have conditioned economists as well as the general public not to take such warnings about a deteriorating environment too seriously. And, indeed, it can now be witnessed how economists rather generally, with some exceptions (including the present author), tend to belong to the "optimists," who are inclined to discount these warnings as exaggerated.

One such early conditioning sequence of events was the

refutation by experience of Malthus' theory and the implicit forecast that what he called the tendency of "geometrical" growth of population, if not checked by "moral restraints," would come to press on the agricultural resources of land. These Malthusian thoughts were accepted by Ricardo and the whole early school of classical economists. They provided the basis for Ricardo's harsh theory of wages and of distribution in general. Indeed, they led him to vaguely envisage as a result of development the stationary state, with rising land rates, falling profits, the ending of real capital accumulation, and wages becoming stabilized at the production costs of the labor force, all based on a balance of the forces of growing scarcity of land and the tendency toward population increase.

Quite contrary to this gloomy forecast—except indeed for the underdeveloped regions—the era from Malthus up to the present has been one of historically unprecedented economic growth and also gradually rising levels of living, even in the lower income brackets. This has happened in spite of periodic interruptions by depressions and even devastating wars. Growth generally accelerated after World War II.

In hindsight, it is possible to account for the major alterations that had this result: among them, rapid technological advance in agriculture as well as industry; from the middle of the nineteenth century, the huge imports of food to Britain and Western Europe generally from the emigrant settlements in the areas of the New World where the natives were not so numerous and could be killed off or segregated in various ways; and, still later, the spontaneous spread of birth control.

Another series of experiences conditioning us to "optimism" has been the following: Through all my working life as an economist, there have been fears about the pending scarcity of raw materials. Even the Atlantic Charter contained a passage expressing this fear and requesting free access to raw materials. From time to time, there have been large-scale studies giving similar warnings, among them the *Paley Report* in the Fifties and, more recently, the report on *Resources and Man* by the National Academy of Sciences in the United States.

But in actuality there has always been a good supply of raw materials. Indeed, the development prospects for underdeveloped countries have continually been endangered by oversupply and the low prices of the primary products, depending on land resources, that make up the bulk of their exports. Again, it is possible *ex post* to explain why these newer fears have so far not been justified by later developments. A main cause has been the never-ending discoveries of new supplies of raw materials, particularly of oil and various metal ores. In addition, there have been technological inventions making it possible and economically profitable to create economies in the use of raw materials and also to replace some of them by less scarce raw materials or by manufactured products produced from them.

Because we in the developed countries have been permitted to retain that important element of the faith in human progress prevailing in the era before World War I, we have all come to trust in continuous and boundless economic growth. In that respect, there has been no difference between developed countries with different political systems. And after the hurricane of liberation from the colonial power system that swept over the globe after World War II, the ruling elites of the underdeveloped countries raised demands for development, basing their planning on the same faith in the unlimited space for growth, provided they could overcome the lack of capital and other obstacles and inhibitions to development.

2. The Seriousness of Present Anxieties

We have so often heard people cry wolf that we have become accustomed not to take them seriously. From my studies, though naturally inexpert, of what my colleagues in the natural sciences have more recently reported, I have, however, become convinced that we must finally recognize and prepare for the fact that there are limits to a growth whose component elements all follow an exponential curve.

A main reason why I am inclined to take a more gloomy view of the future than most of my economist colleagues is that I foresee that, this time, an unsteered, natural development will not save us. We would need to take planned government actions on a large scale to defend our environment. And even if we came to develop a theory for such planning, I mistrust both the will and the capacity of governments to decide upon and effectuate such planned policies to the extent needed. I shall return to this point later.

All estimates upon which the warnings of depletion and pollution are founded are utterly uncertain, as another of the lecturers in this series, Professor René Dubos, has authoritatively explained: "The existing knowledge of the natural sciences is not sufficient to permit the development of effective action programs." Many of these estimates are still of a highly controversial nature. In particular, further discoveries and inventions can only be very broadly surmised. Future policies, which might even come to steer and thereby influence the scope and direction of science and technology, are in principle not possible to predict, as they will depend upon the way in which people choose to act and react. History is not a blind fate.

But these reservations against the inexcusably careless manner in which so-called futuristic research is now often pursued do not decrease the need for long-term planning. What happens in our children's time and even further ahead, if this type of exponential economic growth continues, does matter to us as citizens of our nations and of the world.

And, as has been demonstrated in a broad way, the reservations about the uncertainty of all forecasts I have piled up merely imply that the future, when uncontrolled growth comes up against serious limits, is somewhat indeterminate, but usually within the range of only one or at most a few generations.

In any case, with the unprecedentedly rapid and still accelerating growth of the world's population, which we must now take as fairly certain to continue for many decades—to this I shall return—we shall invite catastrophic developments, unless we are prepared now to introduce and enforce various restraints on, and deflections of, production and consumption and, indeed, our ways of life. If we in the developed countries were alone in the world, but still had free access to the primary products that underdeveloped countries are now exporting, the threatening consequences of uncontrolled growth might not disturb us too much for several decades ahead, provided that we took reasonable measures against pollution. But the situation in the underdeveloped world is very much more serious and the impending dangers more immediate, as I shall point out later.

3. Gross National Product

As usual, the economists have reflected and rationalized in their work the common inclinations among the general public in the societies they are living in and servicing. At the same time, they thereby support in a mighty way the psychology and ideology of continuous and unlimited economic growth.

There are, in particular, two traits in modern economic theory that reflect this accommodation to prevalent thinking and that consequently have to be given up, or altered in a radical fashion, in order to build up an "economics of an improved environment," to quote the title given me for this lecture.

One is the gross national product concept, or national income, which is a derivation, and the use made of this concept. As I pointed out in Chapter 10, Section 1, it is no exaggeration to state that modern economic theory has more and more organized itself around this concept. I stressed that GNP is a flimsy concept in developed countries and, for various reasons, even very much more so in underdeveloped countries. These defects stand out as particularly relevant in regard to problems of a long-term character, such as those I am discussing now.

I must add that attempts to define a broader concept of "social utility," including not only production, but also all other social indicators, are doomed to remain on a level of useless speculation that is not even conceptually valid. There is no logical way of constructing an objective index of "gross national happiness."

In addition to this comes not only the lack of reliable quantification of all the things that are deemed desirable or harmful, but also, more fundamentally, the almost total absence of quantitative knowledge about the coefficients of interrelations among the various factors determining the movement of the social system as a whole. This becomes particularly apparent when, as certainly we should, we include living levels, attitudes, institutions, and political forces as they operate in circular causation with cumulative effects, which governs the movement of the social system.

In the very short-term economic analysis—and in developed countries though, as I firmly hold, not in underdeveloped countries—the GNP as now calculated may nevertheless have some indicative value, at least in the very short run. In all countries, many individual figures from national accounts relating to ingredient elements may also be of use. But for long-term problems, focused on the facts of depletion and pollution that are excluded from the calculations, the GNP has to be thrown out as entirely inadequate to reality.

This is the more serious as the GNP concept is now seen as being of central importance in economic analysis of the development problems in both developed and underdeveloped countries. Indeed, this use of the GNP has become the expression and justification of the psychology and ideology of continued unlimited growth I have mentioned.

4. The Rome Report

At this point, a few critical remarks should perhaps be added on the recently published so-called "Rome Report," *The Limits to Growth: A Global Challenge.*[2] It will probably have the useful effect of popularizing the ecologists' broad warnings of the necessity of giving up our expectations of continuing on the road of unrestrained growth. But to the serious student the report has grave defects in its very approach to the problems of both present trends and the possibilities and means of altering these trends.

To begin with, the Report uncritically accepts the GNP concept. Also, for the rest, it builds upon, and aggregates in the most careless way, data that are extremely uncertain both in regard to economic growth itself and to its various components. The data concerning the threat of pollution and depletion are equally unreliable. Even a popular presentation should contain a reminder of this, particularly as it is of importance for the use of these data in a system analysis. The authors are, in other words, overselling their product in regard to the validity of the basic data.

Much more fundamental is the question of the realism of the Report's global "world system analysis." This analysis implies, to begin with, a non-consideration of the enormous and increasing differences and inequalities within

countries and still more among countries (see below). To
explain this, the Report states that "inequalities of distribution are defined as social problems" and then placed outside "the world simulation model," which only "calculates
the maximum possible behavior of our world system," provided that there is "intelligent action on world problems,
from a worldwide perspective."

An economist working on these very problems will be
hard put to it to give any intelligible meaning to this assumption of perfect harmony in the world. Still less will he
be able to outline how it could be brought about. Particularly in a simulated system analysis, it is simply not possible
to get away from "the social problems" merely by stating
that they are not taken into account. The ecosystem has to
be studied as part of the social system I have mentioned.

More specifically, the Report places outside the "interactions" within the "world model" attitudes and institutions,
indeed even the process of price formation, while politics
is represented only by stating a number of the results of
highly abstract policy alternatives. Their system is, therefore, far from inclusive enough to have meaning.

The birth rate, for example, is quite rightly a factor, and
a very important one, within their model. But it is certainly
not a function only of the other factors within that model
and the interrelations among them all. As we who have
studied the demographic development in the several regions of the world know, the movements of these factors
are not even among the most important determinants of
the birth rate. And the importance of them is not through
the simple interrelations of the model. Indeed, those interrelations are fictitious.

Under these circumstances, the use of mathematical equations and a huge computer, which registers the alternatives of abstractly conceived policies by a "world simulation
model," may impress the innocent general public but has
little, if any, scientific validity. That this "sort of model is

actually a new tool for mankind" is unfortunately not true. It represents quasi-learnedness of a type that we have, for a long time, had too much of, not least in economics, when we try to deal with problems simply in "economic terms."

In the end, those conclusions from the Report's analysis that are at all sensible are not different and definitely not more certain than could have been reached without that elaborate apparatus by what Alfred Marshall called "hard simple thinking aware of the limitations of what we know."

5. The Competitive Market Model

The second trait in economic theory I referred to which implies an accommodation to the psychology and ideology of unlimited growth is that, fundamentally, economic analysis has retained its character of being carried out in terms of a theory of price formation in competitive markets. The preferences of all concerned are expressed in aggregate form by their demands and supplies. Production and resource allocation are steered by relative profitability.

With regard to depletion and pollution, a main fact is, however, the very heavy discounting of the future at the present time, represented by interest and profit rates. This implies that the time horizon becomes much narrower than should be accepted by our collective society, which must consider developments decades and centuries ahead. When, as has happened, economists argue that, as resources become scarce, the cost of these resources will rise so that depletion is avoided, they are not taking into account the fact that this reaction does not come early and strongly enough to be rational and sufficient in order to avoid depletion.

Price formation in markets is biased and does not give the "right" signals to business concerns or to individual consumers. Consumption, production, technology, and resource allocation expand in directions and with a speed that result in depletion and pollution. This, together with the population growth, is, in fact, how we happened to arrive in the present situation.

It is true that, from the neo-classical authors on, we have made reference to what they called "externalities," by which was meant the incidental effects at large of the economic subjects' acting according to the competitive market model. But it is not unfair to state that particularly the negative externalities of depletion and pollution have practically never been made the object of economic analysis, but remained, until very recently, one of our several empty boxes.

What is needed to realize the goals of society is a large-scale correction of the process of price formation, conditioning production, investment, scientific and technological research, and consumption to take a different course and also, in regard particularly to pollution, to get the whole population to behave differently in regard not only to what they demand for consumption, but also, for instance, to how they behave in the matter of wastage and refuse.

There are, in principle, two means of introducing and giving effect to policy measures against depletion and pollution. One is direct government regulation of people's behavior, forbidding them to do certain things and directing them to do others. The second way is that of price policies, inducing, by means of charges and/or subsidies, the price formation to give different signals to consumers and producers.

Now it can be said that economic theory is already well adapted for accounting for such alterations by policy measures of what is a "may" or a "must" in the economic behavior of all participants in the process of price formation, and in addition what things actually come to cost and what income an activity renders. Price formation is, of course, never thought to work within an abstract society but in an actual national community which has laid down its parameters. Economic theory is, for instance, not helpless in dealing with the effects of protectionist policy measures or of labor legislation, the latter ordinarily containing both types of interference in the process of price formation.

The rule is, however, that the effects of these interferences have been rather marginal, leaving the process of price formation to be ruled mainly by spontaneous demands and supplies, which operate within the established parameters. The new restraints and deflections, rationally motivated by considerations of long-term effects of the trends toward depletion and pollution but infringing upon people's impulses to follow their individual short-term preferences, must in comparison stand out as radical.

This exposes first a serious political problem. How is it possible to move from a general awareness by the public of the dangers ahead, and by the policy-deciding instances acting on behalf of the public, to a preparedness to impose the controls needed? This would ideally imply a centrally imposed and enforced planning of almost all economic and, indeed, all human activity. Implied also is an equally serious administrative problem: How can the controls be applied so that policy decisions really become effectuated, and how can that be done without necessitating a huge policing and controlling administration which would be financially too expensive and also too obnoxious to the people?

I shall return to these two major problems, the political and the administrative, at the end of this chapter, where I shall attempt to characterize present policy trends and make a short-term forecast of what will actually evolve in the way of realizing the ideals of the movement that has brought into being the United Nations Conference on the Human Environment.

I should like to add here that, from the point of view of the administrative problem, there is every reason to operate as far as possible through price policies and other general controls, which impose much more easily manageable demands on administration, than through direct discretionary government interdictions and prescriptions. On this particular point, I believe I can speak for the whole profession of economists. But we would deceive ourselves if we believed that the goals could be reached without direct administrative controls also, for instance in the vast field of waste disposal or in regard to international treaties directed toward the control of pollution transmitted through water and air.

I feel sure that economic science will increasingly be able to lay the foundation for such radical central planning, which may be rational enough to meet the pending dangers of depletion and pollution. It would imply, however, such alterations in our approaches that we would have the right to talk about a "new economics." To what extent such a development of our theory would influence government policy is another matter, however.

The concept of the GNP, and the whole structure of theoretical approaches built up with the GNP as a central axis, will have to be dethroned. And the process of price formation will, by policy interventions, have to be even further removed from being essentially concerned with aggregated individual preferences represented by supply and demand.

As economists as a rule are a rather conservative lot insofar as the main structure of their conceptions and preconceptions is concerned, it was not to be expected that they would have been in the vanguard for such a fundamental change of society and of their own science. The main pressure will, in the future years, as well as up till now, have to be exerted by those natural scientists who are studying the ecosystem.

I have here focused attention on the imperfection of the competitive market model in regard to depletion and pollution. I should add that the conservative attachment to this model on the part of conventional economists has been seriously wrong for many other reasons, among them, in particular, the market power of big business enterprises—see the excellent 1972 presidential address to the American Economic Association by John Kenneth Galbraith, "Power and the Useful Economist"—if that power is not checked and controlled by the state. But this assumes an alert, enlightened and politically activated citizenry.

6. In the Communist Developed Countries

So far I have had in mind the developed Western countries, including also Japan and the two small Australasian developed countries. It could be expected that the problems would have taken a different shape in the East European Communist countries with their centralized and comprehensive planning.

We might first note that, at least until recently, their planning has been directed almost solely toward economic growth. In that respect, they have not been different from the Western countries, even though they have defined the GNP somewhat differently. A change, implying increasing considerations to the problems of depletion and pollution, is now under way. These countries should more easily be able to move further in that direction as they have only to incorporate new goals for the central planning that already exists.

This does not mean, however, that they have escaped, or even can escape, the two serious problems, the political and the administrative ones, that I briefly characterized in regard to the Western countries. Indeed, if they have not been more successful in speeding up economic growth, the main reasons are, I believe, the necessity to take into account the inclinations of their consumers and, even more, the top-heavy, hierarchically structured bureaucracy which they created for implementing their central planning.

In these countries, prices are, in principle, not left free to be the result of a market process of price formation, but are centrally decided upon, as part of the planning. In regard to the determination of prices, their economists have not been very successful in explaining and motivating it by a clear-cut theory. In all these countries there have been intermittent attempts to allow space for a somewhat freer play of supply and demand in markets, thereby decentralizing decision-making in the interest of efficiency and rational resource allocation.

I foresee that it is probable that the European Communist countries will retain their central planning, increasingly directing it not only toward growth but also toward improving the environment, at the same time giving price formation a somewhat freer play. Meanwhile, under the influence of the environmental crisis, the Western countries will be compelled to move toward more central planning, while retaining as much of a market economy as possible. This will tend to decrease the distance between the two types of economies. And there are other developments working in the same direction.

Fundamentally, the threatening advance of depletion and pollution gives rise to very similar problems, and even the needed policy adjustments and administrative difficulties are broadly similar.

7. Two Disregarded Conditions

In the global perspective, it is the great majority of people living in the underdeveloped countries that are most seriously and most immediately threatened by the environmental crisis. There are, among other things, two important facts which lead to this conclusion.

For one thing, all the underdeveloped countries are located in the tropical and subtropical zones, while all industrialized countries are to be found in the temperate zones.

By its direct and indirect effects on human beings, animals, soil, and various materials, climate is generally a serious impediment to development, although one can read hundreds of books and articles on the development problems of these countries without finding any reference to climate as slight as, for instance, to the "soft state" and corruption.

In regard to pollution, and to a certain extent also the depletion of resources, particularly in agriculture, climate implies that these countries stand more defenseless against destructive forces. I would be prepared to exemplify this thesis in breadth and depth, but in this brief chapter I have to abstain from doing so.

The second important fact, much more important even than climate, is the population explosion.

I find it a serious defect of the Founex *Report on Development and Environment,* presented as an expert document to the United Nations Conference on the Human Environment,[3] that these two major problems of climate and population are not given their due importance. It is, unfortunately, not true that the problems of environment in underdeveloped countries are simply related to underdevelopment on the one hand and development on the other.

8. The Population Explosion

In one sense, the population increase is the key factor in the environmental problem. Natural resources have to be considered in relation to the size of the population which is to be provided for. And pollution is also in many ways a function of the density of population.

The world population may already have reached the 3 billion mark in 1970. It is estimated that it will increase by another billion by 1975 and reach 7 billion by the end of the century. If, at the present time, the underdeveloped countries may be estimated to have two-thirds of the world's

population, by the end of the century their population might
have increased to four-fifths. At that time, the population
in the developed countries may have gone a long way toward a stationary condition, while the population in underdeveloped countries will almost certainly continue to increase further—tending to result before long in a world
population of 10 and gradually 15 billion and more. During
the seventies, at least, the population increase in the underdeveloped countries, taken together, is bound to accelerate.

This exercise in extremely loose estimates is intended
only to convey a broad perspective of trends in the population field. The driving force behind this development is
largely what happens in underdeveloped countries. There
the braking distance is long, and would continue to be
even if birth control were soon to become widespread. This
is due to the youthfulness of the populations, which is a
result of earlier and still persistent high fertility.

In general, the spread of birth control to the masses in
these countries is an exceedingly difficult task. It will not
happen spontaneously, as it did in the developed countries.
I cannot enlarge upon this subject in this context, but must
restrict myself to two crucial assertions.

First, it must be said that the oft-repeated cry, not least
in the recent debate on the impending environmental crisis,
that policy should be very "strict," sometimes explained to
imply "compulsory rationing of births" or something on that
order, is totally unrealistic.

What a government, which we assume has decided to do
its utmost to spread birth control among the masses, has to
attempt is to reach out in the villages and the city slums
where people are often illiterate, very poor, underfed, often
not in good health, and, as a result, generally apathetic.
There it has to get the individual couples to radically change
their most intimate sexual behavior. That is one area where
"strict" orders from above do not have much effect and
where "compulsion" is simply not workable.

Secondly, there is very little the developed countries can do to assist governments in the underdeveloped countries in carrying out this policy task, other than giving contraceptives, which they mostly should be able to produce themselves, some equipment, jeeps to be used by the family planning staff, and so on. The common clamor that "we" should place a high priority in our aid policy on family planning again demonstrates lack of realism. There is only one major aid we can offer, viz., that our scientists perfect even more the already vastly improved technology of birth control.

9. Increasing Inequality

It is clear that the unprecedentedly rapid population increase in underdeveloped countries, which will continue for decades, or at least for more than a generation, places a great impediment in the way to development. Though this is not the place for entering more deeply into that problem, I must mention as another serious impediment to development the trend in most underdeveloped countries toward increasing inequalities (see Chapter 6).

Population growth alone has in many ways the effect of increasing inequalities, particularly in agriculture. But in addition to this, there are gross inequalities that are ordinarily not being counteracted effectively by reforms regarding land ownership and tenancy, the school system as inherited from colonial times, the assessment and collection of taxes, and many other aspects of the institutional structure. In a "soft state," it is also people with economic, social, and political power who can most easily enrich themselves by unlawful means of various types—among them, plain corruption, which seems to be on the increase almost everywhere.

Egalitarian reforms in these and other respects are not

felt to be in the short-term interests of the upper strata, which mostly have the power in these countries, whatever their system of government. As in colonial times, it is also almost inevitable that both governments and businesses in developed countries have, through all their relations, come to support these strata, which have not been enthusiastic about egalitarian reforms, but have stood against them or distorted them to favor the not-so-poor.

I have, through my studies, come to the conclusion that the trend to greater inequality must be broken and that egalitarian reforms in the fields alluded to are not only in the interest of greater justice but a prerequisite for rapid and sustained growth. Up till now, whatever development most of the underdeveloped countries have had has mostly enriched the tiny upper strata, including the so-called middle class of "educated" and occasionally also the small group of organized workers in large-scale industry, but left the masses of people where they were. That the Founex Report is entirely silent on these and related problems is understandable and typical.

This trend to greater inequality in most underdeveloped countries, and the certainty in regard to them all of a very rapid increase of the labor force and the entire population, make it probable that we will have to expect an unfortunate development in the Seventies, which the United Nations General Assembly has courageously named the Second Development Decade: the increasing under-utilization of labor and, as a result, great misery among the rapidly swelling masses in the rural and urban slums.

In some parts of the underdeveloped world we might then not be far from the crisis point, where, for certain broad strata, the Malthusian checks come into active operation. Except after natural catastrophes, such a development will ordinarily stretch over a period of years with minor ups and downs. And it may not show up for a long time in the mortality statistics, which, with the great weakness of statistics on illnesses, is commonly also used as a measurement of morbidity.[4]

But a large and growing part of the poorest strata in a population may be diseased, or at least lacking in normal vigor, and may become even more afflicted, while the mortality rate is still decreasing due to the cheap and powerful medical tools made available after the war. They might continue to live and breed only to suffer debilitating conditions of ill health to an ever greater extent. Sooner or later, however, the death rate is also going to rise.

10. The International Equality Issue

The environmental problem, particularly in regard to the depletion of irreplaceable resources, is nowadays discussed as a global problem. But there is a distributional issue involved: Who has the power over the resources? The disregard of this issue makes many of the current brave and broad pronouncements utterly superficial and misleading, indeed meaningless. To give meaning, concreteness, and relevance to our pronouncements on the global problem of resource depletion, we have to decide on a basis for drawing our inferences, a definite condition in regard to the distributional issue.

It is customary to say that the 20 or 30 per cent of mankind living in the developed countries now dispose of some 80 per cent or more of the world's natural resources for their own use. Much of this 80 per cent of the world's resources is imported from the underdeveloped countries, where now two-thirds, and soon a greater proportion, of all people live. (I am quoting estimates that roughly illustrate a fundamental element of inequality in the world today.)

International trade in resources and products near the raw material stage has, in some respects, rather sinister consequences. As my compatriot Professor Georg Borgström has reiterated, thereby doing public enlightenment a service, underdeveloped countries are continually exporting large quantities of high-quality, protein-rich food products to make overeating possible in the affluent developed countries, and sometimes to provide food for dogs and other domestic animals, or to be used as fertilizers. Thus fish meat, for instance, is imported from African and Latin American areas, more critically short of protein than even South Asia. In the United States and Europe it is then used to feed broilers and livestock.

The result is that the inhabitants of the rich countries take an altogether disproportionate share of protective food available in the world and use it in a less economical way than would be necessary in the underdeveloped countries, at the same time as they generally use up an equally disproportionate share of grains for feeding purposes.

But even aside from that type of export from underdeveloped countries which deprives them of primary products from land and sea that they badly need themselves for feeding their largely undernourished, malnourished, and rapidly increasing populations, the fact must be spelled out that the small minority of people in developed countries appropriate and use for their own production and consumption an entirely disproportionate and steadily increasing part of the world's resources. One broad inference is that any hope that the living levels in underdeveloped countries would ever even approach those in developed countries would presuppose a radical increase in their use of irreplaceable resources.

Particularly with the now growing awareness of their threatening depletion, this would, in turn, necessitate acceptance of a substantial lowering of living levels in developed countries. I see few signs of such a change, even among the most ardent advocates of the necessity of taking a global view of the use of resources, and certainly not in the announced aid policies of any developed country.

My main point, however, is the purely logical request that any discussion of threatening depletion of resources in global terms, if it is not to remain on a level of general and unclear phrase-mongering, must define a stand on the distributional issue. Is it our assumption that, in the interest of greater equality in the world, there should come to be a more fair distribution of resources between developed and underdeveloped countries in order to make possible a corresponding speeding up of their development? Or is the assumption instead that the present proportion appropriated by developed countries is going to be upheld and even gradually increased with their rising levels of living, including the large imports of resources from the underdeveloped countries?

The second alternative on the distributional issue—that of a *status quo*—is apparently taken for granted. This should then in all honesty be stated. And the word "global" should be used with more care, spelling out that tacit assumption.

As I have already hinted, there is also a tremendous difference in timing, when, in particular, the race between agricultural resources and population size may result in a catastrophic situation. In some underdeveloped countries that time might now be approaching for large masses of their inhabitants, while developed countries would even be in the position to continue to decrease the areas of cultivated land as well as the labor force employed in cultivating it. A simple juxtaposing of population and arable land for the world as a whole is, therefore, a meaningless and misleading exercise.

In regard to most other resources and, in particular, all sorts of minerals, the main efforts to economize their use must take place in the developed countries, where most of them are actually being used up. Any success in this direction would then, for many of these materials which are imported from some underdeveloped countries, imply a decrease of export incomes for these countries. It would lower exports and, whatever prices are established by price policies in the importing developed countries themselves in order to bring down their use, lower prices on the "world market," which is in this case the export prices for the underdeveloped countries depending on these exports. Again, a "global" analysis in aggregate terms of total world resources and the use made of them is grossly misleading and, in fact, meaningless.

11. The Political Prospects

I shall end by asking: What are the political prospects for governments coming to apply policy measures to improve environment or, to begin with, to prevent its further deterioration?

I am not rising to futuristic heights, least of all trying to press my estimates into quantitative terms, for which there is no basis, and stretch them over decades ahead. I am considering present trends and their possible or probable continuation in the near future—say the next ten years.

Even with the tasks so humbly perceived, I make no claim to infallibility. From study and from some experience of how politics evolve, I have learned that people's actions and reactions, collectively as well as individually, will always be more or less unexpected, and the more so the further ahead we gaze. As I have said, history is not predetermined.

I shall be thinking first of national communities in the developed Western countries, but shall later consider briefly other countries and international relations.

The awareness of the threat to our environment has recently intensified, partly under the influence of the preparations for the United Nations Conference on the Human Environment. Under the leadership of its Secretary General, Maurice F. Strong, this preparation has become, in fact, a worldwide educational movement.

In many of our countries, urging government action for the protection of environment has become almost a matter of competition among political parties. We should not hide from ourselves, however, that what I have called the psychology and ideology of unrestrained economic growth has meanwhile retained its hold over people's minds as powerfully as ever. And in national communities with a competitive market economy, every single group is bent upon, and organized for, continual pressure for getting their incomes and their levels of living raised, with little or no visible intention of changing the direction of their consumption demands.

There are, in particular, few or no widespread thoughts on the costs and restraints that are implied in the application of the new policies, and no great preparedness in any group to participate in paying these costs and submitting to these restraints. Such inconsistency in popular conceptions of policy issues is nothing extraordinary, but rather a universal pattern of the way politics are conducted in our type of countries.

Meanwhile, however, we already see governments sponsoring studies and setting up agencies for environmental controls. I foresee that, without too much resistance, we shall everywhere in the Western world have ever more effective control of all sorts of novel chemical and biotic concoctions that for some time have increasingly gone into the supplies offered by pharmacies and into food production as coloring or to improve taste. Their numbers are rapidly increasing, and up till now no more than a fraction of them is said to have been reliably tested for possible toxicity. The same is true of the increasing variety of washing detergents. The capacity of national research institutions is

increased by borrowing from what is done in other countries. These new discoveries are not kept secret as are often
the results of research and development work in industry
and, in particular, in the military field.

The restrictive controls over these types of manufactured
substances will be the more readily accepted by the public,
because of the steady stream of new research reports on
the damaging effects of one after another of them. I can
foresee, in the not very distant future, legislation that will
lay the burden of proving them harmless upon the producer
or seller. They form too small a fraction of business to be
able to offer much resistance as a pressure group. And the
restrictive controls do not cause many real sacrifices and
costs on the part of the consumers, who might even soon
learn that they are better off with a less variegated supply
of drugs, fancy foods, and detergents.

When, however, we come to restricting the use of various chemicals for raising productivity in agriculture and
forestry, and to preventing the dumping of unprocessed
waste from industrial factories into lakes and rivers and
their poisoning of the air by smoke, then we enter a field
where substantial costs are implied. The more effectively
the controls are applied, the more the costs are increased.
If not absorbed by government subsidies and borne by the
taxpayer, these costs will ultimately fall on the people—as
consumers in the form of higher prices, and as income
earners, mainly the employees, in lower wages than otherwise they could press for.

Only transitionally can these costs be expected to remain
as losses on already invested capital. But considering the
fact that such strong vested interests are involved, it must
be astonishing that these controls have recently been increased and magnified so relatively fast in many developed
countries. Part of the explanation is undoubtedly the publicity about, and people's actual experiences of, for instance,
dead waters where it is not safe to swim and where fish are

disappearing or have become so contaminated that they cannot be eaten without health risk. In regard to these types of controls we are, however, only beginning something that we have good reason to continue. And the controls will be expensive.

In advanced welfare states like Sweden, interest will increasingly be directed toward improving conditions in factories in order to protect the health and happiness of the workers. This movement is becoming coordinated with the strivings for an "industrial democracy," giving employees a larger say in directing industrial activity, particularly, but not only, in regard to working conditions. Industry will cooperate, partly under compulsion from government regulations, sometimes sweetened by subsidies in various forms, and partly, undoubtedly, because of social responsibility. But it all means heavy costs.

In these countries, too, there will be increasing popular pressure for the protection of flora and fauna in order to serve the pleasure and well-being of the people. This is not without its costs, either.

All these policy measures as here exemplified are directed against pollution in the widest sense of that term. In a world where raw materials can be imported and are continually cheap, the threatening depletion of irreplaceable resources will hardly become an effective motivation for national policies. Exceptions to this rule are the water, land, and energy resources within a country, in regard to which, restrictive planning is usually also required in order to avoid or decrease pollution. Some saving of resources will also follow the reclamation and recycling that is often implied in preventing wastage from industry or human conglomerations from polluting our environment.

Besides entailing costs, policy measures taken to preserve and improve our environment will regularly restrain people's freedom to do what they please. This is what I referred to as the administrative problem. Insofar as the

policy measures are restricted to charges and/or subsidies
of a generalized nature, the administrative problem should
not be too heavy a burden to shoulder for a government of
a developed country, although the sometimes high profits
to be gained by circumventing these controls may create
temptations similar to those causing tax avoidance and tax
evasion. General regulations restraining and redirecting investment and production in industry and commerce and the
municipalities' ways of dealing with wastage will also not
usually raise insurmountable administrative difficulties.

But when it comes to regulating the individual behavior
of ordinary people and, to some extent, also of the really
small-scale enterprises—for instance, in what manner they
dispose of all sorts of refuse and how they generally behave
toward nature—there are limits as to what the government
can do both in the costs implied in policing the regulations
and in the acceptance by those being controlled. Such limits on the practicability of exerting authority to discipline
the behavior of masses of people are already severely hampering policy.

12. Difficulties Ahead

The primary difficulties are, however, the political ones:
how to get people to permit the government to initiate the
policy measures in the first place.

Take a special case—automobiles. Our nations will probably accept ever more effective controls of the production
of automobiles, aimed at making them safer and less polluting. The increased costs, ultimately to be borne by the
consumer, will, in the generally inflationary climate of all
developed countries and with the high priority given to
that type of private consumption, be not too grudgingly
tolerated.

But this is only part of the problem. All big cities suffer

from severe automobile overcrowding. Not only is the air polluted by exhausts, but their transport situation is in a mess, without any government or municipal authority having felt it possible to restrict effectively the use of automobiles in cities. Owners and would-be-owners are by far the biggest "political party" everywhere.

And in no developed country, as far as I know, has it proved politically possible to get car owners to pay the full costs, including also the heavy investment costs for roads and for adjusting cities to the cramming of cars in the streets, the costs implied for all delays caused to people in the cars and on the streets, the costs of policing the traffic, and the very heavy public and private costs caused by accidents, not to speak of our now also having to pay for the pollution of the air.

General declarations in favor of "a new style of life," directed toward "the quality of living," while giving up consumption of a lot of basically less necessary commodities, has a general appeal for any public. But the accustomed "style of life" has a strong survival force, particularly in a competitive market economy, where every group is bent upon defending and raising its incomes and levels of living. Almost our entire institutional structure and attitudes are geared to growth of the old kind. And now comes the additional fact that there are costs implied in the policy measures needed for defending and improving environment. No group is, as yet, really willing to pay these additional costs.

It is true that in the longer run these costs may be profitable and result in higher productivity. But initially, they are heavy, and they come first, far ahead of the returns. They are in the nature of "investments."

We might at this point note that none of the developed countries has managed to prevent inflation and its result in "stagflation" (see Chapter 2). From one crucial point of view, the fundamental cause of inflation is that people are not prepared to make sacrifices in their private consumption large enough to pay for the public expenditures they want made.

The priorities differ. For the forced extra saving implied in inflation, the Americans have got in exchange the moon flights, a huge military establishment, and the deeply disturbing memory of the lost Vietnam war, while we Swedes have, among many other good things, a great number of large and excellently equipped but very expensive hospitals, available free to the entire population. But fundamentally, there is a similarity in the causation of inflation. What the ordinary citizen in our countries wants is higher public expenditures without having to pay for them—that is, to raise public expenditures without committing himself to saving.

It is with this in mind that we have to take into account that the policy measures against pollution imply costs, often of the investment type. Without a fundamental change in people's attitudes, these policy measures will, therefore, add to the forces driving to inflation. From one angle, important to the economist, this is the effect of people's readiness to desire a "higher quality of life" without any infringement on all their other desires. In this respect, every country has to watch what is happening in the others. More rapid developments than in those countries with which it trades imply dangers for its own trade and payment balance.

This relation to inflation will undoubtedly put a hamper on the speed at which policy measures against pollution can be decided upon and applied. And if we should make the assumption, at present rather unrealistic, that a country would become prepared to fight inflation effectively and keep an unchanged value of its currency, it would have to go further than would otherwise be necessary in its restriction of private consumption, if it wanted, at the same time, to pursue an effective anti-pollution policy—or give up that policy more or less completely.

13. In Other Countries

About conditions in the centrally planned economies of the developed Communist countries of Europe, I shall say only that the problem is largely a similar one, except that they are not under the same pressure to care so much about their peoples' reactions. The difference is, however, only a relative one.

As everybody knows, the articulate, educated citizens of underdeveloped countries who represent "public opinion" show less excitement about the environmental problems. The oligarchies that mostly rule these countries, often not truly representing even those upper strata, are equally often much more tightly controlled by the big enterprises, who therefore represent comparatively much stronger pressure groups. And they will be the last to think that their industrialization should now be hampered by controls that were not applied in the developed countries when they were industrializing.

In agriculture, in particular, where there is both depletion and pollution on a large and damaging scale, policies to prevent a deterioration of the environment are intimately related to other needs for radical reforms, in regard not only to population control but also to landownership and education among other things. As these reforms are ordinarily not attacked with much vigor, the environmental reforms also tend to fall under the table.

It is as a result of the discussion in developed countries that the problem is now broached even in underdeveloped countries. Then, naturally, the talk turns to the possibility that developed countries will inaugurate policies to defend

themselves against pollution reaching them through imports. To this I shall come back.

14. Mansholt's Dream

There are intergovernmental problems related to the defense and improvement of the environment. Let me first
consider these problems as they appear within a political
bloc of developed countries which, being like-minded, could
be assumed to offer the greatest opportunities for intergovernmental cooperation. I am here in a position to cite an
important and widely noted policy statement by Dr. Sicco
Mansholt, until recently President of the EEC Commission.[5]

It is, indeed, radical in its tenets. He argues for "a strictly
planned economy" for the Community of West European
States, a "European plan" that would make planning "highly
centralized" and make it "respected when national economic
plans are drawn up."

For this planning, the GNP would be "abandoned" and
replaced by a mystical "GNU (utility)." This latter concept
is not defined, except by a reference to "Tinbergen's idea of
Gross National Happiness," with the added reservation
that "it is still not known whether one can quantify this
utility." As I have already observed in Chapter 10, Sections
4 and 5, it is not only a question of quantification: even
conceptually this idea is not logically tenable.

The purpose of this severe planning is to reach "a non-
polluting system of production and the creation of a recy-
cled economy." Particularly as counteracting the depletion
of resources is also a goal, Mansholt foresees "considerable
reductions in the consumption of material goods per inhabitant, to be compensated for by the extension of less tangible goods (social forethought, intellectual expansion, organization of leisure and recreational activities, etc.)." As
there will then be "a sharp reduction in material well-being

per inhabitant," Mansholt also finds reasons for egalitarian reforms that aim "to offer equal chances to all."

Mansholt argues "that the Commission could make concrete proposals" for this overall centralized planning and apparently also believes that these would be accepted by the member states. I am an old planner, with the roots of my thinking firmly in the Enlightenment philosophy and, in particular, the thinking of the early socialists in France and England, whom Marx later called "utopian." But experience and study have taught me the very narrow limits for effective planning and plan implementation in our type of national communities. Already, stopping inflation and restoring a stable value of our currencies seems at present an unrealistic goal for planning. And we may note that economists generally are not even seriously pursuing that goal any longer, but are content to warn of the danger of getting out of step with the general trend toward inflation in other countries (Chapter 2).

That Mansholt is building a castle in the air should be clear from what I pointed out in the last sections. Peoples and governments do not become different just by joining in the community of states, the bureaucracy of which Mansholt is heading. Rather, the commitment to seek common solutions of problems will necessitate considerations being given to the government that is slowest to move and thereby often prevents other governments from proceeding faster and further. Of this Mansholt has himself had several experiences.

This would not prevent the EEC from occasionally being able to provide the matrix for intergovernmental negotiations within their subregion, directed, for instance, toward getting the West German government to take action against the poisoning of our common atmosphere by the Ruhr industries.

In regard more particularly to planned policy actions against depletion of resources, which figures so prominently

in Mansholt's philosophical tract, I doubt whether any government action is likely or possible in any country as long
as there is a world market for these resources—with the
reservation made in the next to last section for a few of
them that are nationally based and in regard to which controls are often needed already to decrease pollution.

The possibility of imposing a common central planning
of pollution controls upon the European Communist countries participating in the Warsaw Pact should be somewhat
greater, since they are all planned economies (though even
in that subregion it will meet resistance). Among underdeveloped countries regional cooperation is generally
nowhere highly developed. As, moreover, the pressure for
environmental controls is weak within them all, I cannot
foresee much prospect for any such cooperation.

15. Worldwide Cooperation?

Coming then to the still broader problem of a worldwide
cooperation to protect and improve our environment, it is
difficult to see the prospects as being bright. We have behind us a number of conspicuous failures to reach intergovernmental agreements in fields where common interests
should be very strong and even more urgent in character.

In regard to the negotiations on armament controls,
which the United Nations Charter placed high on the
agenda for the new world organization, we have so far
reached only "cosmetic" agreements, which have not
stopped the armaments race nor affected the competitive
arming of underdeveloped countries, mainly by the two
superpowers. The results of the SALT talks can unfortunately not be expected to effectively stop the armaments
race, but only slightly to redirect it. The two superpowers
have reasons of their own to play them up. They have already followed that line in a strange collusion, for instance

in regard to the partial test ban, which, as we know, has not prevented them from pushing ahead faster than ever with underground testing.

As I pointed out in Chapter 9, Section 5, the balance of terror between these superpowers has so far prevented outbreak of open warfare between them and also among developed countries generally. We cannot forget, however, the armed aggression against Czechoslovakia by the Soviet Union. The other superpower, the United States, has committed military aggression in Indochina, where, besides other horrors, it represents an unprecedented gross destruction of the environment for many millions of very poor people.

Armed conflicts within or between underdeveloped countries are continually flaring up, and the parties to the conflicts are regularly being aided or even spurred by developed countries, principally again the two superpowers. The machinery for the prevention or peaceful settlement of conflicts in the United Nations is increasingly becoming bypassed and obsolete.

On the subject of these serious failures of intergovernmental cooperation, one has only to refer to the publications of the Stockholm International Peace Research Institute [SIPRI].[6]

Globally, the aid to development of underdeveloped countries, which never amounted to much, has been decreasing quantitatively for at least a decade, and its quality has been deteriorating. This serious development is largely hidden from the general public by a gross falsification of the statistics as published by the governments in most developed countries and by their organization, OECD and its Development Assistance Committee (DAC) (see Chapter 6, Section 13).[7]

Commercial policies in developed countries have in various ways been discriminating against exports from underdeveloped countries and are still doing so on a large scale.

An effective way of aiding them would be to end these
discriminatory policies and, indeed, generally to make commercial policies work instead in their favor. It can be proved
that such a change of commercial policies would, in the
long run, be in the interest also of the developed countries
themselves (see Chapter 6, Section 12).[8]

The third meeting of UNCTAD, which ended last year,
has not demonstrated much willingness on the part of most
developed countries to move in this direction in regard to
commercial policies, and very little preparedness to raise the
quantity and quality of financial aid.

The two political blocs had not been able to agree on
letting East Germany participate in the United Nations
Conference on the Human Environment, which, in turn, led
the Soviet Union, together with its closest allies, also to
stay away from the Conference. This happened in spite of
the general expectancy that East Germany, together with
West Germany, will have entrance to the United Nations
within the next year. It has been part of the tactical game
of the blocs and demonstrates a cynical lack of interest in
the purpose of the Conference.

This, in addition to the desperately precarious situation in
the underdeveloped countries to which I have alluded in
earlier chapters, together formed the world political climate
for the Conference, which met in Stockholm. It was prudent
that we felt happy that the Conference could preserve the
momentum in the awakening of interest in the environmental problem, plan for a permanent agency for continuing the work, build a substructure for carrying it out in the
regions and subregions under UN auspices, organize the
gathering and analysis of crucial information and, in addition, outline a few badly needed treaties in regard to intergovernmental cooperation in preventing the pollution of air
and water.

In the case of pollution, however, intergovernmental action will be severely hampered by collision of interests,

particularly those between developed and underdeveloped countries. To take one example, if the former countries are stamping out the use of DDT and other similar harmful agents, they might find it natural to set up trade barriers against imports of food and other commodities containing them.

As long as science and technology have not yet produced effective and equally cheap substitutes for DDT, underdeveloped countries may find that they cannot afford to abstain from using them. Even if that were to become their policy, the developed countries could not, in fact, protect themselves very effectively by trade barriers, as DDT also spreads through air and water. Developed countries could, however, find additional reasons for trade barriers by using them for protectionist purposes or as a pressure on underdeveloped countries.

This is meant only to exemplify, by an abstract example, how interests conflict over the pollution issue. This does not imply that it should not be possible in some cases to find compromise solutions advantageous to all parties.

But none of the broad pollution problems is simple. For reasons already alluded to, pollution does not stand out as a major problem to those who are politically powerful in most underdeveloped countries. They will therefore have to be offered inducements, or be put under pressure, to go along. In regard to the depletion of irreplaceable resources, I must confess that, as long as they are flowing in international trade, I cannot conceive of any possibility even of approaching agreed policies. As I said, in the individual developed countries I cannot foresee any interest in taking action against depletion, even nationally, except in very limited fields, and of course still less in the underdeveloped countries.

And I see no political mechanism through which action could be taken for preserving resources. We do not have a world government, still less a world government having the power to enforce planning on a world scale of the use of resources. What we have are agreed matrices for government cooperation. This would do, perhaps, but only if they were used more effectively for intergovernmental agreements on important issues such as those that concerned the United Nations Conference on the Human Environment.

16. Conclusions

As I come to the end of this chapter, I realize that what I have said adds up to what is usually characterized as a "pessimistic" view. Personally, I am against both "pessimism" and "optimism," which to me only represent differently directed biases. As a scientist, I want simply to be realistic.

Let me add that, though I have had to express rather somber views, this does not lead me to defeatism. A scientist's faith is that realistic research leading to true knowledge is always and everywhere wholesome, while opportunistic illusions are damaging. Without that faith, which is *a priori* to all his exertions and can never itself be proven in that general form, there would be no incentive to labor on.

I have been taking the shorter view of the immediate future. If we are given time, we might be able to change political attitudes among peoples and even political conditions in countries. A realistic analysis should only urge us to strive harder and be prepared for pressing radical reforms.

As regards the environmental problem, it does matter that pending dangers are drawn to the attention of everybody. People are generally not entirely cynical, though they are ignorant, shortsighted, and narrowminded. This implies that they can, to some extent, be brought to act against what they have become accustomed to feel to be in their own short-term interests.

Nationally, this implies being really prepared to accept a "new style of life." We all feel hopeful that the youth now growing up in the developed countries will have other ideals than those now motivating our policies. We also hope that they will have more of a heart for the misery in underdeveloped countries.

Internationally, it means that we could become prepared to permit the intergovernmental organizations within the United Nations system to work more effectively as matrices for government cooperation. This would also require abstention from pressing for short-term and often narrow and even misconceived interests. It is clear that, internationally, this would in the first place again demand greater generosity on the part of people in the developed countries.

From that moral issue we cannot escape. Economics is a moral science, which, in principle, though with faulty logic, was recognized by our predecessors a hundred and two hundred years ago, but is now mostly forgotten.

Chapter 12

GANDHI AS A
RADICAL LIBERAL[1]

1. The Liberal Legacy

MOHANDAS GANDHI's moral personality was a gem, faceted with immense richness. He will appear differently when viewed by different observers, depending upon where they stand and the background against which they perceive him.

The present author was for many years involved in a study of South Asia's and, in particular, India's problems of underdevelopment, development, and planning for development. My value premises in this study were the rationalistic modernization ideals[2] as they had emanated in the early European era of Enlightenment and been preserved and developed in liberal thought everywhere. Together with Jawaharlal Nehru, Gandhi walks through my book as a spiritual leader upholding these ideals in a quite consistent way.

Viewed in this setting, Gandhi stands out as a radical and over-optimistic liberal of the post-Victorian English variety, though molded by the Indian tradition and translating those ideals into folksy language. I realize that this characterization does not exhaust what can be said about Gandhi's world outlooks, but I do believe that it catches a significant and important trait and belongs to a fuller view of the "father of the Indian nation."

2. Civil Disobedience

Gandhi's political tactic of civil disobedience and noncooperation with the colonial power structure was, of course, to him based on a philosophy in line with his moral imperative of nonviolence. His absolutist concept of this imperative was not endorsed by the rationalistic intellectuals in the Congress movement. That is evident from criticisms by Nehru and other contemporaries.

But to them, too, the application of the principle of nonviolence seemed a rational means for a very large and very poor people to use in attaining national independence with a minimum of sacrifice from the British—with their specific ideals and inhibitions. Unlike so many of Gandhi's other political views, it did not even prove over-optimistic.

3. A Radical Leveler

Gandhi spoke up for the "dumb semi-starved millions scattered over the length and the breadth of the land in its 700,000 villages" and he perceived their situation to be the result of systematic "exploitation." He saw clearly what later would become so forgotten in India, as in the whole Western economic literature, viz., that greater equality was not an aim in competition with economic progress but, instead, a necessary condition for it.

Until Gandhi's crusade, social and, in particular, economic equalization had not been discussed much, either in India or anywhere else in South Asia. Gandhi's egalitarianism became one of the links between him and the rationalistic intellectuals of Nehru's type who, unlike Gandhi, were relatively unconcerned with religion. Together they persuaded Congress to accept a radical variant of modern liberal ideology. Confirmed at the Karachi session in 1931,

it demanded that "in order to end the exploitation of the
masses, political freedom must include real economic freedom for the starving millions."

In line with the golden-age myth, which Gandhi no more
than any other Indian leader—not even Nehru—could
entirely forsake, he held that a "purer" and functional caste
system could once upon a time have been a beneficial social
organization. But the present caste system was to him a
horror and had to be suppressed. He also stood for the liberation of women from their shackles. He cried out against
child marriage and the religious and social compulsion hin-
dering remarriage of widows. On all these questions,
Gandhi was the opposite of a traditionalist.

In regard to the distribution of income and wealth,
Gandhi's views were radical. Often he spoke as if he demanded complete economic equality, but his thinking became blurred with his concept of trusteeship: The rich
could keep their wealth if they acted in the interests of the
underprivileged. This notion was a practical compromise,
mainly motivated by his rejection of violence and his realization that the rich would not willingly give up their
possessions (see below, however). It was so flexible that it
could serve as a justification for gross inequality. But
Gandhi also demanded a moral revolution, a change of
heart among the rich. Nehru, who doubted the likelihood
of such a conversion, criticized Gandhi for inconsistency in
regard to economic equalization.

4. Gandhi's Over-optimism

Gandhi remained optimistic on this score and often gave
expression to his conviction of a radical improvement of the
economic conditions of the poor, once India had become
independent. He was equally optimistic about the rapid
disappearance of caste and other social inequalities.

This optimism was founded on two judgments, which can now be seen to have been mistaken, but which were largely shared by Nehru and the rationalistic intellectuals in the Congress movement. One was that the British colonial rule over India had so suppressed the forces for economic progress that once the shackles of imperialism were removed, rapid economic progress would ensue and increase the elbow room for rich and poor. The other judgment concerned the political democracy that would come with independence and its expected revolutionary effects on Indian society.

To Gandhi, a radical change in the social and economic order was, indeed, the meaning and essential purpose of overthrowing foreign rule. Without it, independence and democracy would be an empty achievement. But Gandhi took for granted that once the power was transferred to the masses of the Indian people, these masses would assert themselves and carry out the economic and social revolution.

The rich and mighty would have to give up their privileges and do it willingly and peacefully. In his words: "Economic equality is the master key to nonviolent independence. . . . A nonviolent system of government is clearly an impossibility so long as the wide gulf between the rich and the hungry millions persists. The contrast between the palaces of New Delhi and the miserable hovels of the poor, laboring class cannot last one day in a free India in which the poor will enjoy the same power as the richest in the land. A violent and bloody revolution is a certainty one day unless there is a voluntary abdication of riches, and the power that riches give, and sharing them for the common good."

That independent India should be a democracy based on adult franchise, Gandhi held as above dispute, and so did Congress as a body. The economic and social revolution to him then became simply an inference of the extreme degree of social and economic inequality existing there as a start.

5. Grass-Roots Democracy

Not as a qualification but as an amplification of the democratic principle, Gandhi was adamant in demanding that a maximum of the political power should be dispersed and reserved for local and functional communities, and on this point also he won adherence in the movement he led.

He feared centralization of power, even if founded on a majority vote, and wanted the villagers to be the makers of their own destiny, with only general rules laid down from above. This view had, with Gandhi, a moral basis in his concept of the dignity of individuals and his vision of their having an opportunity to organize their life together in a way that was conducive to peaceful cooperation, progress, and happiness.

Gandhi clearly perceived that development is basically a human problem concerning attitudes and institutions. It must imply that people everywhere begin to act more purposefully to improve their living conditions and then also to change their community in such a way as to make these strivings more possible and effective. The efforts in India to institute "democratic planning" or "decentralization" through various forms of cooperatives and agencies for local self-government have been an outgrowth of this Gandhian ideal that democracy is built "from below."

We can now see that when these policies have not, as yet, been very successful, a main explanation is that the social and economic revolution that Gandhi, like Nehru and the whole radical wing of Congress, so confidently had expected to follow independence and general suffrage, did not materialize. The attempts made to cultivate a grass-roots democracy in the event came to bypass the equality issue and so were emasculated. Effective cooperation assumes greater equality, among many other things. This critique of mine, would, I am sure, have found favor with Gandhi.

6. The Blending with Traditionalism

In practically all fields, Gandhi was thus an enlightened radical liberal. He demanded also a revolutionary change in the direction of education and not simply the sluicing of more children and youths through an unreformed school system inherited from colonial time and serving the interests of the metropolitan power and that Indian upper class which had flourished under its protection. In this, he was in line with the most modern contemporary philosophers of education, particularly prominent in the two countries where thinking in this field was already ahead of the rest of the world, namely, the United States and later the Soviet Union.[3]

He stood, by words and personal example, against that serious obstacle to development which persists in the contempt for manual work. Much of the educational reform he propagated had a major aim of elevating to its proper level the dignity of labor, all labor. He saw clearly its relation to the issue of social and economic equality, and he never tired of stressing this fact.

As Gandhi stood so undeniably on the side of the poor and downtrodden, he dared also to be more outspoken than any other Indian leader after him—with the occasional exception of Nehru—in upbraiding his people for laziness and for not keeping themselves and their surroundings clean.

Blended with all these highly rationalistic opinions of Gandhi, which make him an outspoken radical liberal, he held at the same time more traditionalistic views that, seemingly at least, are contradictory. His hostility to modern industrial technology and to machines and, more generally,

his pro-rural and anti-city bias were sometimes expressed in
terms which are hardly compatible with enlightened liberalism. But the recognition in recent years of the very predomi-
nant importance of agriculture in economic development
and also of the primary necessity to put to work under-
utilized labor resources in the cause of development, has, to
an extent, proved these ideas of his to be less irrational than
they seemed to be at a time when development was narrowly defined as industrialization and when it was believed
that industrialization would rapidly create new employment
that would make possible the "skimming off" of the "labor
surplus" in agriculture.

Even at the culmination of that era—approximately in
the years when the Second Five-Year Plan was being prepared—the planners found it rational to make a compromise with Gandhian ideas, viz., to reserve a large area of
production of consumer goods for traditional labor-intensive
technology.

In regard to central state planning generally, where
Indian policy has seemed to deviate most conspicuously
from Gandhi's teaching, there may now be forewarnings of
an evolution of thinking that comes closer to Gandhi's own.
The plans produced in predominantly financial terms have
turned out to be fictitious and misleading. Consequently,
India is beginning to recognize the necessity of perceiving
development as a process encompassing the entire social
system. This was Gandhi's view, though he never elaborated
it in clear terms. In this view, he was far ahead of the approach to planning that has been applied in India as well as
other underdeveloped countries. It is only in the last few
years that economists more generally have understood the
need for a "unified approach."

To Gandhi, politics should be rooted in morals. In this
respect, he only emphasized truly liberal principles, from
which too many writers, particularly among the economists,
have in the postwar era tried to run away. More question-

able—from a liberal point of view—is Gandhi's insistence on basing morals on religion. But by his religious syncretism, stressing the affinities between all religions, he gave preponderant weight to the "higher" ideals which all religions have in common and which are generally humanitarian and rationalistic, while playing down the importance of rites and taboos which are diversive and arational, if not irrational.

His reverence for sexual abstinence, however, and his consequent hostility to contraception are definitely anti-rationalistic elements in his moral philosophy. If adhered to, they would have become the more blatantly illiberal when the population explosion gathered momentum, but that occurred only after his death. Similarly, his support for cow worship—and sometimes idol worship—stands out as contradictory to his enlightened liberalism.

7. If Gandhi Came Back

Everyone who has studied Gandhi's teaching in depth must have pondered over what his intellectual, moral, and political reactions would be if he returned to his India after more than twenty years of independence. Certainly, he would have to confess to himself that the unbounded optimism that inspired him and his contemporaries in the Congress movement during the struggle for independence had been mistaken.

The social and economic revolution he had looked forward to following independence has been, first, postponed and, later, shelved altogether—except for some continued rhetorical exuberances in public speaking. Instead of the economic equalization he had seen coming, inequality gaps have been widening; the concentration of financial power has increased.

Against the clear condemnation in the Constitution and special legislation, which had been adopted under the in-

fluence of the legacy from Gandhi, caste as a social institution has shown obstinate persistence and may even have
gained in importance in some fields. The rise in the freedom
and status of women which he advocated has, for the most
part, remained a rather empty prescription—except in the
top social strata.

The land and tenancy reforms have been little more than
a sham, and there has been no fundamental reform of education, which still serves to preserve the gulf between those
who work with their hands and those who, having acquired
the badge of education, are not willing to do so. The efforts to
lift up rural life—agricultural extension, credit and other
cooperatives, community development, *panchayat raj*, and
so on—have, contrary to proclaimed objectives, mainly
favored the better-off.

And so the masses of people in the villages, where now,
as in Gandhi's time, more than 80 per cent of the people
live, have mostly remained in relative stagnation. The landless and poorer half of the villagers—Gandhi's dumb semi-
starved millions—may be worse off in some respects than
they were a quarter of a century ago and are certainly not
decidedly better off.

Undoubtedly, the still unhampered population explosion
has contributed in a mighty way to the severity of what,
measured by Gandhi's predictions and honest expectancy,
he would now see as large-scale failures. It is open to speculation whether Gandhi, when facing the population explosion and the cattle explosion, would have modified his
views on contraception and cow slaughter. As rational liberalism was a major element in Gandhi's thinking, this does
not seem entirely excluded. In any case, he would probably
not have laid a main emphasis on these issues, but looked on
them as peripheral to the general failure in the field of
politics.

The development of Indian politics since the attainment
of independence, which he himself barely survived, Gandhi

would in all certainty have censured severely. He would have seen it to be afflicted with a progressively worsening moral illness, spreading out in the entire polity and society like a cancerous growth, to which the increase of corruption and the swelling volume of "black money" bore testimony.

He would have seen another sign of the downward trend of political life in the increasing prevalence of violence— on the one side, riots, usually without a major and rational political purpose, and police brutality on the other. Violence, as is often pointed out, has reached a higher level than it did during the struggle against the British, which Gandhi on the whole succeeded in keeping disciplined— though the British should be given part of the credit for it.

He would probably have judged the ailment of Indian politics as an *ex post* justification of his recommendation, at the time when India set sail as an independent state, that Congress should stay out of politics, not remaining a political party, but becoming a voluntary organization for social improvement. When Nehru and the majority of the Congress leaders chose to act differently, this was motivated by their correct view that a functioning democracy needed political parties and that there was already in existence the Congress with an effective machine which could become a national party. Its domination undoubtedly made possible the first ten years of relatively successful government in the country. But it was also during those ten years that the postponement of the social and economic revolution was becoming accepted, the revolution that would have been necessary if the exalted hopes of Gandhi, Nehru, and many others were to have materialized.

8. What Would He Have Done?

If Gandhi could return to India after almost a quarter of a century, he would thus have to confess that he, together with most leaders of the Congress movement, had been grossly over-optimistic. It is equally certain, however, that he would stick to what were his fundamental valuations, rooted as they were in his moral convictions and in his religion. It is unthinkable that today he would remain silent and idle. He would again take to the roads and village lanes and begin anew his crusade, seeking to change the social and economic conceptions of the articulate upper middle classes of his nation, but at the same time trying to stir up the masses from their torpor. And he would have followers from many diverse backgrounds, now as then kept together as a unified force by his faith, resourcefulness, and humor.

Often, when laboring with India's staggering development problems, I have felt inclined to believe that what that great country needs today, more than foreign aid and day-to-day adjustments of policies to meet the recurring emergencies, is spiritual leaders approaching Gandhi's greatness, his love, and fearlessness. Together with all the patriots who would undoubtedly come to surround such leaders, they might electrify the nation to undertake, late but perhaps not too late, the revolutionary changes in social, economic, and political institutions, attitudes, and practices which are now so desperately needed.

Chapter 13

THE FUTURE OF INDIA[1]

1. A Glorious Epoch in Indian History

DURING THE NINE MONTHS following the turn to terroristic suppression of the people in East Pakistan by the military regime in West Pakistan, three developments in India have deeply impressed thoughtful people all over the world, independent of the policies followed by their various governments, and have earned India respect and, indeed, admiration.

One, India ungrudgingly received the swelling stream of refugees from East Pakistan (eventually numbering almost 10 million), gave them shelter, fed them, and cared for them as well as she could, with little aid from abroad.

Second, India succeeded, on the whole, in preventing conflict between the refugees and her own poor people. In spite of the Hindu-Moslem element of tension, stemming from the communal composition of the refugees and inherent in any confrontation with Pakistan, India succeeded in this crucial period in avoiding much religious rioting in and around the refugee camps and also in India at large.

Third, for nine months India kept away from open warfare against the West Pakistani occupation army in East Pakistan, in spite of the clear and accumulating aggression and brutality against the people there, leading to the many millions of refugees being driven over the frontier. India was vainly pleading, and hoping, that governments abroad —and particularly Pakistan's Western political and military ally, the United States—would exert effective pressure on the rulers in Islamabad to stop the invasion and make a political and military retreat.

That their oppressive policy toward the people of East Pakistan was doomed to complete failure should have been obvious to everybody who knew anything about conditions and developments on the Indian subcontinent. Even without much knowledge, it should have been possible to understand that no government anywhere can rule a people that almost unanimously stands up against it. The policies of the rulers of Pakistan were thus not only cruel and criminal, but stupid and foredoomed to total defeat.

With the continued stream of millions of refugees to India and the absence of any effective pressure from abroad on the Pakistani government to change its suppressive policy in East Pakistan, open warfare was inevitable. The controversy about how it eventually started and with whom is to me rather meaningless. In a sense, the causes were the terrorist actions of the occupation army in East Pakistan month after month and the millions of refugees continually being driven into India.

I could, as a fourth reason for worldwide admiration of India's conduct, point to the well prepared and efficient way her military forces finally brought about the liberation of East Pakistan with a minimum of destruction and sacrifices of lives.

There has been much speculation in the United States and everywhere in the West, that the rise of the East Bengalis against the rulers of West Pakistan was in the narrow nationalistic interests of India. And the inference has been drawn that it must have been instigated by the Indians. As one who has over the years been discussing Indian foreign policy with Indian leaders, I can give personal testimony that what they always feared was an upheaval in East

Pakistan that could upset the balance in the peninsula and even create trouble in India, particularly in West Bengal.

When the uprising finally came, it was not inspired from India but caused by the ill-considered, selfish, and in the end brutal policies of the West Pakistan rulers. There was no prior machination from India. India simply had to react to the conflict when it occurred. And, as I said, she reacted with admirable charity toward the refugees and with reticence, firmness, and, in the end, courage and determination toward the military clique in West Pakistan.

2. India's New Role

I had been asked in spring 1972 to comment upon "India's new role after victory." In answer, I first wanted to state that my sincere hope was, and is, that India's role will unfold itself as a continuation of her old and often declared policy lines from Jawaharlal Nehru and, indeed, Mohandas Gandhi. The glory of India's heritage from the liberation struggle and the first decades of her political independence was her firm adherence to the ideals of the secular state and, in foreign policy, her renunciation of power politics, which is the deeper meaning of Nehru's policy of nonalignment. Both these ideals are certainly well founded upon rational consideration of what is good for India and the world. But with Gandhi and Nehru they had also a deeper moral motivation.

Bangladesh as an independent country is now an accomplished fact. Against the background of what has happened in the past few years, and indeed ever since Partition, there could have been no other outcome. The recognition of Bangladesh by the whole world was bound to come. However, no country is starting out with greater initial political, economic, and administrative difficulties.

India cannot escape playing a prominent role in getting

Bangladesh on its feet. In the Western press there was much speculation that India would now fall for the temptation to power politics. I trusted her leaders when they declared that India had no plans to expand her territory toward Bangladesh and no intention of keeping her army there longer than needed. India will also have to continue to undertake economic sacrifices.

As things developed, I also believed that Western countries could now no longer keep aloof, as they did up till the brief war, but would have to come forward with substantial aid. Even the United States could not do otherwise. The Kissinger-Nixon policy in regard to Pakistan—and India— had met with complete failure. It also had America's intellectual and moral elite against it from the beginning. They were not in power, but could not be silenced. Now the Nixon government will have to radically change its policies toward the countries on the Indian peninsula. And it will have to be an unconditional retreat.

China must feel unhappy for having given her sympathy and support to a reactionary and oppressive dictatorship. This is not in line with China's interest in standing for liberation movements in the underdeveloped world. There is, however, no rational reason for hostility between China and India. China's interest in rebuilding the transit road in the uninhabited northeast corner of Ladakh should certainly not be an important issue. India can now afford to see that it was not without fault that that issue was permitted to result in a war.[2]

What remains of Pakistan—that is, West Pakistan—has to go through a most difficult period of adjustment. Again I would trust India to allow her vastly increased self-confidence to result in magnanimity instead of modeling her actions on old-fashioned power politics. As all Indian leaders have always said, and are saying now, there are no inherent reasons for hostility between India and her neighbor to the west.

In the wake of the war there are difficult problems to settle between India and Pakistan—the prisoners of war, whom India, in her consideration of Bangladesh, has not yet felt she could release, some removals of population groups, etc.—but it should be possible to solve these problems, assuming good will on both sides.

I cannot feel entirely hopeless about the future of the new Pakistan. The country has received a shock, which in this case may have been fortunate for her policies and her future. She has encountered some new problems to tackle but also been relieved of some vexatious old ones, and the net result is not necessarily negative. The army has lost prestige and everybody wants a parliamentary system of government, which Pakistan has never really had. Nobody wants to be ruled any longer by martial law.

President Bhutto comes out as a new man in many ways, and is energetic and bent on internal reforms. He heads a new people's party that shows a relative unity and discipline that no political party has shown earlier in Pakistan's unhappy history. Bhutto and his party are radical in regard to educational reform, land reform and the control over industry. A new generation of economists is available for the Planning Commission, after the American advisers have already earlier been dismissed. They take a pragmatic but at the same time courageous attitude toward the economic problems of the country. I hope and believe that the country can now be kept together in spite of some tendencies toward disintegration. The Kashmir issue has been de-emotionalized. And everybody knows that Bangladesh now is independent.

With all the many interneighborly problems that still remain to be solved, I would thus look upon recent happenings as providing a basis for building up more peaceful relations in all South Asia and with China. And everything I know convinces me that the hopes I have expressed above are shared by India's now responsible political leaders and in the first place by Prime Minister Indira Gandhi. The victory of India in the recent conflict has vastly increased their opportunities for moving in this direction.

3. Rejecting Power Politics

I should not be honest if I did not express a slight anxiety I have, that India might now become tempted to play power politics. As we all know, a certain exalted and self-righteous pomposity in thought and speech is not altogether absent from the attitudes of some Indians in the top strata and, as I pointed out in *Asian Drama,* their behavior has sometimes made India less popular in the neighboring countries.[3]

More specifically, I feel a little disturbed by some Indian writers, who now indulge with obvious pleasure in the thought that India is now a great power in the region, implying that she will have to play out a role in that capacity. Generally, I feel dissatisfied that so relatively many Indian writers accept the type of thinking that has unfortunately, since World War II, become prevalent in the United States, where considerations of power and the balance of power have been substituted for the higher, more specifically the moral, consideration that has guided the social sciences since Enlightenment (Chapter 14, Section 2).

In these Indian writings, demands have often been made that India must now keep up the military might and the heavy defense expenditures which, for good reasons, have been expanding all the time up till the last crisis and the brief war with West Pakistan. It is in line with that type of thinking that proposals have been made that India should become a nuclear power.

Prime Minister Indira Gandhi, however, has consistently argued a contrary thesis: that India does not want to be a dominant power in South Asia and, in particular, does not want to play power politics; that she looks forward to friendship and cooperation even with Pakistan, which has now become so much weaker; and, generally, that after this last war she wants India, which should now feel so much more secure, to use all opportunities to create goodwill, understanding, and collaboration in all matters with the whole region and with China. She is emphatically against outside great powers meddling with the affairs of the countries of the region and trying to use them as pawns in their conflicts. She is well aware, and stresses it, that she is thus following out the ideals of her father, Jawaharlal Nehru, and indeed of Mohandas Gandhi.

As an economist, aware of the great poverty of India as well as that of all the other countries in South Asia, I must express my earnest hope that she will win over a handful of power-hungry intellectuals and politicians, often active in her own Congress Party. She has directed India's planning toward stamping out mass poverty. This is, under any conditions, a most difficult goal to attain. It is altogether incompatible with rising armament expenditures, or even, I am afraid, with retaining them at their present very high level. Nothing would be more sensible than an armaments reduction conference of the countries on the Indian subcontinent. Its success would depend on keeping the superpowers at a distance.

In this direct way, India's craving for development is crucially dependent upon the success of her attempts to inaugurate an era of peace in the region, leading to a mutual reduction in armament expenditures, maximum friendly cooperation among all the countries there, and keeping the intrigues of the outside great powers, in particular the superpowers, from interfering. Even a lower level of foreign aid would not be too high a price to pay for being left alone politically more completely.

The danger in India is understandably seen to come from the United States, particularly if the latter should come to plot with China, at which point even the Soviet Union

would be spurred to defend its interests within the region.
This has been underlined in several of Indira Gandhi's policy
statements.

4. The Need for a Social and Economic Revolution

Having studied the development problems of the region as
an economist, I must stress that India, Pakistan, and
Bangladesh together constitute the greatest conglomeration
of very poor people in the world. India ought certainly to
welcome foreign aid, provided it is given without political
strings. But much more important will be her internal policies. She needs far-reaching radical reforms, and they must
be directed toward creating greater equality.

From my studies of the development problems in underdeveloped countries, I have reached the conclusion that there
is not, as so many of my colleagues have assumed, a conflict
between the goals of economic progress and of social justice. On the contrary, radical egalitarian reforms, well
planned and well coordinated, are a necessary condition for
sustained economic advance and development. (In Chapter
6, Section 2, I give the general reasons for this conclusion.)

In India, as in most other underdeveloped countries, we
face a strange paradox in regard to the quest for greater
equality. On the one hand, policy declarations have continually stressed the need for greater equality and, in particular, for raising the levels of living of the masses. That type
of declaration can also be found in India's Five-Year Plans.
It is known that Jawaharlal Nehru, as the head of the Planning Commission, was the one who, often at the last minute,
insisted upon their insertion, mostly in the introductions.

On the other hand, economic and social inequality is
not only gross and harsh in India, but seems generally to
have been on the increase. Policy measures declared to be

taken in the interests of the poor are mostly not implemented, or they turn out in practice to favor the not-so-
poor. Through studies by Indian economists carried out
over many years, we have been made aware that whatever
development there has been in India has mostly enriched
only the top strata, the urban "middle class" of "educated,"
what in India is called the "rural elite," and, to some extent,
also the relatively few organized workers in large-scale industry and transportation. Swelling masses in the rural and
urban slums have been left in misery.

What India needs is a radical reversal of that trend. She
needs honest and effective reforms. "Cosmetic" treatment
would not be enough.

When the Prime Minister wants India to direct her domestic policies toward the radical goal of exterminating
mass poverty, she is indeed faithfully following out ideals
cherished right from the fight for independence. As I
pointed out in Section 3 of the last chapter, Mohandas
Gandhi was a radical leveler, and he never doubted that
when India had once freed herself from colonial bondage,
and her destiny was being decided by free election of the
people, the result would be a social and economic revolution.

The torch was then taken over by Jawaharlal Nehru, who
never tired of preaching the same gospel. And the whole
articulate class of India has never given up the claim that
India should be a "welfare state," should move toward a
"classless society," a "socialist cooperative commonwealth,"
and establish a "socialist [or socialistic] pattern of society."

It is in line with that great tradition that the Prime Minister is now moving. Her difficulties in reaching further than
her father are immense. They consist in an often inarticulate
but nevertheless forceful resistance, ultimately based not
only on passivity and inertia, but also on the short-sighted
vested interests of those who are not poor. These forces are

well represented in her own Congress Party, and they are particularly strong on the state and municipal levels, where actions have to be taken and implemented.

5. The Reforms

The quest for land and tenancy reform was raised in the period before Independence, already then in the radical terms of "land to the tillers." Throughout the twenty-five years that have since elapsed, that radical expression has continued to be heard.

But the legislation on land and tenancy reform has contained all sorts of loopholes, and it has not been effectively administered and implemented. Not least in this field, India has remained a "soft state." The interests of the landless laborers have been almost totally disregarded.[4]

In Indian agriculture, the yields are very low; the labor force, which is rapidly growing, is tremendously under-utilized; in spite of the fact that over 70 per cent of the labor force has to earn its living in agriculture, the use of the land is extensive and not, as usually assumed, intensive. Too few are working at all, they work for too short hours during the day and too short periods during the year, and they do not work intensively and effectively. That is what in the literature is inadequately called "unemployment" and "underemployment."

Land and tenancy reform must now be taken seriously and rethought. Concrete policies should now be inaugurated to change the "relation between man and land" which give man the opportunities and incentives to work more and to work more effectively, and to invest whatever he can dispose of, in the first place his own labor, to improve the land. And legislation should be clear-cut and it should be honestly implemented.

There are several ways of changing the relations of man

and land for this purpose. Choices have to be made between alternatives that need to be studied and clearly stated. There are in India plenty of reports on this issue, which need only to be reconsidered from the point of view that now, finally, they should result in policies to be effectively carried out. They should establish greater justice, but at the same time result in a substantive and general rise of productivity.

Without an effective land and tenancy reform, the "green revolution" is bound rather to increase inequality in the rural sector (Chapter 5, Section 5). And all other efforts toward rural uplift—community development, cooperatives, and local self-government—will continue to be emasculated and, in particular, be ineffective from the point of view of greater equality.

In regard to education, Nehru's demand was for a total revolution of the educational system as inherited from the colonial era and its adjustment to serve the interests of the metropolitan power and the Indian upper class, including the so-called middle class. But such a revolution is exactly what has not been carried out. The school system has, without much reform, been allowed to expand where the pressure was felt to be strongest, mostly from the upper and middle classes. Adult education has been dealt with in a way one of India's great educational authorities, J. P. Naik, has characterized as "criminally neglectful."

The Education Commission published in 1966 a truly excellent report. It ended the report by stating that "the future of the country depends largely upon what is done about education during the next ten years or so." More than half of that period has now gone by without much action on that front, so crucially important not only for social justice, but for economic progress and development as well.

Another important report, by the Santhanam Committee on Prevention of Corruption, was published in 1964. It stirred up some public discussion for a short time, but few of its policy recommendations have been acted upon. Even although laxity and licentiousness will spread and influence the behavior even of people in the lower strata, they will mainly be exploited for unjust enrichment by persons who have economic, social, and political power. To stamp out corruption is therefore important for attaining greater social justice. At the same time, however, corruption is weakening and distorting all efforts for planning and implementing policies for economic advance and development.

Corruption has, in fact, been permitted to increase. The parallel economy of the "black money" has been swelling. It distorts all planning and at the same time poisons the political life, as the political parties—and not least the Congress Party—and occasionally individual politicians are induced to take a share of the cheap and hidden resources. I consider a determined and unsparing struggle against corruption and all the other sequels of the "soft state" indispensable and vital for securing a happy and secure development in India.

The population explosion tends by itself to increase inequality, particularly in agriculture, at the same time that it impedes development. The arrested development, particularly as experienced by the masses of people, in turn implies an impediment to population policy. When India, in spite of long and energetic efforts, has met great difficulties in attempting to spread birth control among the masses, this is in my opinion due mainly to the fact that for such a policy to be more successful in changing motivations necessitates that these masses experience a dynamic society where their living conditions and economic opportunities improve substantially and can be expected to continue to improve. All the reforms I am discussing here must be looked upon as a package in the sense that they need each other in order to be successful.

I shall not enlarge upon this abstract exemplification of reforms in the interests of both social justice and economic progress. These interests are not, as some biased economists have believed, incompatible, but complimentary and, indeed, mutually supporting.

Some, but by no means all, of these and other reforms in the interest of equality entail fiscal expenditures. Even when they do to some extent, I believe that, if well planned and coordinated, they belong to the most profitable investments the country can make. But the period of gestation may be a fairly long one. This is the reason they raise the demand for a certain restraint upon consumption in the upper strata.

It is a fact that from an egalitarian point of view India's industrial development has been directed too much at providing consumption goods for these strata. This becomes an almost automatic effect of scarcity of foreign exchange that has brought the government to restrict importation of less necessary goods. The production in India of such goods thus often gets sky-high protection (Chapter 5, Section 11). To break this tendency would require stern and effective handling of the investment and production controls, guided by firm planning. To combat mass poverty without redirecting consumption, and production of what directly and indirectly serves consumption, is impossible.

This direction of production also reflects the increasingly unequal incomes for different strata. The distribution of the tax burden—which is heavily regressive because of forced saving due to inflation and the preponderance of indirect taxation—must be reformed. And it is not enough, or not even productive, to raise the taxation rates for rich people, as long as tax assessment and tax collecting is so utterly ineffective. And again we are back to the need to overcome corruption and the softness of the administration.

In this way all reforms are interconnected. To liquidate mass poverty and at the same time to spur economic development is a herculean task. But a really vigorous effort must be undertaken if India is to have a good future.

6. No Dearth of Intellectual Capacity

After her inspired and successful leadership in the conflict with the military junta that had ruled Pakistan, and by her party's overwhelming victory in the more recent elections, Prime Minister Indira Gandhi has emerged as a more powerful political leader than ever her father was or, during the liberation fight, even Mohandas Gandhi. She has demonstrated an ability to overcome those who stand against her, and to get things done according to her aims. That her aims are in the direction of radical reforms, I have no doubts at all.

The spiritual consolidation and the enhanced self-confidence of the Indian people should now be on her side when trying to carry out radical reforms that her father could only preach in general terms. Nevertheless, she has great difficulties ahead, as I have already pointed out. She will need all her strength to win out in the struggle for reform against much passivity, and, indeed, strong resistance, not least within her own political party. As desperately serious as is India's situation, Indira Gandhi stands now as her country's great chance, perhaps its last, to enter an era of rapid and sustained development, while retaining parliamentary democracy.

The fact that in India there is no dearth of intellectual capacity of the highest order should also inspire hope. All the arguments for the radical reforms that I have found wanting have been authoritatively stated and developed by supremely competent persons in leading positions in their fields. And India's excellent publicists have used the freedom of the press to bluntly expose dishonesty and ineffectiveness in policies and politics. It is only the legislation and the implementation of the laws that have largely been permitted to be insufficient and sloppy.

The dream of one scientist who is also a devoted friend

of India is that the multitude in that country of highly competent intellectuals and professionals—among whom I also reckon many of India's industrial leaders—who see the truth, will firmly grasp the new opportunities, courageously bury petty and short-term private interests, and join together in a national movement for justice and growth. It is that type of huge and devoted brain trust that the Prime Minister needs to push India to give reality to the ideals of Mohandas Gandhi and Jawaharlal Nehru. It would not be a break with inherited ideals, but a determination to see them materialize in practical action.

7. *"Revolution from Above"*

Such a "revolution from above" has sometimes, but very seldom, taken place in the world and been successfully carried to an end. In order to succeed, it has in any case to become supported by sufficient "pressure from below."

The fight for liberation had precisely this character of being led by an elite, but sustained by their stirring up support from large masses in the nation. It was then made possible by the historical accident of Mohandas Gandhi. Also the issue, political independence, was simple to grasp, even for the masses. The adversary, the metropolitan power Britain, was more easily visible. And Britain was in two minds from the beginning and was ultimately not prepared to fight the rebellion with all the might it could have mobilized.

To fight poverty and inequality can never in the same simple way command the support of the whole nation. Those who have to climb down from privileges and open up monopolies—including officials and elected representatives on the local, state, and national levels—will not easily be moved to line up for the radical reforms implied. This holds true even though, as I believe, rational consideration of long-term interests, including interests in national advancement and political stability, should easily balance individual sacrifices.

Many who are not really at the top of present-day Indian society but are themselves rather poor (most of the so-called rural elite of petty landowners, merchants, moneylenders, and local officials) are undoubtedly more reactionary than people in the top urban strata.

Added to this, both the goal and the means for radical reform are vastly more complicated and difficult to grasp than merely driving away a tiny group of foreigners as in the liberation struggle. Every single one of these reforms has to be presented and discussed in rather technical terms. This gives much greater opportunities to resist what is actually being considered and launched.

The poor, on their side, are downtrodden, hungry, ill-housed, and disfavored in regard to education, health, and everything else. And to them it must be even more difficult to see and feel their rational interest in specific reform proposals. The masses are not rational on questions greater than their daily worries. Unfortunately, it is a fact that the masses are normally passive to the point of submission. Many may even consider their lowly status in society to be ordained by God, or the gods, and by their karma.

This last point is apt to stress the crucial importance of education in the national reform program. Indeed, were it possible to educate a sizable portion of the masses to see their own true interests and to organize with a view to asserting them, nothing could resist a reform movement in India, particularly as the upper strata are not of one mind, having themselves been the harbingers of the modernization ideals from the Western democracies and the Soviet Union, among which the equality doctrine has a prominent place.

Strategically, the educational reform is therefore of crucial importance. It should lay stress on primary education, literacy, and the building and spreading of new rational

attitudes. The training of teachers must be radically improved, and their social and economic standards raised.
The secondary or tertiary schools, where teachers themselves become trained and educated, should be the "power
plants" that generate moral and intellectual energy among
their students to prepare the people for the "social and cultural revolution" the Education Commission pleaded for
as needed for the "social and economic revolution" they
saw as the goal.

Unfortunately, even if such a radical reform of education
were courageously speeded up, it would take a whole generation before it could bear fruit. The educational influence
to be expected of the people's participation in local, state,
and national elections is undoubtedly real, but it is also a
rather long-term development. The need for the beginning
of radical reforms is, however, immediate. If educational
reform is delayed, India's situation might deteriorate di-
sastrously—there the Education Commission was right.

For this reason, adult education becomes tremendously
important for building the basis for the economic and social
revolution needed to save India. Adult education should be
closely related to, and be an extension of, the activity in
the schools. In the villages, where practically all are func-
tionally illiterate, it should be questioned whether the
pattern as inherited from the colonial era, with schools for
children and perhaps now some classes also for adults, is
really the appropriate one. Perhaps whole families or, indeed, whole villages should be taught together. This suggestion would have had Mohandas Gandhi's sympathy, and
he sometimes hinted in that direction.

In the effort to educate the whole people, the universities
and the students should become actively engaged. This
would also end their isolation from the nation and
give them a new purpose in life. The early vision of Jawaharlal Nehru that the millions of "educated unemployed"
(in reality they are simply miseducated) should be per-

suaded to go out into the villages to teach the people to
read and write and reckon, instead of living purposeless
lives in the cities and swelling by their pressure the lower
echelons of useless persons employed in administration.

Educating the nation in this broad way would itself
amount to a people's movement being directed toward
radical reforms. But without determined and courageous,
charismatic leadership, the task of a "revolution from
above" sustained by "pressure from below" is a hopeless
undertaking. It must be attempted, however, as the alternatives would be disastrous.[5]

8. The Alternatives

The first alternative is to proceed as India has been doing
since Independence. The rudder can certainly be moved
even more to the Left, as Prime Minister Indira Gandhi
already has managed to do. But those in power, at all levels
right down to the villages, are well trained in emasculating
reforms and even turning some of them into means of increasing inequality. Corruption and collusion are only
two of such means. As the reforms are framed in legislation,
the laws and regulations themselves often imply the invita-
tion to such a perversion.

India has become the one country in the world that has
succeeded in marrying excellent declarations for greater
equality agreed upon by almost everybody, including, since
the fight for independence, the clamor for a "social and
economic revolution," with policies that in practice have
not prevented ever greater inequality. The mental state of
most intellectually alert persons in India contains serious
signs of schizophrenia, with which they apparently manage
to live happily and undisturbed.

An alternative to a serious beginning of radical reforms

in India is undoubtedly that the alert groups in the nation accept with considerable satisfaction Indira Gandhi's general proposals for equality and a planning directed toward an extermination of mass poverty, but, at the same time, see to it that nothing of great importance happens to the structure of the society in which they are privileged. This is what I meant by my warning against "cosmetic" reforms.

Under the pressure of the rapid increase in the labor force, which will, whatever happens, continue till the turn of the century and beyond, the under-utilization of that labor force will tend to rise, resulting in a continuous increase of the miserably poor in the rural and urban slums— unless large-scale rationally planned and vigorously implemented radical reforms are really carried out.

Whether such a development, in turn, will result in an uprising of the poor masses, which stands as the second alternative, is uncertain. There are indications that poverty by itself breeds intensified passivity. In any case, when riots occur, they tend to be inflamed by ethnic and communal fanaticism and/or the drive to steal from each other. As noted in Chapter 6, Section 3, they are then not only useless but inimical to a rational, organized movement to press for equality and progress.

But, of course, there can be efforts from above the masses of poor to organize a revolt of those masses or strategic segments of them. The several Communist parties in India have not shown much ability to act in this capacity. Generally, the educated youth can become radical but—contrary to what happened long before the October Revolution in Russia—they shun the idea of going out to the people in the villages. The best choice for Indian Communism would in all likelihood be to act as a driving force helping to push radical reforms through Parliament. And even in that capacity it has not been working very effectively.

Even if this were to change, a Communist revolt would

be suppressed. A more authoritarian regime is, in fact, more
likely in India than a Communist takeover, though it would
hardly happen except if a Communist takeover were a serious
prospect, which it is not today.

We should remind ourselves that in the only two very
large countries where the Communists have come to power
and functioned as a state building force, Russia and China,
it was not an instantaneous affair, but prepared for decades
—prolonged in Russia by the NEP period until the first
Five-Year Plan, and in China by everything that happened
before and after the Long March. The revolt generated in
the course of long and devastating wars, where military intervention from abroad—in China, by Japan and by the United
States' active support of the Kuomintang, which from an
initially revolutionary liberation movement had developed
into a thoroughly corrupt, feudal dictatorship—forcefully
contributed to national consolidation along a radical line.
That Communism would have won in the absence of these
extraordinary circumstances, which are not present in India,
is not likely.

And India is in such a desperate situation that she cannot
afford a period of breakup, with all its serious effects on the
economy, while waiting for an orderly Communist regime
to become effective. This is a reason why, if the prospect
of a Communist revolt became real, practically the whole
class of intellectually alert people would line up behind a
more authoritarian regime. But, as I said, a Communist
takeover is not a very serious possibility.

9. Conclusions

This is all in the nature of speculation, though founded on
evidence for which I cannot find room in this brief chapter.
Its simple meaning is that political revolution in India is
not a real alternative to evolution by radical reforms in-

troduced from above but supported by pressure from below, instigated by education of the masses. The more actual
alternative to an effective radical reform policy is to allow
mass poverty to remain and even to encompass an ever
larger part of the nation.

Chapter 14

TOWARD A
BETTER AMERICA[1]

Implied in the title is a sense of dissatisfaction with things as they are in present-day America, both in regard to internal conditions and policies and in regard to the role played by the United States in world affairs. In both respects, I share this critical view. Implied also, however, is the conviction that policies can be altered and that America would then be a better America. I share this conviction also.

1. A Personal Declaration

I feel a need first to insert a few personal remarks in order to "define the situation" of my addressing American youths on the state of their country—to use the terminology of W. I. Thomas, the grand old man of American sociology in his time, who in my own youth honored me by his friendship. The accidents of my life and work have led me to a deep identification with the inherited ideals and aspirations of the American nation—what I once called the "American Creed."

Even though, ever since the American Revolution two hundred years ago, these ideals and aspirations have been highlighted in the United States more expressly than anywhere else and, indeed, laid down as the law of the land, they are our common legacy from the era of Enlightenment: justice, liberty, and equality of opportunity. By accidents of environment and inclination, I had myself in my early youth drunk deeply of the political optimism of Enlightenment. How the Enlightenment philosophy came to acquire its particular position in the new nation's conscience, I have sketched in the first chapter of my book, written thirty years ago, *An American Dilemma: A Problem of Modern Democracy:* "American Ideals and the American Conscience."

Having become so involved in the problems of this country, and so identified with its moral commitment, has implied that, perhaps more than any other citizen of a foreign country in this generation, I have felt it natural to express freely my views on American issues, without any restraints due to my not being an American. And my right to do so has, in the United States, been generally accepted—probably to the great astonishment of all those abroad, who are less familiar with one of the finest traditions of this country: the openness for criticism by a foreigner when he speaks in line with the moral legacy I hinted at.

For more than two decades, and on some issues concerning internal conditions and policies for three decades, my views of the United States have been severely critical. Even those who were inclined broadly to share my views have said that in my writings I tended to be ahead of my time. But this is exactly why I have always felt myself, and do today, to be speaking to, and for, the openminded among America's youth.

At this particular juncture, the generation preparing to take over the responsibility for this country certainly needs to be ahead of its time. If the nation is not to go downhill into reaction and disaster, the many serious mistakes in policies, committed by the older generation, must not be perpetuated. A new and better America will require the

determined will to make fundamental changes in policies
now being pursued. This is how I feel when, as now, I am
speaking to a youthful audience.

2. After World War II

I must first touch upon United States foreign policy. As I
shall hint at later, it has of late also gravely distorted its
policies at home.

At the end of World War II, the United States reached
a high point in its international position. It had earned the
gratitude of the world by going into the war and decisively
contributing to the defeat of the fascist powers.

Unlike all the other countries in the Great Alliance, it had
not seen destruction at home. In fact, the war had accomplished what the New Deal never succeeded in doing,
namely, overcoming the Great Depression of the Thirties,
with the result that the United States emerged after the
war richer than ever before.

The United States felt itself—and was for a time—overwhelmingly powerful. The dangerous concept then took
hold over the nation that the world had now entered the
"American century," when United States policies would be
the determining influence for world development. Everything would then depend on how these policies were
shaped.

I know enough about the American people to be able to
testify that the main motivation for the financial aid given
the West European nations under the Marshall Plan—much
more unselfish than any aid later bestowed upon underdeveloped countries—was a positive one of genuine compassion and solidarity with these nations who had suffered
so severely in the war, and from where so many in the
American nation traced their ancestry.

But already before the Marshall program was launched,

the cold war had begun. It developed by what I call circular causation with cumulative effects, whereby in both blocs those who goaded its intensification could always count on a hostile move from the other side, which had to be met by a counter move.

In America, this soon reflected itself in a veritable nightmare of an imagined Communist world conspiracy against the United States and the entire "free world." Anti-Communism had already been used as a complementary motivation for Marshall aid, which at that time I saw as a dangerous and ill-boding portent.

At home, during the shameful McCarthy era, the completely frantic idea that the few Communists in this great and powerful country could overthrow constitutional government by violent means became for a time almost a national ideology. It affected the intellectual life of nearly the entire nation and also left its mark on scientific literature and on teaching at all levels. At the same time and to an even greater extent, it was a popular belief among the masses.

Under the influence of the cold war and this ominous change in the political climate, military considerations began to overwhelm all thinking about international issues. In the political sciences and even in economics, where traditionally the humanism that was a legacy from the Enlightenment era had set the tone, strange models of power and power balances began to invade and sometimes to dominate the field of study. The writings too often testified to the fact that the students felt themselves called upon to stand, not simply for truth-seeking, but for the national cause, understood in the crude way that had become established in the sickness of extreme nationalism.

3. The Emerging Foreign Policies

"Containment of Communism" increasingly became the
supreme motivation of United States foreign policy. As I
mentioned in Chapter 9, Section 2, it pressed upon the
unwilling West European countries and the entire non-
Communist world the so-called strategic embargo, which
in reality was a wholesale trade discrimination against the
European Communist countries and later China. Working
as an independent economist but carrying the responsibility
of being Executive Secretary of the United Nations Economic Commission for Europe (ECE), I foresaw from the
beginning that this economic warfare was doomed to failure, even in the short run, besides being damaging to world
interests.[2]

The United States armament expenditures were rising,
occasionally coming to claim more than half of the federal
budget; military bases were set up all over the world, en-
circling the Communist countries; political and military
alliances with all sorts of governments were part of this
encirclement policy.

In the underdeveloped world, support was given to
crudely fascist regimes, creating an image of the United
States as standing for suppression and reaction on a global
scale. In the end, this caused liberal congressmen to react
in disgust against the foreign aid program which had been
so grossly distorted.

Most of the anti-Communist alliances, particularly in the
underdeveloped regions, are now becoming inactive. Even
the authoritarian regimes that the United States has been
pampering often find them uncomfortable. Behind this development of their sympathies was also dissatisfaction with
the often highhanded manner of the United States government in dealing with its allies. It continually talked of

"bilateral aid," "cooperation," and "partnership" but too often insisted on having it all its own way.

And so the United States government was more and more often forced to go it alone. For its forcible interventions in several Latin American countries, it could not even reckon on wholehearted and common support in the region itself, while the rest of the world stood aloof and censorious.

For its escalating war in Vietnam—enlarged under the Kissinger-Nixon regime to involve the whole of Indochina and Thailand—it could rely only on active support from some of the totally dependent satellite governments in the region, and for this it had to pay heavily in cash. Most unfortunately, Australia and New Zealand were also persuaded to send troops. Now that the conservative governments in these two countries have been brought down, this is the end of their allegiance to American policy in Southeast Asia.

Otherwise, none of the governments of the United States' allies in Europe or in Latin America and Asia—besides the governments mentioned—would dare to send a squadron to help the United States in Vietnam. The only effect of the United States pressure upon the governments of these countries was a relative suppression of their peoples' protests against its warfare in Vietnam. In spite of this inhibition, however, popular protest has everywhere been mounting for many years.

Facing defeat in Indochina and increasing resistance in Latin America and, at the same time, having both its capability and, still more, its motives and, of course, its methods of warfare, severely censured throughout the world, the United States several years ago became more morally and politically isolated than most Americans were prepared to realize.

4. Hubris

What caused this stupendous failure of the United States'
foreign policy was its government's insolent claim, by virtue
of its might, to a right to police the world on its own terms,
using totally inconsiderate means of warfare, and while so
doing, to be immune from generally recognized moral
injunctions. This was what the Greeks called *hubris*, and
they held that when it was not stopped it always led to
self-destruction.

During World War II, I wrote *An American Dilemma*, a
book devoted to America's internal problems of justice,
liberty, and equality. I was led to consider in the last chapter of that book the role in the world that I foresaw for the
United States, when it became "America's turn in the end-
less sequence of main actors on the world stage." I wrote
then, and I want to repeat it:

> America has now joined the world and is tremendously
> dependent upon the support and good will of other coun-
> tries. Its rise to leadership brings this to a climax. None
> is watched so suspiciously as the one who is rising.

I criticized the idea that I found common in America
even then, namely, that financial and military power could
be a substitute for the moral power of having earned the
good will of decent people throughout the world. Without
followers, the leader is no longer a leader, but only an
isolated aberrant. And if he is strong, like America, he becomes a dangerous aberrant, dangerous for himself and the
world.

This is unfortunately how America has been increasingly
looked upon abroad. The excellent American journalists
posted abroad have not been very effective in informing
the public about how enlightened public opinion in all
countries now views the United States. In the political

climate and under the influence of militarist thinking in terms of power and power balancing to which I referred, they and the publishers of newspapers and journals and the managers of radio and television stations are exercising self-censorship, of which I could give many examples. Even those of them who share my critical views apparently feel that Americans are tired of hearing about how people abroad view their country.

Government officials and businessmen abroad often have reasons of their own not to be too explicit on this point. It is mainly their inhibited opinions that, in the present political climate in the United States, have been recorded. But in all Western countries, and also to a varying extent in other countries, the views of informed citizens at large are, in the longer run, decisive.

As I sit writing these lines on Christmas Eve 1972, I am listening to radio reports about the renewed terror bombing, resumed a week ago and carried on more recklessly than ever before, of the residential quarters of Hanoi and other densely inhabited parts of North Vietnam—killing and wounding thousands of innocent men, women, and children, destroying homes, churches, pagodas, schools, hospitals, foreign embassies, and, incidentally, also touching one camp where shot-down American pilots are kept. The big hospital maintained by Swedish charity has been hit by bombs dropped in five consecutive attacks, killing some fifty doctors, nurses, and patients. As Sweden has an embassy in Hanoi, I can get authoritative and fairly complete information about these outrageous war crimes, with which the Nixon government has been celebrating the feast of the messenger to humanity of peace.

This has finally shocked the world to full indignation. In the churches, prayers are being offered for the victims of these terror actions—and, in the Christian tradition, also for the so severely misled American people and their rulers.

Not only the Pope, but governments all around the world,

denounce the United States' stepped-up aggression in Vietnam. The Swedish Prime Minister talks of the evil of collective torture and says that the memories connected with the names Guernica, Oradour, Babi Yar, Katyn, Lidice, Sharpeville, and Treblinka now have an added name: Hanoi at Christmas 1972. Similar condemnations are coming from the other Scandinavian countries—already in October the Danish Prime Minister had opened the third session in Copenhagen of the International Commission of Enquiry into United States War Crimes in Indochina—as well as from Belgium, Holland, Italy, India, Canada, and many other countries. The language used is no longer diplomatically muffled. Even business people are now uneasily silent, if not actually joining the protesters.

Even if Britain's Conservative government, following a pattern established by the previous Labor government, is silent, as are of course the governments of Turkey, Greece, Spain, and other countries under dependent fascist rule, this does not give a true representation of how their peoples feel.

For ordinary people around the world, the heartfelt disgust for Nixon extends to those who are his tools or instigators and, indeed, to the American nation, which did not prevent his election to four more years as the President of the United States.

The world fully understood the desire on the part of the United States to get back the American prisoners of war, but not its demonstrated lack of concern for the many more Vietnamese in the prisons of the Saigon government and for the misery of all the refugees. When occasionally American war criminals have been brought before court, we have also witnessed grave falterings of the judicial process, directed toward protecting them from justice. To the world the "gooks" are human beings like all of us and also like the Americans.

This is also a question of generation. My generation,

which felt sincere admiration, appreciation, and gratitude
to the United States for what it did to win the war, and
afterwards to aid the economic reconstruction of Western
Europe, is passing. We are succeeded by a new generation,
which has no memories of the war years and the years
immediately following the war, when America was great
in its devotion to high ideals.

When I travel over the world, talk to people, and read the
press and literature from many countries, I find to my deep
dismay an ever wider spread of hate-America feelings. It
is a mistake to believe that this is simply the result of
Communist propaganda. I cannot, of course, harbor such
feelings—no more than can American liberals who share
my views and my anxieties. But I have to recognize them as
facts. They continuously decrease the real power of the
United States in world affairs.

When Mohandas Gandhi taught that we should hate the
crime and not the criminal, he expressed a humanitarian
and rational moral principle that now is gradually winning
observance in the laws of the most advanced welfare states.
The world today is so filled with hatred that most certainly
we must try to follow this noble moral injunction. But it
becomes difficult, particularly for the youth in the world, as
long as the guilty continue on their criminal course and stay
in power.

5. The Legacy of the Vietnam War

I am convinced that the Vietnam war, and the way it is
brought to an end, will stand out as of crucial significance
in the history of the world and, in particular, of the United
States. In this volume I shall not recapitulate much of what
I have written on this issue over the years. In addition to
sections in *Asian Drama*,[3] they consist of papers I have
written and statements I have made as Chairman of the

Swedish Vietnam Committee, encompassing the overwhelmingly great majority of almost all alert citizens in Sweden, heard through their organizations, and also as Chairman of the International Commission of Enquiry into the United States War Crimes in Indochina—responsibilities I have for reasons of conscience felt I should not decline, even though they took me away from my ordinary work.

Instead, I reproduce what two highly competent and morally responsible Americans have succinctly expressed in a recent issue of *Foreign Affairs*.[4]

The first quotation is from an article, "After the Cold War," written by the former diplomatist turned scholar, George F. Kennan, who, as is well known, carried responsibility for the early formulation of the containment policy of the United States:

> As for Vietnam, the less said at this point, the better. In this, the most disastrous of all America's undertakings over the whole 200 years of its history, the United States has not only contrived to do a great deal that is unconstructive in the immediate past but has precluded itself from doing much that is constructive for some time into the future. The only graceful and halfway posture it can adopt will be one of total withdrawal, followed by silence and detachment, leaving initiatives to others.

In the same issue Hamilton Fish Armstrong, the editor of this authoritative periodical for many years, celebrated his leaving that responsibility by writing an article called "Isolated America":

> The war in Vietnam has been the longest and in some respects the most calamitous war in our history. It has rent the American people apart, spiritually and politically. It is a war which has not been and could not be won, a war which was pushed from small beginnings to an appalling multitude of horrors, many of which we have become conscious of only by degrees. The methods we have used

in fighting the war have scandalized and disgusted public opinion in almost all foreign countries.

Not since we withdrew into comfortable isolation in 1920 has the prestige of the United States stood so low.

. . . The risk today is not that the American people may become isolationist; the reality is that the United States is being isolated. . . . Not, in the experience of the present writer, since the Harding era when we denied our enlightened self-interest and retreated from responsibility in our foreign relationships, while confessing to scandal and tawdry commercialism at home, has the world had such a poor opinion of us.

. . . It is now one of the two superpowers, unassailable in nuclear strength. Nevertheless its political power is less than its material power, and its prestige is tarnished.

The end of our long-time friendship with India came about as a by-product of our efforts to please the People's Republic of China by averting our faces while the army of China's protégé, Pakistan, bloodily repressed a revolt in the eastern half of the country.

Our isolation from other peoples is the reverse of fifty years ago; today we are the object, not the subject. . . . recovery can come only slowly as a result of a multitude of actions that could give our country a sense of direction again.

The task is, in fact, to prepare a radically changed posture in American foreign and military policy that would give the United States back its honor and gradually decrease its moral and political isolation in the world. That is primarily the task of American youth. However much it can mean that ardent reformers among the middle-aged and aging stand up and protest, such a very fundamental change must be firmly anchored in the new generation that is gradually stepping into power and responsibility.

The change will not be without its price. With my views about what America has been, is, and should aspire to be, it is not enough for the United States to get out of Indochina, however important and urgent this is, on the grounds that the war cannot be won—implying also that it was a mistake from the beginning to get into it. A majority of Americans arrived at this conclusion several years ago. But more than that, the largest possible number of Americans must also go through an intellectual and moral catharsis and recognize that the war has been immoral, illegal, cruel, even hideously criminal in the eyes of international law. Otherwise, the United States will not regain the confidence and trust of good people everywhere in the world.

More important, more primary, is that the American nation needs to go through such a catharsis in order to be at peace with itself. Living on and just forgetting the Vietnam war and the crimes committed against the Vietnamese people and humanity is not possible, unless the nation accepts a serious break in its history and flagrantly give up its most cherished ideas and aspirations. As Norman Thomas said in his last message to American youth: "You should not burn the flag of the country you love. You should wash it."

The present policy does not satisfy even the primary request to honestly recognize total failure and end the military involvement. To have an "honorable end" of a thoroughly dishonorable war, implying continued backing of an American puppet government in Saigon, now even in the last hours being armed to the teeth by the United States, is not acceptable.

The Nixon government's attempts to begin restoring more normal relations with China can be welcomed, but only as a confession of a wrong policy pursued for more than twenty years. The nation should not be permitted to indulge in complete forgetfulness of how the United States government, under the pressure of McCarthy and the China lobby, was responsible for the break with China in 1950, accompanied by total discrimination against China in trade and all other matters. This policy, or some adaptation of it, was also pressed upon other countries. Meanwhile the world was flooded by a willful campaign aimed at depicting China as a slave society. Experts in the State Department who knew better were dismissed; more discerning professors at the universities had to crouch down or remain silent.

China was kept out of the United Nations by the United States, often using arm-twisting of other, more or less dependent governments. This, and the fact that President Nixon was himself one of the most reckless instigators of this policy, cannot, and should not, be forgotten. The happy laughter that greeted the United Nations Assembly's restoration of China's membership angered Nixon and some others in the United States, but it was a testimony that it was not forgotten.

Generally speaking, a nation facing world opinion is not permitted, any more than an individual in court, to forget the acts and events leading up to the present moment. I am not speaking merely as a moralist but as a realist. New and changed policies are not firmly founded, if the facts of the earlier policies are not recognized and remembered. Germany, Italy, and Japan were brought to face their recent history and did go through their catharsis. The United States will not escape having to do the same.

6. Foreign Aid

It took a considerable time before the need for financial aid to the underdeveloped countries was recognized in the United States and other developed countries. The generosity of Americans that had marked Marshall aid to West European nations had by then largely evaporated.

Increasingly less and less of the aid was given as straight grants, and the aid was increasingly tied to American exports. As I have shown in another book, published a few years ago, and referred to above in Chapter 6, Section 13, the figures for aid were grossly juggled in an opportunistic manner. Much less than half, and probably not even a third, of what is recorded as aid in American and OECD statistics can honestly be counted as genuine aid.

This development reflected the intensification of the cold war. To the American electorate, aid was presented as being "in the best interests of the United States," and stress was laid on the political, military, and strategic interests of having allies in the cold war. This meant that aid was directed mainly to thoroughly reactionary regimes that could usually be counted on to be most firmly anti-Communist.

The American people do not believe in that motivation for aid. The political and military failures in Southeast Asia and Latin America, which received most of the aid, have contributed to the growing unpopularity of foreign aid in the United States. The whole program of aid to underdeveloped countries was brought near collapse in the autumn of 1971. The aid is bound to be scaled down in the years to come, at the same time as the need for aid is becoming ever more palpable.

Again, this is a policy that must be radically changed. Speaking as an economist who has studied this problem, my conviction is that the only motivation that can appeal to ordinary people is compassion and solidarity with people living in great misery. Americans are basically not less charitable than other people, but, as I can testify, ordinarily just the opposite.

7. Pending World Dangers

Even aside from the stupendous fact of Vietnam, the whole world and every individual country on "this spaceship earth" is in a most perilous situation, facing dangers greater than at any earlier period in mankind's history.

To the new and largely unprecedented dangers belong the rapidly proceeding poisoning of the environment in which we are living. Of this we have all been made aware. To avert disaster, large-scale and radical policy measures are called for. As pollution does not stop at boundaries, these new policies require not only national policies, but also courageous international cooperation (Chapter 11).

The same is true of the threatening depletion of the world's natural resources. A sinister aspect of this problem stems from the fact that the minority of mankind in the United States and other highly developed countries consumes such an inordinate part of the total resources. This makes sustained development of underdeveloped countries very questionable, if we in the developed countries are not prepared to shift and scale down our consumption and production. Again there is a need for international cooperation, if disaster is to be prevented.

The spread of the use of dangerous drugs is a third such new danger rising on our horizon. It is foreseeable that the progress of chemical and pharmaceutical research will make available ever more tempting but damaging drugs and make it possible to produce them not only in factories or laboratories, but in kitchens. In general, we know that very much more effective international cooperation is needed in order to make our national policy measures productive of results.

Then we have the stupendous dangers, of which we all have been aware for a longer time, of the armaments race. Not being able to go into that problem in this book, I only want to say that intergovernmental negotiations have as yet produced agreements of only the "cosmetic" type and have had no real effectiveness in stopping the armaments race between the two superpowers, nor put a reliable check on the proliferation of countries having atomic weapons. Technical developments will soon make atomic weapons cheap and available to any country. And fears have been recently expressed that, in time, guerrillas will be able to have them.

The superpowers have not been willing even to outlaw chemical weapons by giving new force to the Geneva protocol (which the United States almost alone has declined to ratify). On this question, the malignant practices followed by the United States government in the Vietnam war have created inhibitions.

Since I am addressing an American audience, I must express my opinion that the United States government has short-sightedly allowed pressure groups, pursuing vested interests and appealing to nationalist sentiments, to prevent it from doing its utmost to seek international agreements in this field. For documentation, I can here refer to the voluminous publications of the Stockholm International Peace Research Institute (SIPRI).

In my lifetime, the world has drifted into two world wars, planned by no one. We might now be on the uncharted course toward a third and more final world war, in which, incidentally, the United States will not, as in the earlier ones, escape destruction and the slaughter of its own civilians.

8. At Home

Meanwhile, America is facing huge unsolved problems at home. Let me touch upon only one of them, the poverty problem.

The "unconditional war on poverty," planned by President Kennedy and after his death proclaimed by President Johnson, was from the beginning underdimensioned in view of the magnitude of the problem, spurious, badly planned, and not well administered. But we could have hoped that it was a beginning, from which something bigger and more effective could have emerged. But under the moral, psychological, and financial pressures from the escalating and in the end totally unsuccessful Vietnam war, the steam went out of the anti-poverty program in the middle Sixties. There were also additional reasons for this development, which I will have to leave uncommented in this brief chapter.

The living conditions for the desperately poor in the rural and urban slums—of whom only a third at most are Negroes—are for the time being nowhere substantially improving. In some respects and in some localities they are even deteriorating still further.

There is an urgent need for rationally coordinated reforms in many fields, including the almost complete rebuilding of the cities and the provision there of parks and open spaces, the break-up of residential segregation, and a radical change in transportation policies.

The metropolitan areas must be redistricted for administrative and fiscal purposes. The typical pattern at present is to divide the center of the city, inhabited mostly by poor people, from the suburbs, where the more well-to-do live. Even after the creation of more functional, and usually bigger, administrative units, their systems of taxation, like those of the states, must be reformed to permit larger taxation intakes. And even after such administrative and fiscal reforms, the federal government must undertake much larger financial contributions.

When broadening the fiscal basis for policy in this way, minimum standards of schooling and all community services must be made more uniform, and the standards enforced.

Most important is the curative remolding of the human beings inside the slums, and the integration of slum dwellers as productive and self-confident citizens into modern industrial society. Raising the levels of schooling can only be part of the large-scale rehabilitation of those who have inherited poverty and all the debilities that, as both causes and effects, are related to poverty.

The costs of these radical reforms are in the order of trillions of dollars. And the healing process will take at least a generation, even if begun with courage and determination and pursued persistently. The estimates now and then publicized, that the problem of poverty and its effects on human beings can swiftly be solved by some $10 or $20 billion a year, are ridiculously inexpert.

I feel sure that the expenditure for extinguishing poverty in America will in the long run prove to be a remunerative investment. But, for a long time, it will require sacrifices by the majority of Americans who are well off, and also the abstention from expensive conspicuous public consumption, such as moon flights and too heavy military expenditures.

There are many vested interests working to prohibit the needed reforms. As I see it, they are not rooted in the "free-enterprise capitalist system" but in the selfishness of broad strata of the American people and their distorted feelings of priorities, which are reflected in the decisions of Congress.

Nevertheless, I cannot be pessimistic about America. It is not a tenable position for the United States to be that country among the rich countries that has the most and the worst slums, the highest rate of unemployed and unemployables, and the least developed health services, and that is the most niggardly toward its old people and its poor children who are so many, as well as being the country that leads the whole Western world in violence, crime, and corruption in high places.

9. Reflections in the Field of Foreign Relations

The present situation of the United States stands out as ironically tragic, when we remember how the founders of the republic viewed the opportunities of the independent nation they established through the Revolution. In their view, its influence abroad was to be exerted not by might and domination but by demonstrating to the world how a people that had thrown off the shackles of tyranny and inequity could, through its free institutions, provide happiness for all its citizens.

With this aspiration, the United States became the first modern democracy. And until recent decades its statesmen and thinkers repeated through the generations their adherence to the faith that it was the United States' chosen destiny to set a shining example to the whole world of what a free nation could aspire to. The reality became very different.

A particularly disturbing fact is that the common knowledge abroad of the serious defects of United States internal conditions and policies becomes increasingly related to the drift of its foreign policies. This is a new feature in the world's feelings toward the United States.

For two decades after finishing my book about the Negro problem, I could to my satisfaction bear witness how the shortcomings in this field were viewed everywhere with a sort of friendly understanding. The world saw that the country was up against serious difficulties, but appreciated that there were forces in America trying to overcome them. As late as during the Little Rock episode, when I happened to be traveling widely in South Asia and Europe, I found that this was then the common view.

This has now radically changed. I believe part of the explanation is again the Vietnam war. An association is made in the minds of people between the United States government's cruel behavior toward innocent, and very poor, colored people in Vietnam, on the one hand, and, on the other hand, the plight of the Negroes in America. The race riots have added fuel to the fire, and this has again fed the hate-America campaign.

Particularly during the period of the Nixon government, which has so obviously not done its best to back the civil

liberties movement and generally to improve conditions for
Negroes, this campaign has gathered momentum. Again, it
is not simply Communist-inspired. Even in the liberal and
conservative press in practically all countries where there is
some freedom of the press a highly critical view is now
taken of the development of race relations in the United
States, often amounting to siding with the few among the
Negroes that have preached violent uprising.

This is all part of a world development of great importance, and the American people should be made aware of
it. The United States' military policy abroad and its internal
conditions are now increasingly combined to give a picture
of the evil of the government and of the nation that backs it.
This makes me, an old friend of America who cannot be a
defeatist, sad and anxious. To answer the world with anger
is not a rational reaction, however.

10. The Delusion of Richness

All Americans, whether they are conservatively inclined or
liberals—yes, even the radicals—have a false view of their
country as immensely rich, richer than all other countries.
This view is founded on flimsy GNP figures, as I pointed
out in Chapter 10, Section 6.

More realistic calculations should take into account how
much of the United States' GNP consists of payments for
the public and private, direct and indirect costs of the rural
and urban slums, and generally for incomes that represent
costs and losses in a less well organized society. Subtracted
from GNP should also be the expenditures serving no productive purposes, such as the moon flights, for a time the
development of supersonic planes—the overflight of which
the Swedes will forbid, as they have forbidden professional
boxing—and, of course, the excessive expenditures for wars

and preparations for war that are a consequence of the
United States' misled foreign policy.

Even more important is the fact that American affluence
is heavily mortgaged. America carries a tremendous burden
of debt to its poor people. That this debt be paid is the wish
not only of the do-gooders. Not paying it implies grave risks
for the social order and for democratic government as we
have known it.

The common idea of the immense richness of America
has the serious implication that it is apparently not assumed
that very much shall be done to begin to pay this debt to
the poor, while continuing large-scale conspicuous consumption of the types exemplified.

11. Warning Against Defeatism

I have been painting with a wide brush, but I believe I have
been telling what is essentially the somber truth.

It is an understatement, bordering on the blatantly ridic-
ulous, to say that the situation in the United States and in
the world, which youth is inheriting from its elders and that
it will have to master, is one of mounting difficulties and
grave pending dangers. When now, at the end of this brief
chapter, I venture to give my advice on how young Americans should react, I speak with humility, but also with
great seriousness.

First, I would warn against defeatism. I cannot be pessimistic about America. I have never been one of those
people who now and then over the decades, as I can well
remember, have said that "it can happen here," not even
during the time when McCarthyism was laying itself as a
dampening pressure over the nation's life.

I speak to youth, and I must insist that it is your country.
You will soon have the land, the buildings, and all the rest,

including the Congress and the Constitution. You will
gradually inherit all the power to do with the country what
you please. You have the responsibility for what the future
will be. History is not a predetermined fate. The future will
be as you will make it.

It is not a revolution America needs, least of all a violent
revolution, but large-scale, indeed radical, reforms. They
should be rationally conceived and should with utmost care
preserve and protect the methods for peaceful change that
in the Western world we have gradually developed over
centuries of democratic growth.

One of the dangerous effects of a *laissez-faire* policy,
which permits problems to remain unsolved and to become
intensified, is that groups of people and sometimes whole
nations come to lose their confidence in peaceful change
through democratic and nonviolent means and so become
desperate and apt to resort to force. It implies a disbelief in
the power of thoughts and words, which the student least
of all should share. Such a distrust is what I call defeatism.

The Bible warns against trying to drive out the Devil by
Beelzebub. It also warns that he who lives by the sword
shall perish by the sword. Riots lead to repression, violence
to counter-violence. If there is anarchy, and if it is allowed
to spread and grow, at the end there is nothing left but the
police state.

12. Conclusions

In its foreign relations the United States must feel the responsibility of being one of the super-states, but at the same
time realize its dependence on the rest of the world. It cannot afford moral and political isolation.

The leadership the world now needs from the United
States must spring from clear thoughts, rational analysis,
and devotion to peaceful living and to development. It

should be possible to move more courageously toward putting a stop to the armaments race and toward giving the poor colored nations of the world trade outlets and substantial financial aid, directed toward social as well as economic advance and not only toward strengthening the reactionary oligarchies.

In the United States itself this would assume public education and not only the half-truths and often blunt lies of official propaganda, and also a resistance to nationalistic pressure groups at home and vested interests. The universities should have an important role in calling forth the much needed intellectual and moral catharsis even in this field of international relations as in the national one of consolidating the American people.

It is on America's youth that we must pin our hopes. America and the world are not in a healthy state. It is your duty, individually and collectively, to strive *against* further deterioration and *for* initiating reforms, which, as I said, must be courageous and far-reaching in all fields, but should be founded upon rational analysis. And you can take your stand on those ideals of justice, liberty, equality, and brotherhood, to which, in the beginning of this chapter, I referred as your spiritual legacy of ideals and aspirations.

These ideals need to be purified and fortified. In particular, general community interests must be stressed, as against the anarchistic tendency to rugged individualism, which in America is such an unfortunate heritage from frontier society.

Liberty should thus not imply the freedom for every crank and criminal to buy and possess a murderous weapon. America is paying a heavy price in asocial violence for its eccentric liberty doctrine in this respect.

Nor should liberty be allowed to mean that a majority of the people is left free to become ever more affluent, while a minority, and a large minority, is pressed down into an alienated underclass. Collusion between people to exclude

certain ethnic or religious groups from living in their neigh-
borhood, working in their profession or trade, sending children to their schools, or from eating in their restaurants and
buying in their shops, is not a legitimate exercise of liberty
but an insolent infringement on other people's rights to
liberty.

There must be equality of opportunity in the pursuit of
happiness, or else this nation will disintegrate into factions
among which there is no national solidarity. Minimum standards in health and educational facilities and more generally in living levels and in employment opportunities must
be established, enforced, and paid for. In these respects,
the United States is still a comparatively backward country.
And this is the main reason for the lack of true liberty for
all in America.

Again, in the international arena, the United States
should not interpret its national liberty as the right to do
what it pleases as a simple exertion of its might. Attempts
to follow that ill-considered line—as in Vietnam—lead to
gross policy failures and are now threatening to leave the
United States isolated in an indifferent and gradually ever
more hostile world.

And the United States must end motivating what it is
prepared to do for aiding the poor countries by trying to
convince itself that it is being done for a national political
purpose—"in the best interests of the United States," or
even "for the security of the United States." That type of
motivation for foreign aid is neither effective in calling forth
a national sacrifice at home or in other rich countries, nor
is it soliciting good will in the poor countries.

The international leadership needed from the United
States must be in the form of vigorous attempts to strengthen
international compassion and solidarity, necessary to build
up intergovernmental cooperation within the United Nations for disarmament, global peace-keeping, and joint

responsibility for the development and welfare of the poor countries.

Of such true internationalism we have, in the last two decades, heard too little. National selfishness is as dangerous for building up a peaceful, progressive international community as rugged individualism is for consolidating the nation state at home.

I have a strong belief that the United States' national and international problems can be solved by pressing on for an ever more faithful realization of our inherited ideals of justice, liberty, equality, and brotherhood. And our hope must be that the coming generation will, more devotedly and effectively than their elders, see the light and do their moral duty.

13. I Believe in America

Let me at the end render my reasons, why I am not a defeatist, why I do not despair about America. Among the nations I have come to know, none is more prepared and accustomed to revise and change its views and policies. Americans are in that sense more dynamic than any other nation. Anybody that thinks back on American history can illustrate this thesis by numerous examples.

For my part, I see this distinctive character of American thinking and acting as part of its puritan legacy. That legacy has certainly not always been productive of wholesome effects. Much of the naïve self-righteousness that many Americans, to the world's annoyance, are apt to demonstrate is similar to the frame of mind of the people sitting on the benches in the temple feeling superior to the sinners outside who have not received the grace of redemption. And much excitement about sex in America has very apparently the character of puritan backlash.

But another puritan trait is that the American nation more than any other can have conversions, indeed radical conversions, and then change course. McCarthyism had a sudden end because the American people finally turned against it. Responsible for this development were the few of the nation's spiritual and political leaders who dared to stand up against the powerful demagogue.

The self-examination that the American nation now urgently needs to undertake will soon, I hope, acquire momentum and strength and have a similar result in changed opinions, though it will have to go deeper and extend over a wider field.

In the Preface to *An American Dilemma,* a book in which I was compelled by my professional standards to "record nearly everything which [thirty years ago was] bad and wrong in America," I saw clearly the importance of conversion in that country's development: "the role of ideals in the social dynamics of America."

And I must confess that "after having become an expert on American imperfections," I had "come to love and admire America next to my own country." In spite of the cruel disappointments accounted for in this chapter, I persevere in these sentiments, trusting that America's youth will try anew to give more reality to what has often been referred to as the "American Dream," which was never ruthless and selfish exertion of power but a striving toward greater human perfection in the nation and the world.

GUNNAR MYRDAL'S
AN AMERICAN DILEMMA—
HAS IT BEEN RESOLVED?[1]

THE TOPIC of this article was assigned me by an American magazine in which it was published. I agreed to write it because, even though it had to be very brief, it gave me the opportunity to correct at least a few lingering misunderstandings about my old book.

But first, it is, of course, an absurd idea that an issue like that of the Negro problem in America, rooted in centuries of a tragic and often even hideous history and still injecting its peculiar effects into all social, economic, and political relations in the country, could be "resolved" like a mathematical problem or an engineering project. Even after another thirty years we shall still live with it, though it will have altered. I do hope that the changes will proceed more rapidly than in the last five to eight years, and that they will go more consistently in the direction of an ever better fulfillment of American ideals and aspirations. But this will depend upon what policies the American people will come to follow, individually and collectively.

1. The Fad of Futuristic Research

I must confess that I feel a little embarrassed when I am praised for having predicted so long ago what was going to happen in the field of race relations. Such predictions cannot be made. As I stated in 1942, when I ended my work on the book: "History is not the result of predetermined fate. Nothing is irredeemable until it is past. The outcome will depend upon decisions and actions yet to be taken."

As a scientist, I am critical of the present fad of futuristic research. Much of it is pretentious nonsense. And I often feel ashamed of what some, even in my profession, present as prognostications, equipped with figures and diagrams.

In any case, *An American Dilemma* was not in that sense futuristic. It was an analysis of facts and the causal relationship between facts as they stood at that time, that is, at the end of the Thirties and the beginning of the Forties. For this analysis data had also to be brought in on the development up till that time. On this basis, ongoing trends of change in various respects could be ascertained.

The study accounted for the reasons why some of these trends could be expected to carry on for decades. This applied, for instance, to the increase in the Negro labor force and also the migration from southern agriculture to cities, particularly in the North and West. These forecasts could be based on demographic data up till the time of finishing the study and on an analysis of the ongoing changes in the agriculture of the southern region. But for most of the observed trends of change no such long-term predictions could be made.

It is perhaps human and understandable that I get even more irritated when, instead of being praised for unbelievable prevision, I am criticized for not having foreseen all that has since then happened. Some years ago, a professor from California wrote a long article in the *New York Times Maga-*

zine on "Where Myrdal Went Wrong." He is a historian, I am told, and should have some insight into the complex and capricious way his nation's destiny is linked from year to year. What sort of philosophy on his own work does a historian, or any social scientist for that matter, have when he apparently assumes it would have been possible to foresee what would happen during three decades to come? And with what care does he read a book he criticizes?

As I mentioned, it was possible to foresee the continued large-scale Negro migration to the northern and western cities, as to the southern ones. But how could anyone in 1942 foresee that America would permit the stupendous and still continuing deterioration and ghettoization of its cities? And that this would happen in a country where, at the time, the science and art of city and regional planning were already so advanced?

2. The Reception of the Study

The book was, in its time, favorably received, even in the South. The reviewing there was handled by the southern liberals, who traditionally enjoyed high status and dominated the region intellectually. Reactionaries of Senator Eastland's type do not read books, particularly not heavy ones like mine. They awakened only after the Supreme Court's decision on the school segregation issue, as the Court had quoted me in support of their conclusion that "separate cannot be equal." This critique spread to articles in the newspapers and some journals, as, for instance, the *Saturday Evening Post,* and had echo in speeches in Congress and Congress Committees. I and my collaborators in the study, among them Ralph Bunche—and incidentally also my wife, Alva Myrdal, by the application of what was then called "guilt by association" (she and I were at that time senior UN officials)—were gratuitously accused of being Com-

munists, which in the years of lingering McCarthyism was
still in the United States a commonly used device to get at
what the reactionaries considered as dangerous liberal
thought. It was, of course, beneath me ever to respond to
this type of argumentation, even though it slipped into
documents of the United States Congress.

But I made an interesting observation, which tends to
show that the leading reactionaries, who were writing and
speaking accusingly, had not even then studied the book,
but were relying on some underlings to provide the text.
There was a queer textual conformity in the formulation of
the accusations made in such diverse fora. The same few
quotations were used everywhere, and invariably they were
misquotations, usually by taking out only a part of a sen-
tence or a part of an argument. They thus succeeded, for
instance, in proving to their own satisfaction that I was an
enemy of the American Constitution!

In all America there were at the time of the publication
of the study only two groups who were hostile: Communists
and fellow travelers, who had every reason to be in opposition, as I pointed to a way of ameliorating the situation
without revolution; and Catholics, who became upset by
the position I took in regard to birth control. (When, later,
McCarthyism broke out, and the liberals so often wavered,
more often, incidentally, than conservatives of the old type
like Senator Taft and many not particularly liberal university professors, I could in my conversations with my anxious
liberal friends jokingly congratulate myself for having what
they did not have: several Communist books and articles
and, indeed, a solemn Communist Party decision, condemn-
ing me and my book.)

But my question is: Why, in spite of this fairly general ap-
proval, did the book not spur greater scientific exertions to
investigate further the problems of race relations in America? That it should do this was certainly my intention. As I
stated in the Preface, I did not look upon my book as

"final," which in the scholarly world is never the case with any single contribution anyhow.

The fact is, however, that from about the time of its appearance there set in a decisive decline of the interest in the scientific study of race relations in America on the part of foundations as well as the academic community, lasting until after the Negro rebellion more than ten years later. I recall from one of the early years of the Sixties that during a visit by me to the United States a conference was called in New York of professors in the disciplines concerned and responsible foundation officials. There was unanimity in regretting that even up till that time the study of the Negro problem had been downgraded and, in fact, discouraged. This both reflected and contributed to the great complacency of the American public that marked that interregnum, and it certainly had its influence on the way the Negro problem was handled. I did not foresee this development and I dare say neither did any of my colleagues at that time.

A third example of a development that came to deeply influence policies in the field of race relations, particularly in the last decade, and which was unforeseen and, indeed, unforeseeable in 1942, was the course of United States foreign and military policy. As is accounted for in other publications of mine,[2] I belonged to the very few who did not expect that friendly and close cooperation with the Soviet Union would continue after the war, which at the time of the finishing of my study was commonly assumed in the Western countries and particularly in the United States. But I did not, and could not, foresee the steadily intensifying cold war over a long period of time.

And how could anyone foresee McCarthy and Dulles and the evolution of American foreign policy that in the end led to the escalating Vietnam war that has expanded to war in all Indochina and in Thailand? That the moral, psychological, and financial effects of that unfortunate and unforeseeable development were greatly responsible when the air went out of the "unconditional war on poverty" is evident.

Victims of this were, among others, the Negro poor, who might account for up to one third of all the desperately poor in America. For the same reasons, the entire civil rights movement drifted into a backwater.

3. I Did Foresee the Negro Rebellion

At the end of the Thirties, the status of the Negroes in America had remained fairly stagnant for more than six decades, that is, since the national compromise in the 1870s when, after Reconstruction, they were delivered back to the embittered southern whites with no means of defense. Following an all too common predilection among social scientists to extrapolate from past experiences without observing incipient signs of change, the prevailing views of race relations in America among my fellow students at that time were static and fatalistic. In this particular field of social study, Sumner's old dictum that "stateways cannot change folkways" remained the basic preconception.

From my analysis of the forces operating in the American national community, I drew the conclusion that this long era of nearly complete stagnation was coming to an end. I even asserted that "not since Reconstruction had there been more reason to anticipate fundamental changes in American race relations, changes that will involve a development toward American ideals."

On this point I proved to be right. In hindsight, it is now apparent that, at about the time I was writing my book, there were forebodings of a dramatic break, speeding the development of the Negro status upward in almost all respects. This trend has continued, and it even accelerated up till at least toward the middle of the Sixties, but has thereafter taken a more uncertain and disparate course. For a brief account of what this new development actually implied in various fields, I can now refer to the Twentieth Anniversary Edition of the book (1962), to which one of my two principal assistants, the late Professor Arnold Rose, contributed a postscript on what had actually happened in the intervening twenty years.

There have been friendly persons who have seen my book as a main cause of this break. This should be heavily discounted—though the book may have had some importance by affording rational reasons for a development that went forward more under the influence of the substantial causes I had pointed to. It should be added that even if there has been in most respects a very considerable change upward of the conditions under which Negroes in America are living, they are in general still cruelly inferior to those of the whites.

Likewise, I did foresee the Negro rebellion. "America can never more regard its Negroes as a patient, submissive minority," I wrote. I was perhaps slightly jumping the gun. It would take a decade before the organized Negro protest became an important national concern. The causes for this movement, as I accounted for them at that time, were broadly the incipient changes toward improvement of Negro status. They are summarized in the last chapter of the book.

On the basis of my analysis, I even foresaw that the Negro rebellion would have its start in the South. I certainly recognized the crucial importance in Negro life in that region, where the great majority of Negroes still then lived, of the church as the one and only form of social organization where Negroes in all strata were joined. I saw the church as rather passive, however, and did not foresee the active role it would come to play in the Negro rebellion.

This characterization was, I believe, correct at that time.

What I did not, and could not, foresee was the arrival on the scene of dynamic church leaders—in the first place, Martin Luther King, Jr., who almost transformed the Negro church into an effective fighting organization with considerable discipline, a program, and a tactic.

4. Value Premises Do Not Mean Optimism

Even my social science colleagues have often not understood the research technique I have argued, and myself tried to use, of working with explicit value premises, tested for relevance, significance, logical consistency, and feasibility. This technique is used to serve three purposes. It helps to purge as far as possible a scientific investigation of distorting, usually incognizant, biases. It determines in a rational manner the statement of problems, the approach, and even the definition of main concepts. It moreover lays a tenable logical basis for reaching rational practical and policy conclusions.

When I found the ideals I called the "American Creed"— justice, liberty, and equality—to be the relevant and significant value premises for my study, this did not mean an undue optimistic and idealistic bias for which some of my colleagues, not only those of a "Marxist" inclination, have occasionally upbraided me. Value premises represent nothing more than the viewpoint necessary to have a view. They determine the questions for which answers are requested. They do not close the researcher's eyes to any relevant facts, least of all discouraging facts. They do not by themselves imply "optimism."

The Negro problem, like all other political problems, is fundamentally a moral issue, and this is brought forward by not escaping the duty to state value premises for research. The problem comes to stand out as a "dilemma." This is realism, not idealism. Those of my colleagues who believe that they are particularly "hard-boiled," because they overlook the fact that human beings are struggling for their consciences, are simply unrealistic.

It is also realistic to become aware of the fact that ideals, like the American Creed, are not without importance in social causation. Human behavior is never determined by simple and solid "attitudes," but is always in the nature of compromises. And behind these compromises are also the general and "higher" valuations, together with the specific opportunistic prejudices and interests on a "lower" level.

When, in the first and successful phase of the Negro revolt, Congress accepted civil rights legislation, more radical than anybody a few years earlier would have believed possible to have passed, the congressmen did not act out of selfish interests (in this case, fear). The explanation is that America had been challenged by the Negro rebellion in terms of its official and living ideals.

And America simply cannot even now, without a serious break with all its inherited aspirations, take over South African *apartheid* ideology and so legislate the segregation which is creeping upon it as a factual development. Ideals, when they are rooted in institutions like the Constitution, and have a place also in people's hearts, are real forces, though not the only ones, sometimes not even the most powerful ones. That is the dilemma, which is not a capricious invention of mine, but a description of the real situation.

5. The Negro Rebellion Conveyed to the North

While for the South I had foreseen the rising Negro protest and, following it, increased tension between whites and Negroes, for the North I had expected a more quiet development. I even foresaw a decrease in the social and economic discrimination against Negroes, that even there was in operation, in spite of their having enjoyed for generations, and in some places always, the vote and the formal civil rights Negroes in the South had to fight for.

My conclusions were, as always, founded upon study of the then visible trends of change. And from a short-term point of view the conclusions were correct. There were a number of forces which at that time moved the social system, particularly in the North, in a direction favorable to the Negroes' aspirations for greater equality.

World War II, into which the United States was becoming drawn, was a war for democracy. In fighting that war, it had to stand before the whole world as defending racial tolerance and racial equality against the Nazis. The fact that the Japanese in their propaganda utilized anti-white feelings in Asia made it even more important to stress the racial equality doctrine. For good reasons whites in the North at that time found it easier to do this wholeheartedly.

Moreover, the war accomplished what the New Deal had failed to accomplish, namely to create a brisk demand for labor, all labor. During the Great Depression, the Negro immigrants from the South had been given doles but not much employment. Now they and also the newcomers became employed. In a full employment economy, white workers had less reason to keep Negroes out of employment and out of the unions.

The war years and perhaps a few years afterwards will probably stand out as the last time up till now when the American economy reached down to provide employment rather freely for all workers, even for Negro workers. Not only the high levels of unemployment becoming customary in the postwar era, but also the effect of another development came then to work to the disadvantage of Negro labor. Rising levels of capital intensity in industry, automation, and general rationalization tended to decrease the demand for much of the type of labor many Negroes could offer.

I have in another publication shown how these new trends and also the spread in majority America of a better education tend to create an "underclass" of labor who are not "in demand" in modern society.[3] Negroes coming from the rural South or growing up in the miserable environmental conditions of the city slums tend to belong to that class, together with many other poverty-stricken groups in the United States. It took a long time before American economists became moved to recognize what in the United States is sometimes called "structural unemployment" in the slums.

Even the industries began to move out of the cities. This whole development was pushed by the unforeseen and unforeseeable reluctance to find effective means to stop the deterioration of the growing slums, to which I have already referred.

When the Negro protest reached the North, where now more than half of the Negroes live, it changed character. It had not the clear targets it had had in the South: to get the vote and break down Jim Crow. It had to fight a whole diffuse social system, grimly disfavoring Negroes.

That system is not "capitalism," as so many of the young leaders of the Negro rebellion and even many radical whites have come to believe. Money does not smell. In my contacts with businessmen in many fields—bankers, insurance people, industrialists, and directors of department stores—I have been told time and time again that they have nothing against employing Negroes, and I believe they are telling the truth. What holds them back are the considerations they have to take about the attitudes of customers and co-workers.

I certainly have my criticisms to direct against the "capitalist system," in particularly against the form it has taken in the United States. But the responsibility for the exclusion of Negroes from work, or certain types of work, does not belong to that system, any more than does the responsibility for the trade discrimination against underdeveloped countries (Chapter 6, Section 12).

The system the Negro rebellion is up against is a "societal" system. The driving forces are attitudes of white people, mostly themselves far from rich, many even as poor as the poor among Negroes. Those attitudes cause them to commit millions of individual acts of discrimination and segregation. They are often not conscious of what they are all doing and still less aware of the consequence for the Negroes. At the same time, these forces emasculate and make legislation against these acts more or less ineffective.

But I am now far away from the things I could study intensively thirty years ago. In particular, magnitudes have changed to an extent implying qualitative alterations in the problems.

6. A System Analysis

Let me finally point to a few general traits of my old study that I believe still stand as correct even in the vastly changed situation today. It was focused not on the Negro people in the United States, as much of the literature at that time was and still is, but on what is commonly referred to as "race relations." In their basic traits, Negroes are inherently not different from other people. Nor, incidentally, are white Americans. But these two groups live, and have always lived, in singular human relation to each other, and this has left its stamp on Negroes as well as whites.

In the American community of thirty years ago, Negroes made up less than 10 per cent of the population, and they disposed of very much less than 10 per cent of everything that gives social, economic, and political power. In both these respects, the movement upward since that time has been slight, though definitely more important in the latter respect. The Negro problem was then, and remains today, mainly a white man's problem. The whites continually live in moral confusion. They proclaim ideals that are bluntly disobeyed in their daily life. This is the dilemma.

In the course of my study it also soon dawned upon me that the Negro problem does not exist as a separate issue, that can be set apart in a scientific study. It is, indeed, one integral part, or a special aspect, of the whole complex of problems in the national community. I found myself writing a book on the American civilization in its entirety, with the stress on conditions in life and work of America's most disadvantaged population group.

This is not least important in the policy issues. It is not possible to rationally plan education for only the Negroes. What is needed is to raise standards for all the children of the poor. Likewise, for technical reasons, improvement of Negro housing can rationally be planned only as part of a general housing policy. The same is true of improvement of all other conditions of life. To be successful in stamping out discrimination against Negroes in the labor market, the condition is a fuller employment economy.

The theoretical method I used in the study of the Negro problem in America was to see the conditions under which the Negro people lived as a part of the entire social system of the country. This system can accidentally be in equilibrium, but normally it should move in one direction or the other, and then the system itself should often turn around its axis.[4]

Between all the conditions in that system there are causal links, most often but not always of the type that a change of one condition tends to move other conditions in the same direction and further changes of the same type in the whole system. I call this circular causation with cumulative effects.

The application of this approach has important consequences even for what would be rational policy. For maximal effect, the efforts should not be directed upon chang-

ing only one condition. Every one-factor strategy—for
instance, claiming the supremacy of the economic factor—is
seen to be erroneous. On the other hand, the effect of
coordinated policies can promise to be much larger than
the sums of the efforts applied.

I accounted for how this general model—which I then
later used in all my other works in different fields—had
been inspired by Wicksell's theory of the cumulative
process of inflation and deflation, which I touched upon in
Chapters 1 and 2.

7. In Perspective

I am now surprised that this old book, which is continually printed without a word, or even the pagination, being changed, is still sold in thousands of copies every year.
I see here a recognition of the fact that, with all the
changes, many general inferences are still valid, and a recognition also that there are advantages of seeing present problems in their historical perspective.

This book has so far been my one and only contribution
to the scholarly study of the problem. Since then I have
worked in other fields, though I have tried to keep informed
about what has been happening in this problem area by
way of a general reading of American newspapers, period-
icals, books, and special research monographs.

And I have now decided to go back to the problem and
write a new book: *An American Dilemma Revisited: The
Racial Crisis in the United States in Perspective.* Many
friends among both academics and persons engaged in
the Negro problem from the practical and policy angle have
generously aided me by sending me additions to my swelling
files of material and by giving me advice.

This new book will not have the comprehensive character of my old book, but be directed upon practical problems

of policy. It is to me a very serious task, and it will probably take me years of preparation. I take the opportunity of mentioning it here, as my remarks in this chapter might induce some more Americans to come to my assistance.

Chapter 16

A BRIEF NOTE ON
MARX AND "MARXISM"[1]

1. A "Bourgeois Economist"?

I HAVE NOTED in introductions to books of mine translated into Russian and published in the Soviet Union, and also in reviews in scientific journals of these and other publications of mine, that my Soviet colleagues have quite generally chosen to classify me as a "bourgeois economist." The implication of this is a criticism of biases on my part of a systematic character.

This criticism stands out as a general characterization of my works, even though Soviet economists have found valuable observations and analyses in what I have produced. When I have been praised for such contributions, their appreciation has often been qualified by the assertion that I "could not avoid" seeing or understanding that things were more or less as they themselves perceived them, sometimes as a result of what I had found. This wording implies that I am nevertheless generally biased, while they themselves, as "Marxists," are purely scientific and unbiased.

Having come to consider myself as something of an authority on the problem of biases in economics, these reactions on the part of my Soviet colleagues have naturally aroused my curiosity. And I shall now permit myself a few critical comments on the topic of Marx and "Marxism."

2. *"Marxism" Not a Technical Term*

I need, by way of background, to explain why I have not found it possible to use "Marxism" as a *terminus technicus,* but have systematically put the word within quotation marks. It is commonly used to characterize more than one approach or theory. And in almost all uses, its meaning is left indistinct.

(1) One clear meaning of "Marxism" would, of course, be Marx's own conception of reality. If this were the only meaning attached to the word, I would be prepared to delete the quotation marks.

Marx's ideas are in some respects difficult to construe, and to an extent they also changed during his working life, which is natural and normal. But "Marxism" in the sense of what Marx wrote can, in principle, be clarified by analytical study. In contemporary writings, this import is seldom or never given to "Marxism," except by some serious students specializing in Marx's writings (see under (5) below).

(2) As I have often pointed out, Western economists have frequently adopted Marx's theories without accounting for their origin or even being aware of it (in this book, touched upon in Chapter 5, Sections 6, 8, and 11, and Chapter 9, Section 4). As this has been done unwittingly and mostly without much exact knowledge of Marx's writings—some authors even explain themselves as "anti-Marxists" in the very context of their plagiarizing him[2]—the theories of this type usually have not been so refined and qualified as Marx understood them. They are often even left merely as implicit assumptions, without having been thought through. When revealed by immanent criticism, they therefore often show up as vulgarizations of Marx. For the same reason, they are ordinarily not recognized as "Marxism" by uncritical readers of their publications.

To trace this "hidden Marxism" and bring this doctrinal

heritage out into the open would be good topics for several doctorate theses.

(3) Perhaps the majority of writers expounding so-called leftist views in the West characterize themselves as "Marxists." When their views in regard to their relation to Marx are so clear that they deserve comment, this relation is seldom correct and consistent (see under Section 3 below).

(4) Particularly in the United States, the term "Marxism" is carelessly used by "non-Marxist" writers as a loose and very inclusive term to characterize all sorts of leftist writings, not least in the underdeveloped countries, usually without attempting to clarify the implied relation to Marx's writings. Much literature on "Marxism" in South Asia is, for instance, of this nature. The concept "Marxism" in this usage is, of course, exceedingly unclear.

(5) On a higher level are the serious studies devoted to Marx's own writings. Some of their authors, but not all, characterize themselves as "Marxists." They then declare their adherence to some specific approach or theory of Marx, which they consider still valid. Again, were they the only contemporary "Marxists," I would be prepared to delete the quotation marks.

(6) Finally, we have the doctrines and theories expounded by writers in the Communist countries and by writers in other countries who follow the party line of the rulers in the former countries. There are occasionally disputes among these writers on minor issues and also a development in time.

Following the political split in the recent decade between the Soviet Union and China, there is, however, a widening gap between what is understood to be the correct "Marxism" or "Marxism-Leninism" in these two countries and in other countries whose governments are politically allied to one or the other of these two very large Communist countries.

Following more specifically the doctrinal development

within the Soviet Union and its closely allied countries
—and reflected also among writers in other countries
who feel affiliated—we can note that all these authors
emphatically announce their works as purely "Marxian."
Actually, however, there "Marxism" is in many respects further removed from Marx's own thinking than even the
thoughts of the "hidden Marxists" in the West, referred to
under (2) above. Thus Soviet "Marxian" thinking about the
"dictatorship of the proletariat" and its duration, the character of the state, and what would happen to it after the
revolution, or civil liberties under Communism, and many
other things, are definitely not consonant with Marx's views.
(There was a brilliant article in the Swedish Syndikalist
journal *Zenit*, No. 3, 1962, by Wolfgang Leonhard, depicting an imaginary conversation between the East German
dictator Ulbricht and Marx and Engels. Everything the
latter two say consists of quotations from their works. The
result is that Ulbricht, who had first greeted them in the
most exalted words, finds himself compelled to put them in
prison as enemies of the state. When they succeed in fleeing
to West Germany they are then dealt with as dangerous
revolutionary "Marxists.")

The diligent attempts at an exegesis of Marx's writings, to
which Soviet economists and philosophers have been driven
in order to reconcile Soviet policies with Marx's ideas, have
been frustrating and emasculating their research efforts.
Together with the severe limitation of the statistical and
other information made available to them by their government, this constraint to be "Marxian" constitutes a main
explanation why economic science in the Soviet Union and
the allied Communist countries has in general not advanced
further.

This also explains why econometrics has in recent years
become such a welcome haven for many of the more
brilliant economists in the Soviet Union. By emulating the
methods, or rather the form of expression, of the well-estab-

lished natural scientists, they escape the necessity pressed upon the other economists to prove statements about economic reality by quoting Marx and Lenin (in one period even Stalin).

(7) Mao is, in the first place, the founder of a positive moral philosophy, embracing all social relations. Under the very singular circumstances that have existed in China for many decades, touched upon in Chapter 13, Section 9, and working within equally singular national traditions in China since centuries, he has succeeded in molding his very large nation to become a "new people," diverging in their patterns of living and working from old China and, of course, from other nations.

Encompassed by this moral doctrine was an ingenious military strategy and tactic, which assured the victory of the Communist Party in China. Also included were certain general lines for economic development planning, which fitted conditions in China and—after many trials and errors —have had considerable success. They are without doubt intellectually superior to the planning directives of other very poor, underdeveloped countries. I only feel flattered that an English student is now preparing a work, "Mao and Myrdal," wherein he shows concordance in regard to main policy conclusions concerning the direction of development planning, though I have not learned from Mao as little as he has learned from me. Neither of these two traits has anything to do with Marx.

Mao's doctrine, as far as planning for development goes, actually shows important similarities to Gandhi's, although Mao, unlike Gandhi, saw power as coming from the use of violence and not from possible resistance. This reflects, in the first place, the different character their liberation struggles had to take (Chapter 13, Section 8). As Maoism—particularly after the Cultural Revolution, which from one important point of view was a struggle between fractions, the orthodox Maoist one on the one hand and various

groups of dissenters on the other—is now in assured posses-
sion of power, and, as even American observers are finding
out, has backing among the masses of people, the difference
does not become so big. A study comparing these two
spiritual leaders of the world's two biggest nations should
be an important research task.

Mao has consistently aligned his teaching to Marx and
Lenin. In the universities and cadre schools the students
have to read their writings. But the connecting link between "Marxism-Leninism" and the "teaching of Chairman
Mao" is regularly missing or utterly loose, often formulated
in uncomprehensible, metaphysical associations of the type
that often creep into religious theology. In North Korea this
intellectual ballast is in the process of being thrown away
and the doctrine directly referred to as the "thoughts of
Kim Il Sung."

The foregoing remarks are only meant to explain why
Maoism will not be discussed as a version of "Marxism."

3. Marx Not a "Marxist"

Marx was, of course, an economist on quite another level
than most writers in the mixed crowd of those who now
call themselves "Marxists." Indeed, their mostly inept attempts to hitch their incongruous thoughts to Marx must be
seen as an offense against one of our great classics.

Behind all Marx's interest in constructing abstract models
for the "laws of movement" of the capitalist society, he was
fundamentally an empiricist. He was therefore against taking anyone as an authority for conclusions about the shape
of reality. At least twice in his writings he expressed scorn
for the "Marxists" of his time. It seems certain that a hundred years later he would be even sterner in his condemnation of the exegetes—in particular the Soviet exegetes who,

in order to come in line with actual Soviet policy, have had to distort his views the most severely.

Moreover, if Marx were living today he, as a hard-working and circumspect scientist, would know and take into account all that we now know but that he could not possibly have known a century and more ago. As a historian and empiricist, he would observe and account for not only what had evolved according to his forecasts, but also what had taken another route.

He would, of course, stand freer from dependency on Hegel and other German philosophers who were more or less his contemporaries. Even more important, he would, I believe, with his critical ability have now freed his thinking from the impact of the mighty tradition of teleological natural-law philosophy, under which both he and his adversaries, the liberal economists of his time, labored, although both he and they repudiated it in principle.[3] This last-mentioned, and main, philosophical influence on Marx's thinking is seldom observed, because so many "anti-Marxists" as well as "Marxists" are still under its spell.

As a hard-boiled analyst, Marx was a severe critic of romanticism and sentimentality. He did not give his backing to revolutionary attempts when the objective conditions for success were not present. If he lived today, he would, for instance, have observed how the technical development of armaments, even those less advanced ones available to underdeveloped countries, has radically increased the power to suppress rebellions by military force.

He would therefore have little in common with the many left-wing youths in the United States and the Western countries generally, who mostly call themselves "Marxists" and who—without danger to themselves—indulge in expecting rapid success for isolated guerrillas, particularly in Latin America. That he would have despised as unrealistic the "Marxists" in the Western countries who wanted to start a revolution there is certain. Some of them are even otherworldly enough to aspire to be "Marxist Marxians."

4. Marx and the Theory of Biases

Marx should be given credit for having raised the problem of biases. When he invented the term "bourgeois economist" and applied it to the classical economists of his time, it implied the accusation that their theories were biased in a way opportune to the well-to-do and socially, economically, and politically mighty of his time. In this he was undoubtedly correct.[4]

If Marx has not played much of a role in my own writings on this issue, the explanation is not only that, as I once figuratively explained, I feel myself "older than Marx," having had, by the accidents of my upbringing and personal inclinations, my thinking directly rooted in the Enlightenment philosophy—as was also the thinking of those gentlemen who made the American Revolution and laid the constitutional and ideological basis for what I have called the "American Creed," and who corresponded with all the great statesmen and philosophers of Europe of their time. More specifically, in relation to what I have had to say on the problem of biases, Marx contributed very little, besides accusing the contemporary classical economists of biases, in which he was correct.

Marx did not see that valuations are always and necessarily conditioning economic research, as there is no view except from a viewpoint and no answers except to questions. This deficiency in his thinking shows up in the facile manner in which he could take for granted that his own views were simply "scientific" and "objective."

Marx, therefore, was not driven to face the problem of selecting value premises, which should not only be rendered explicitly, but whose propriety in a specific situation and a specific problem should be established.

Nor did Marx make a significant contribution to clarify the methodology of immanent criticism, through which, on the logical level, biases can be detected.

Marx still less raised the psychological and sociological problem of the causation of biases, that is, how personality traits, the force of tradition, and the influence of dominant interests and prejudices in the surrounding society acted together.

These four problems were outlined in Chapter 4 and have been touched upon in several other contexts in this book. Having said this about Marx, and so raised a criticism against his books, which I think is valid and correct, I should add that neither did anybody else in his time evoke these very crucial problems in a systematic way.

And I would like to add that it would be worth someone's while to go through Marx's voluminous writings, specifically searching for oblique hints he might here and there have given in the directions I have followed. So rich and fecund with associations was Marx's mind that I believe such a search would be fruitful. This is another suggestion for a doctoral thesis, or several of them.

5. An Institutional Economist

When Marx has to be seen as one of the great classics in the development of economic science, this should be founded, not on his contributions to the study of biases, which were incomplete and shallow, but on his pioneering in institutional economics—after the still earlier and very different Friedrich List. But this is a large topic, and one on which this mention can serve only as a reminder.

Notes and Index

NOTES

Preface

1. Myrdal, *The Challenge of World Poverty: A World Anti-Poverty Program in Outline* (New York: Pantheon Books, 1970).
2. Myrdal, *Asian Drama: An Inquiry into the Poverty of Nations* (New York: Twentieth Century Fund and Pantheon Books, 1968).
3. *Objectivity in Social Research* (New York: Pantheon Books, 1969) belongs in the same category. Similar autobiographical notes are also contained in a postscript to Myrdal's *Value in Social Theory* (New York: Harper & Row, 1958, edited by Paul Streeten) and in the preface and appendices to the new edition of Myrdal's *Vetenskap och politik i nationalekonomin* (Stockholm: Raben & Sjögren, 1972), originally published in 1929 and appearing much later in English (London: Routledge & Kegan Paul Ltd., 1953; Cambridge: Harvard University Press, 1965) as *The Political Element in the Development of Economic Theory*.

Chapter 1. Crises and Cycles in the Development of Economics

1. This is an adaptation of a reply made at a luncheon for the author and Alva Myrdal given by the American Economic Association at its annual meeting in New Orleans on Decem-

ber 28, 1971, and published in the *American Economic Review, Papers and Proceedings*, Vol. 62, No. 2, May 1972, pp. 456–62. The article reappeared in amended form in the *Political Quarterly*, January 1973.

2. Myrdal, *Prisbildningsproblemet och föränderligheten* [Price Formation Under Changeability] (Uppsala: Almqvist & Wiksell, 1927).

3. Original Swedish edition *Vetenskap och politik* (Stockholm: Norstedt, 1929).

3a. Myrdal, *Sveriges väg genom penningkrisen* [Sweden's Way Through the Monetary Crisis] (Stockholm: Natur och Kultur, 1931) and a number of articles.

4. Myrdal, *Monetary Equilibrium* (London: William Hodge, 1939); Swedish original "Om penningteoretisk jämvikt," *Ekonomisk Tidskrift*, 1931.

5. G. L. S. Shackle, *The Years of High Theory. Invention and Tradition in Economic Thought 1926–1939* (London: Cambridge University Press, 1967).

6. Myrdal, "Konjunktur och offentlig hushållning" [Short-term Economic Development and Public Policy], Bihang till riksdagens protokoll 1933, 1:a saml., bilaga III. See also *Sveriges väg genom penningkrisen.*

7. Myrdal, *Kris i befolkningsfrågan* (Stockholm: Bonniers, 1934).

8. In 1937 I wrote a book proposing radical changes in Sweden's agricultural policy, which I looked upon as social policy; while the steady decrease of the labor force was going on in agriculture, those remaining there should not be pressed down to become an underclass. In my opinion their income levels should be raised, not by price support, but by direct state subsidies.

In this context I also proposed for the first time that children should be given a free meal and also that families under a certain income level should be allowed to buy food at reduced prices. In spring 1938, when I visited America, Mordicai Ezekiel brought me together with Henry Wallace, who was then Secretary of Agriculture. The book and a report from a public committee, of which I had been chairman and which had endorsed my proposals, were rapidly translated in condensed form. I have added this note as it might be of some historical interest. From this Swedish publication and my conferences with Wallace and his officials emerged the food-stamp plan, which I understand is still badly needed and in practice.

Chapter 2. "Stagflation"

1. Not published before.
2. *Varning för fredsoptimism* [Warning for Peace Optimism] (Stockholm: Bonniers, 1944).

Chapter 3. The Place of "Values" in Social Policy

1. Adapted from article published in the first issue of the *Journal of Social Policy,* Cambridge University Press, January 1972.
2. *Objectivity in Social Research* and other sources referred to in that book, particularly *An American Dilemma: The Negro Problem and Modern Democracy* (New York: Harper & Row, 1944), Introduction, Section 2, Appendices 1 and 2.
3. Myrdal, *Economic Theory and Underdeveloped Regions* (New York: Harper & Row, 1971. [Original edition: London: Gerald Duckworth & Co. Ltd., 1957]), Part 2.
4. *The Political Element in the Development of Economic Theory,* Chapter 2.
5. *Objectivity in Social Research,* Section 22; *Economic Theory and Underdeveloped Regions,* Part 2, *et passim;* and *The Political Element in the Development of Economic Theory.*
6. Myrdal, *Beyond the Welfare State* (New Haven: Yale University Press, 1960), pp. 56ff. *et passim.*
7. Alva Myrdal, *Nation and Family* (New York: Harper & Brothers, 1941. [Paperback edition: MIT Press, 1968]).
8. *Beyond the Welfare State,* Chapter 10, p. 117, *et passim.*
9. *The Challenge of World Poverty: A World Anti-Poverty Program in Outline,* Chapter 11.

Chapter 4. The Need for a Sociology and Psychology of Social Science and Scientists

1. Adapted from an opening address at the Annual Meeting of the British Sociological Association at the University of York, April 11, 1972. Published in *World Development,* No. 3, 1973.
2. *Asian Drama.*
3. *The Challenge of World Poverty.*
4. Chicago, April 1972.
5. For a recent condensed account of the problem, in which earlier

sources are referred to, see *Objectivity in Social Research,*
particularly Sections 13–14.

6. *Objectivity in Social Research,* particularly Sections 22 and
   23; *The Political Element in the Development of Economic
   Theory; Value in Social Theory; Economic Theory and Underdeveloped Regions,* Part 2.

7. *An American Dilemma: The Negro Problem and Modern Democracy,* particularly Appendix 2, pp. 1035ff.

8. *Economic Theory and Underdeveloped Regions,* pp. 132ff.

9. *The Political Element in the Development of Economic Theory,*
   Chapter 2.

10. I might be permitted in this connection to make a contribution to
    the growing treasury of Keynesiana:
        "Some time soon after the publication of his *General Theory,*
    Keynes visited us in Stockholm and spoke at a gathering of the
    Club of Economists, which had been founded when, toward the
    end of World War I, Knut Wicksell moved to Stockholm from
    Lund as professor emeritus; at the time of Keynes's visit,
    Wicksell had already been dead for some ten years.
        "Not surprisingly, Keynes had chose as the topic of his talk:
    'Heresies in Economics.' After his talk one after another of the
    youngest members of our Club took the floor and accused
    Keynes of being too classical on this or that point. To this day
    I do not know if there had been a planned conspiracy to tease
    Keynes in his favorite pose as the great heretic, or if it just
    happened so.
        "Keynes met his young critics with open delight, implying that
    the criticism directed against him for being too classical, though
    exaggerated, was a particularly bright and amusing idea; only
    gradually did he show some easily understandable irritation, as
    the discussion put him more systematically on the defensive
    against a group of youngsters who stole his pose." (Quoted
    from *Economic Theory and Underdeveloped Regions,* footnote
    p. 130.)

Chapter 5. The World Poverty Problem

1. This and the following chapter are adapted from a feature
   article in the *1972 Yearbook of Encyclopaedia Britannica,*
   Chicago, 1972.

2. *Asian Drama,* Prologue, Section 2, *et passim.*

3. *The Challenge of World Poverty,* Chapter 1.

4. *Asian Drama,* Chapter 21, Sections 6 and 7.

5. *Ibid.,* Appendix 1.

6. *Ibid.,* Chapter 14, Section 2, and Appendix 10.

7. *Ibid.,* Appendix 3, Section 3.

8. *Ibid.*, Appendix 2, Section 21.
9. *Ibid.*, Chapter 14, Section 1, Appendix 2, Section 3.
10. *Ibid.*, Chapter 14.
11. *Ibid.*, Chapter 13, Section 17, *et passim.*
12. *Ibid.*, Chapter 14, Sections 6–8.
13. *Ibid.*, Chapter 24, Sections 7–9.
14. *Ibid.*, Appendix 3.
15. See, for example, *Asian Drama*, Chapter 11.
16. *Ibid.*, Appendix 2, Section 21.
17. *Ibid.*, Chapter 21 and Appendix 6.
18. *Ibid.*, Appendix 5.
19. *Ibid.*, Appendix 7.
20. *Ibid.*, Appendix 3.
21. *Ibid.*, Chapter 29, Sections 4–7.
22. *Ibid.*, Appendix. 4.

Chapter 6. The Need for Radical Domestic Reforms

1. See Chapter 5, footnote 1.
2. *The Challenge of World Poverty*, Chapter 3.
3. *Asian Drama*, Chapter 24.
4. *Ibid.*, Chapter 24, Section 5.
5. *The Challenge of World Poverty*, Chapter 4.
6. *Ibid.*, Chapter 5.
7. *Ibid.*, Chapter 6; *Asian Drama*, Chapters 27 and 29.
8. *Ibid.*, Chapter 7; *Asian Drama*, Chapters 31–33.
9. *Asian Drama*, Chapter 19 and Appendix 8.
10. *The Challenge of World Poverty*, Chapter 9: *Economic Theory and Underdeveloped Regions*, Chapters 2–5, 11.
11. *The Challenge of World Poverty*, Chapter 9.
12. *Ibid.*, Chapters 10 and 11.

Chapter 7. How Scientific Are the Social Sciences?

1. Adapted from the Gordon Allport Memorial Lecture, Harvard University, November 4, 1971; also published in the *Journal of Social Issues*, Vol. 28, No. 4, 1973.
2. *The Political Element in the Development of Economic Theory*, Chapters 2, 4, 5, and 8. See also Paul Streeten's appendix to the English version.

Chapter 8. Twisted Terminology and Biased Ideas

1. Adapted from an essay contributed to a volume in honor of Raúl Prebisch, *International Economics and Development* (New York: Academic Press, 1972). See also interview published in CERES, Vol. 4, No. 2, March–April 1971.

Chapter 9. Politics and Economics in International Relations

1. Adapted from an unpublished lecture at the XIVth International Seminar for Diplomats, Schloss Klesheim bei Salzburg, Austria, July 30, 1971. See also "Political Factors in Economic Assistance," *Scientific American*, Vol. 226, No. 4, April 1972. (The author is not responsible for the statistics and diagrams accompanying this article.)
2. Stockholm: Almqvist & Wiksell, 1968.
3. "Twenty Years of the United Nations Economic Commission for Europe," *International Organization*, Vol. 23, No. 3, 1968.
4. *The Arms Trade with the Third World* (New York: Humanities Press, 1971; Stockholm: Almqvist & Wiksell, 1971). The Institute had to produce its own statistics, as the exports and imports of armaments often do not appear in statistics on trade.

Chapter 10. "Growth" and "Development"

1. Adapted from an article in a special issue of *Mondes en développement*, No. 3, 1972, a collective study of development theory, edited by Professor François Perroux.
2. Leipzig: Wintersche Verlag, 1918, pp. 27ff. (British edition: *Theory of Social Economy* [London: Unwin, 1923].)
3. Cassel looked upon business fluctuations, which he declined to study earlier than from the 1870s, as fundamentally reflecting the readjustment of the Western economies to continued industrialization. During this transitional period, the availability of a labor reserve in the shrinking agricultural sector conditioned the course of the boom. The cycles also reflected commonly applied policies. Fundamentally, Cassel was skeptical of the type of generalized and solid business cycle theory which at that time was in vogue among economists. World War I, which was then called the Great War (without a number), had in

Cassel's view fundamentally changed all conditions and policies, so that what he had to say about regularities of business fluctuations up till the war was essentially economic history and not a theory that would have much application and relevancy for the future. Even in other respects, this fourth part contains original contributions, now often forgotten.

4. *Asian Drama*, pp. 1969f., footnote 3. I am indebted to Paul Streeten for this footnote and even for reminding me of Cassel's thoughts on this point.

5. *An American Dilemma*, Chapter 3, Section 7, and Appendix 3. See also *Economic Theory and Underdeveloped Regions*, Chapters 2–5, and *Asian Drama*, Appendix 2, Part 2.

6. *An American Dilemma*, Appendix 3.

7. For what follows, see also *Asian Drama* and *The Challenge of World Poverty*.

8. *Asian Drama*, Chapter 11 and Appendix 13.

Chapter 11. Economics of an Improved Environment

1. Adapted from a lecture in the Distinguished Lecture Series, sponsored by the International Institute for Environmental Affairs, with the support of the Population Institute, held in connection with the United Nations Conference on the Human Environment, Stockholm, June 8, 1972. Published in *Who Speaks for Earth?* (New York: W. W. Norton, 1973) and also in *World Development*, No. 2, 1973.

2. Washington, D.C.: Potomac Associates Inc., 1972.

3. UN document A/CONF. 48/10, December 22, 1971.

4. *Asian Drama*, Chapter 30, Sections 1 and 12.

5. I am quoting Mansholt from the *Guardian*, London, April 11, 1972.

6. Particularly *World Armaments and Disarmament, SIPRI Year-book 1972* (New York: Humanities Press, 1972). A new year-book will be published in May 1973.

7. *The Challenge of World Poverty*, Chapters 10 and 11.

8. *Ibid.*, Chapter 9.

Chapter 12. Gandhi as a Radical Liberal

1. Adapted from a paper contributed to *Mahatma Gandhi 100 Years*, edited by S. Radhakrishnan (New Delhi: Gandhi Peace Foundation, 1968).

2. *Asian Drama*, Prologue, Section 9, and Chapter 2. The assertions

about Gandhi's opinions expressed in this chapter are documented in various places in that book.

3. *Ibid.*, Chapter 33, Section 5.

Chapter 13. The Future of India

1. Adapted from two articles: "India's New Role Following Victory," published in the Indian press for Republic Day, January 26, 1972; and "Growth and Social Justice," the *Economic Times Annual*, October 1972; also to some extent from the manuscript of the introductory lecture at the Second One Asia Assembly to be held in New Delhi February 5, 1973.

2. *Asian Drama*, Chapter 5, Sections 6–8.

3. *Ibid.*, Chapter 3, Section 5, *et passim.*

4. *Ibid.*, Chapter 26, Sections 12–18; *The Challenge of World Poverty*, Chapter 4.

5. For this and the following section, see *The Challenge of World Poverty*, Chapter 14, and *Asian Drama, passim.*

Chapter 14. Toward a Better America

1. The title of one of the addresses I have given in recent years to student audiences at a number of universities in the United States. None has been published before.

2. *Challenge to Affluence* (New York: Pantheon Books, 1963), Chapter 9, pp. 116ff.

3. *Ibid.*, In particular, Chapter 5, Section 13, and Chapter 9, Section 16.

4. Vol. 51, No. 1, October 1972.

Chapter 15. Gunnar Myrdal's An American Dilemma— Has It Been Resolved?

1. Article for *Worldview*, December 1972.

2. *Warnung gegen Friedensoptimismus* (Zurich: Europa Verlag, 1945), Part 2 (Swedish original 1944); *Challenge to Affluence*, pp. 122ff.

3. *Challenge to Affluence*, Part 1.

4. *An American Dilemma*, Chapter 3, Section 7, Appendix 3. *Economic Theory and Underdeveloped Regions*, Chapter 3.

Chapter 16. Brief Note on Marx and "Marxism"

1. Hitherto unpublished.
2. *Asian Drama*, Chapter 14, Section 1, Appendix 2, Section 3.
3. In *The Political Element in the Development of Economic Theory*, Chapter 4, I showed that the classical theory of a real value was deeply rooted in natural-law philosophy from Locke on. The theory is invalid when scrutinized as a theory; it assumes a timeless measurement of value. But when Marx adopted it from Ricardo and construed his theory of surplus value, he was undoubtedly thinking straight, while Ricardo and all other classical economists were swayed by the political forces in Britain at that time and thus biased.
   ". . . Marx's theory of surplus value is not the result of a 'gross misunderstanding.' . . . Marx was right in saying that his surplus value theory follows from the classical theory of real value, admittedly with additions from other sources. . . . For the historian of thought, the real puzzle is why the classics did *not* draw these radical conclusions." (*Op. cit.*, pp. 78–79; cf. 110–112.)
4. *The Political Element in the Development of Economic Theory*, Chapters 2 and 3.

INDEX